# A
# SENSE
# FOR SPICE

# A
# **SENSE**
# FOR **SPICE**

*Recipes and Stories from a Konkan Kitchen*

# TARA
# DESHPANDE
# TENNEBAUM

Westland Ltd

westland ltd
61 Silverline Building, 2nd Floor, Alapakkam Main Road, Maduravoyal,
Chennai 600 095
No. 38/10 (New No. 5), Raghava Nagar, New Timber Yard Layout,
Bangalore 560 026
23/181, Anand Nagar, Nehru Road, Santacruz East, Mumbai 400 055
93, 1st Floor, Sham Lal Road, Daryaganj, New Delhi 110 002

First published in India by westland ltd  2013

10 9 8 7 6 5 4 3 2 1
ISBN: 978-93-82618-49-2

Book design by Lavanya
Photographs by Deepa Netto

Printed at Manipal Technologies Limited, Manipal

DISCLAIMER

The characters in *A Sense for Spice* are often composite and situations have been described with some poetic licence. Names, dates and places have also been changed for reasons of privacy.

Please consult your doctor before cooking the recipes contained in this book if you suffer from allergies. For those with compromised immune systems; pregnant women and senior citizens please avoid shellfish and raw vegetables.

I would be an irresponsible food writer, if I didn't encourage people to eat in moderation but more so to be a thoughtful and compassionate eater. We no longer live in a world where the suffering of animals and the environment can be ignored. Encourage the demand for cage free eggs, cruelty free, free range and hormone free farm products. Seek out organic foods, pesticides hurt consumers but cause havoc among farmers who handle them. Don't buy fish that's caught illegally or off-season. It negatively impacts the breeding patterns of thousands of sea creatures. Encourage small farmers and independent growers so they may continue to be able to till their lands.

**To my grandmothers**

Sarala Kamalakar Rao Kulkarni

Your kitchen was a temple and you, its Devi

Late Vimala Prabhakar Deshpande

For the time we lost and the time we had

# TABLE OF CONTENTS

# ACKNOWLEDGEMENTS

This book would not have been possible without the support of my family, many friends and well-wishers.
I extend my grateful thanks to:
My husband for being the official taster, (some would say victim!) for all the recipes in this book.

My mother and sister, for a lifetime of culinary guidance.

To my father whose rip-roaring cry, 'Enjwaay Boy' before every meal, rings in my ears always, even though he isn't at table with us anymore.

Our four-legged children, Anna and Daisy, for their abiding presence while I typed this manuscript, all hours of the night.

To my editor Renuka Chatterjee who published my first book *Fifty and Done*, ten years ago and with whom I have so enjoyed working again.

To my food editor Sherna Wadia and book designers Lavanya Agarwal and Ahlawat Gunjan, who breathed life, colour and quality into my book.

To Deepa Netto whose wonderful photography makes the Konkan come alive in these pages.

To Abodh Aras and Gauri Welinkar for access to Madhavashram, one of Mumbai's most unique eateries.

To all my household staff for helping me chop, wash and clean while I practised these recipes again and again.

To all my neighbours in Mumbai, New York and Boston, none of whom were spared my test cooking.

The students I taught while living in the United States these past seven years. They came to learn, but they taught me so much, not just about food and cultures but the joy that comes from cooking with passion.

# AUTHOR'S NOTE

It was on a bench in Boston Common, far from the chaos of Mumbai that the idea for *A Sense for Spice* was conceived. Armed with crumbs for my squirrel friends and a coffee for myself, I attempted initially only to translate and contemporize a precious, tattered manuscript of my great-grandmother's recipes, from Marathi to English. But of the many literary projects I began in recent years, this one has changed the most. It grew indulgently into the story of a childhood in family kitchens and then into a study of Konkan cuisine and culture. I embarked upon a journey of discovery that led me through the monsoon-washed plains of the Konkan coast, fishing villages in Karwar, mango plantations in Ratnagiri and chilli gardens in Goa.

My younger sister and I grew up in Mumbai, the urban heart of the Konkan, but we spent many glorious summers in our maternal grandparents' bungalow in Belgaum. Grandpa, we called him Ajoba, moved here with Granny (Nani), after he retired from the Indian navy. A mid-size city on the border of Karnataka and Maharashtra, Belgaum is driving distance from Goa, Dharwad and Karwar. It became disputed territory between the two states after Independence. My grandparents' home was a mix of liberal values, derived from a western education , and of traditional Konkani ways. We ate solachi kadi and apple pie with similar zest and read the Marathi *Tarun Bharat* alongside the local English and Kannada papers.

Growing up where I did, it would seem natural I would write this book but in fact, my interest was fuelled after I married and left India's shores and long after the sweet summers of Belgaum were gone. It started with questions from friends and students in the cooking classes I taught. Genuine questions but embarrassing to me, passionate as I am about local cuisine: 'Is Konkani food the same as Marathi food?', 'Is it similar to Kerala cuisine?' 'Isn't it sweet like Gujarati food?' A ragtag list of fried fish, nondescript coconut curries and the omnipresent vada pao are possibly all many Indians know about Konkan cuisine.

If India knows so little, the world knows even less. For instance, not many people know that the Konkan is the birthplace of the dosa, where it is known as 'polé'. Was Konkani food hampered by its own diversity, its proximity to the more famous Malabar Coast, or its distance from the patronage of Mughal Dilli? Punjab's tandoori paneer, Kerala appams, Tamil Nadu idlis, even the Kashmiri wazwaan have travelled better. Konkani food has remained a cuisine of the common man, the farmer, the fisherman and the nine-to-five office-goer, anchored in an unpretentious reality, like a palm tree to the shore.

But it is in this stubborn simplicity that I unearthed a remarkably contrary cuisine, one that deserves a place in the sun. As you feast on cumin-scented, ghee-drenched varan and linger over silken sol kadi, you will experience a living palate of five hundred years of fusion that is also, in parts, impeccably pedigreed, as perfectly preserved as a limbu lonché, Marathi lemon pickle.

This is how Indians ate before the European ships came with potatoes, tomatoes, and other bounties of the New World; before Afghans and Rohillas on white steeds rode across Panipat, stopping only to hunt and cook game on open fires, even before Alexander's army sowed saffron in the north-western frontier, two thousand years ago. And this is how we eat today, long after these conquerors have vanished into the dusts of time.

Many would argue the exact geography of the Konkan, based on their politics or cultural affinity but for the purposes of this book the Konkan or Karavalli begins in Raigad on India's western coast and ends in Mangalore. Nestled between the Sahayadri mountains in the east and the Arabian Sea to the west, this fertile strip spills into parts of three states: Maharashtra, Karnataka and Goa. It encompasses in its arc Raigad, Thane, Mumbai, Sindhudurg, Uttar and Dakshin Kanara, Goa and Udupi. The Konkan coast is dotted with white beaches, breathtaking forts and important temples and darghas.

Steeped in history, the Konkan was in centuries past a port of Anglo Saxon supremacy, a world stage for treasure hunters and spice traders, and a haven for persecuted communities like the Jews. The Arabian Sea bore on its waters ships and their motley crews and the Konkan conquered them all: sailors and saints, preachers and pirates, mercenaries and farmers.

From this colourful history of continuous migration and conquest comes a profusion of tribes and communities, unusually dense, even by India's polyglot standards, all on a narrow strip of land between mountain and sea.

People who live here, can be called Konkani, even if Konkani is not their spoken language. But beneath this catch-all identity lie diverse ethnicities and culinary traditions.

For instance fish curry in Goa is prepared with vinegar and tomato, while in Karwar, my hometown, only two hours away, the Goud Saraswats, the community I come from, make it with turmeric and coconut oil. In the pages and recipes that follow I will explain how these culinary differences are influenced by varied faiths, social obligations and the distant echoes of history.

Writing *A Sense for Spice* has been a labour of love. I hope that this extraordinarily diverse cuisine, more than a sliver of which you will find in this book, will gain some of the renown it has long deserved and that those outside the Konkan will enjoy the mouth-watering foods I grew up eating and learning to cook. And that together, we can preserve for the next generation the great Indian tradition of cooking with love for those you love. Enjoy it in good health.

Tara Deshpande Tennebaum
Mumbai
December 2012

GUJARAT

MADHYA PRADESH

CHHATTIS

R. NARMADA

MAHARASHTRA

FRENCH SHIP c.1600

THANE

MUMBAI

RAIGAD

MURUD

DAPOL

GUHAGAR

MALVAN

PUNE

CHIPLUN

KOLHAPUR

RATNAGIRI

BELGAUM

DHARWAR

R. GODAVARI

MARATHA CAVALRY 1659

Mughal Emperor
Aurangzeb
c.1618 -1707

ANDHRA PRAD

VIJAYDURG FORT

ARABIAN SEA

R. MANDOVI

R. KALINADI

Kesava Temple
Andhra Pradesh

KARWAR

KARNATAKA

R. GANGAVALLI

Hyder Ali
c.1720 –1782

MANGALORE

Tanjore Temple
Tamil Nadu

c. 1600's, ELIZABETH
EAST INDIA COMPANY

Basilica of
Our Lady of Dolours
Thrissur

KOCHI

PADDY PLANTATIONS

KONKAN COAST

MALABAR COAST

# THE
# **KONKAN**
# TRAIL

Myth and belief are as thick as thieves in the Konkan. The creation of this hilly strip, once the domain of warrior Chhatrapati Shivaji Maharaj, has many versions in Indian mythology and plays a definitive role in its peculiar culinary predispositions. Legend has it that it was whittled from the axe of the Vedic warrior Parshurama.

The story of Parshurama is the story of the Konkan, where kinship and gotra play central roles in the life of its inhabitants, determining how they marry and what they cook. Every Hindu is assigned three distinct social groupings in his lifetime, a gotra, caste and a clan, the latter a group who share a real or perceived sense of kinship. For instance, the Marathas in the Konkan count almost one hundred clans.

Caste, India's ancient and notorious social system is a stifling hierarchy of four immobile stratas or varnas while gotra, a lesser-known social concept outside India that, unlike caste, does not interfere with one's position in society, refers to a group of people descending from the same unbroken line of male ancestor. Inter-marriage between gotras is forbidden but endogamy among clans, is common. The original eight gotras sprang from the loins of the 'saptarishes' or seven preeminent sages, who are believed to be the sons of Brahma the Creator. They include Angirasa, (Lord Buddha is considered a descendant) and most importantly in this context, Jamadagni, father of Parshurama.

One of the interpretations of the holy texts tells us that Parshurama pleased Shiva with his devotion and learnt the art of warfare from him even though the scriptures forbid Brahmins from doing so. When he returned home to Aparant, now known as Goa, he discovered his father had been murdered by Kshatriyas. So terrible was his revenge, he slaughtered every Kshatriya in his homeland. But this left him with two big problems. He no longer had a ruling class to govern his kingdom, and he'd angered many gods, who were threatened by his power. Varuna, god of the sea, decided to submerge Parshurama's hometown. While Varuna planned his attack, Parshurama learnt of the distress of the Goud Saraswats who lived along the Saraswati River in the Indus valley. The river Saraswati had dried up or as fables go, went underground and the families were stricken by drought. The Saraswats were all Shaivites, so it was to Lord Shiva they prayed, to transport them to a more habitable place. Shiva ordered his most loyal disciple, Parshurama, to undertake the task. This command came at an opportune moment. Parshurama would bring the Saraswats to Aparant and entrust them with governing and defending the land in place of the slain Kshatriyas. However, the Saraswats' safety in Aparant was threatened by Varuna's impending Tsunami.

But the God Varuna underestimated Parshurama's power, and was forced to recede. To the Konkanis, Parshurama is their saviour and the Konkan is his 'karma bhoomi'.

From the Konkan's geographical proximity come various tribes: Gambit, Tuleris, Warli, Kulchas, and many sub-communities: Karwaris, Kannadiga, Maratha, Koli, Malwani, Kayastha, Chitrapur and Rajpur Saraswat, Tuluvas, and my community, the Goud Saraswat. Each of these communities has unique customs, different family gods, called Kuladevtas, and gotras but is bound by religious, migratory and culinary ties. The Konkan is peopled by Hindus, Christians and Muslims. Parsis and Indian Jews too, find much of their Indian history in the Konkan.

Culinary identity is based on several factors: the place of one's birth, caste and language. Family background is also an important factor because it determines the deities one worships and affiliations to a matt or religious stream, both of which, involve complex social and culinary obligations. For instance, a Panchamrut, 'panch' meaning five ingredients and 'amrut' the ambrosia of the gods, is prepared differently for holy days by Shaivites in the Konkan and Vaishnavites in the north. In the Konkan it is also called Kayras, a blend of white sesame, tamarind, sugar, coconut and capsicum. In northern India, it is equal parts of honey, ghee, yogurt, milk and grapes or raisins.

Konkani Jewish families, also known as Bene Israelis, have their own mix of Jewish Konkani practices. They speak Marathi and bear Marathi last names like Dandekar and Pirolkar. Their version of pohé, a staple Konkani dish, is called malida and is served on religious occasions. Like local Hindus, they too, use coconut milk but as a substitute for dairy products since Kashrut dietary laws don't permit the mixing of meat and milk.

Konkanis one encounters every day, have singular heritages. Take, for instance, the Sandori Christians from Vasai with names like Vadval, who are traditionally goldsmiths and carpenters, while their proximate neighbours, the Samvedi Christians who bear Portuguese names like Tuscano, Ghosal and Kudel, are farmers whose vegetables you probably buy at Mumbai's Dadar market. Konkani Christians from Mangalore and Goa are Roman Catholic. Konkani Muslims, like the Nayawats, Siddis of Arab and Ethiopian descent, settled here long before Ghazni or Babar set foot in India.

The Koli community, like the Kunbi tribals, are among the oldest Konkan residents. Mumbai's famous 'Koliwada prawns', a staple in seafood restaurants, is named after this fishing community, even though traditional Kolis disavow its authenticity.

I belong to a sub-community of Saraswats or GSB, slang for Goud Saraswat Brahmin. But among the Saraswats, too, there are culinary distinctions between those who cleave to a Konkani background from Goa and those from Mumbai, Ratnagiri and beyond; between the Kannada-speakers from Belgaum, the Malayalee Saraswats from Kerala and the Konkanis from Pune. I myself am a 'hybrid' Konkani – my mother's family came from Karwar and Goa and spoke Kannada and Konkani, while my father's family are Punekars (from Pune), who spoke only Marathi, but both are Goud Saraswat.

The diet of the Saraswats is unusual on account of their origin and migrations. They are among the few pisco (fish-eating) vegetarian Brahmins in the country. The Saraswats deviated from their satvik or orthodox vegetarian diet, which prohibits consumption not only of meat, fish and eggs but onions and garlic. Seafood in Marathi is called 'samudra phalam' or 'jal kaaya', fruits of the sea and is not deemed strictly non- vegetarian.

One theory explains that it was acceptable to introduce fish to an otherwise meatless diet because Kshatriyas, on account of their military duties are permitted flesh. The Saraswats, who had these responsibilities thrust upon them by Parshurama, were allowed to eat seafood. It is not uncommon, however, for GSB women to be vegetarian, since they did not have to go to war! My grandmother and grand-aunts are terrific seafood cooks but are themselves vegetarian.

The Saraswat migrations are well documented with mentions in the Rig Veda, Ramayana, Bhagvad Gita and Zend Avasta. They are described as an agrarian community who valued education and were devout in their worship of family gods. There were five major migrations, prompted by drought, war or religious persecution.

The Puranas date the first migration to approximately 2000-1500 B.C. Two hundred and fifty families came from Central Asia through the Hindukush Mountains. They farmed along the mighty Saraswati River, whose name they came to be known by, near the Indus Valley. Their spiritual guide was Saraswat Muni, a son of the river. The Saraswat settlements followed the river through modern Punjab and Rajasthan to the Rann of Kutch where she entered the Arabian Sea. Settlements were also found in Harappa, Mohenjodaro and Quetta.

Here, we have another interpretation of ancient texts; when water became scarce and farming difficult, Saraswat Muni suggested consuming fish. The Muni, a shrewd man, found a way to both maintain Hindu vegetarian tradition and feed his starving devotees. He pulled fish out of the water and separated the head and tail and gave the Saraswats the middle. He then put the tail and head back together, uttered mantras and returned the revitalized fish to the water.

When the paucity of water became insurmountable, families migrated to four different locations:  Kashmir where they are known as Kashmiri Pandits, Rajasthan, Punjab and Trihotra in Bihar. When the Magadha and Pala dynasties in Bihar began crumbling they moved again, this time to Goa, from the ancient and now submerged city of Dwarka. Goa became the central meeting point of Saraswats who migrated in waves from 700 B.C. to 1000 A.D. Goa attracted migrants for its flourishing trade and benevolent rulers.

The Goud Saraswats prospered in the Konkan region. Coconut, rice and lime became an integral part of their cuisine. In modern times they became accountants, lawyers, bankers, goldsmiths, dentists, teachers and clerks in the cities of Mumbai, Karwar, Raigad, Mangalore, Goa and Cochin.

During the thirteenth century, a significant number of Saraswats who had always followed the Smarta or Shaivite tradition, adopted Vaishnavism under the leadership of Swami Madhavacharya. They also returned to pure vegetarianism.

The fourth migration came in the fifteenth century when attacks by the Khiljis and Bahmanis forced the Saraswats to find cover in Kerala and Tamil Nadu. They also fled to the Vijayanagara kingdoms, seeking protection from southern Hindu kings. Since migrations isolate and separate communities, Saraswats named themselves after villages and towns they settled in, making it easier to identify themselves. Today, a surname in India will tell you a lot about a person's origins. Those who relocated to towns in northern Maharashtra, like Lotli and Pedne are Lotlikars and Pednekars. Kar in Sanskrit means land or place. Those who moved to Rajapur are Rajapur Saraswats with names like Tendulkar, Gavalkar, Ashekar and Shenoy while Chitrapur Saraswats come from Chitrapur Taluk in Karnataka. Every community established a matt, or central temple with a chief priest who presided over all religious matters.

The fifth and final exodus began in the fourteenth century. The coming of the Portuguese to Goa in the 1500s changed everything in the Konkan; the way people ate, prayed, even spoke. The serene coastal strip became a simmering pot of oppression, political feuds and religious bigotry. This forced many Saraswats into Kerala where they now live and are known as Kerala Saraswats.

Vasco Da Gama arrived on India's western coast in search of spices in 1498. Trade prospered and the Portuguese did not proselytize aggressively.

The Jesuits who came to Goa with the Portuguese were admirers of the Konkani language and were interested in imbibing local culture and customs. They translated their own Christian texts to Konkani to better preach the faith. However, the threat of Maratha invasion in the 1500s turned admiration to fear. The Goa Inquisition, the most Draconian phase of Portuguese rule, regarded by Christians and non-Christians alike as a terrible ordeal, began in 1561 and lasted almost two centuries.

In the late 1600s, the Portuguese Viceroy, influenced by Franciscan missionaries banned the use of Konkani, the local Indian language, a law formalized by a decree from King Peter II of Portugal. It became mandatory to speak and learn only Portuguese. Konkani had no prescribed script until the mid-twentieth century. Konkani was written in Malayalam, Kannada and Roman scripts and never had the opportunity to develop a collective, credited literature. Konkani languished in obscurity until it was declared the official language of Goa in 1983 with Devnagiri as its formal script.

The Gambit, Kawar, Kukna, Kunbi and Koli tribals, considered original settlers of the Konkan, speak primitive versions of Konkani. Several other languages are also spoken along the

Konkan: Marathi, Kannada, Malayalam, Bankoti, Samvedic, Tulu, Malwani and English.

Another perceived competitor to the Konkani language is Marathi, the official language of Maharashtra. Contrary to popular belief Konkani is not derived from Marathi or the other way around. Both languages derive independently from Maharashtri, one of the many Prakrit dialects spoken in ancient India. Prakrit is a member of the Apabhramsa school of languages, considered 'not grammatical enough' by Sanskrit scholars. On account of its popularity Maharashtri gained prominence, while Sanskrit waned as a language of daily communication.

The Konkan coast had contact with as many ancient civilizations and European colonizers as the Kerala coast. The Sumerians, Arabs, Persians, Portuguese, Dutch and English all came to this shoreline to trade and conquer.

The Greeks gave us saffron and fenugreek. The saffron flower grew abundantly in the cool Kashmir valley and fenugreek, (methi) is now used more commonly in India than in the Mediterranean.

The Arabs gave us coffee and dry fruits. The British prescribed afternoon tea, taught us all about sandwiches, cutlets, puddings, sausages and soups, many of which thrive on our menus, even today.

Before the British, it was the Portuguese who made the greatest contribution to Konkan's culinary landscape. They brought with them potatoes, 'batata' in Marathi, the Portuguese word for the delicious tuber, red chillies, vinegar, tomato, papaya, corn, capsicum, cashews and sweet potatoes. Today, you cannot imagine Indian cuisine without tomato and red chilli pastes or a Konkan summer without roasted corn. The Portuguese are also credited with teaching Indians how to bake custards and pastries and yeast-leavened breads, still called 'pao', Portuguese for bread, in Goa.

## NOT JUST A CURRY

There are many terms in Konkan cuisine, some Marathi, others Konkani that refer very specifically to the kind of method used to prepare a dish or particular combinations of spices.

A vegetable is called bhaji, a bread, poli and a lentil curry, amti. There are many kinds of polis: sanjori, puran poli and gulachi poli, stuffed with lentils and jaggery; chapattis, vades, purya and more. The term sukké, meaning dry and olé, meaning wet are often added as a prefix to describe a dish. So a sukké kombdi would mean a dry chicken curry and an ole modak would mean fresh, moist dumplings. Gravies too have consistencies. A patal or thin gravy is generally prepared without yogurt, coconut, nuts or flours as thickeners. A 'rassa' is also gravy but generally contains some ground coconut or yogurt. A kadi is a curry but is used to describe a variety of main courses like a fish kadi, a coconut drink like sol kadi, or dahi kadi, a yogurt and gram flour curry. Ambat, meaning sour is another commonly used term. For example a palak ambat is a dish of sour wild spinach. Usal is a lightly stir-fried vegetable where the flavour comes largely from the vegetable itself and a light tempering of whole spices.

Phodni is the Marathi word for tempering equivalent to tadka in Hindi and waghar in Gujarati. The flavour of whole spices is released by frying them on high heat in a small skillet or a tempering ladle in small amounts of oil. This technique is particularly important in vegetarian food where onion and garlic is not employed. Instead hing or ground asafoetida imitates the flavours of garlic.

In Konkan cooking great importance is placed on sensory satisfaction. There is a complex combination of sweet, spicy, salty, bitter and sour. Soft is paired with hard, smoky with sweet and deep-fried with raw. Soft potatoes are paired with hard peas and crunchy nuts with macerated lentils. A savoury dish like pohé is garnished with tart lime and sweet jaggery while spongy items like polés soak up curried vegetables. Crisp-fried bitter gourd is served with velvety, sweet coconut and alkaline turmeric is neutralized with acidic kokum. Carbohydrate-rich semolina and rice are always spiked with protein-rich nuts like cashews and peanuts. A traditional Konkan meal is well balanced with stir-fried vegetables, starches, protein-rich lentils and a raw salad.

## SEAFOOD
Konkan cuisine is distinguished from its close cousin, Marathi cuisine, largely by its seafood. Also, traditional Konkanis use coconut oil in their cooking instead of ghee. Fish kadis made with coconut milk and a ground paste of coriander and dried red chillies, pan-fried fish fillets and shrimp rolled in semolina or rice flour, stuffed crabs, dry coconut clams and deep-fried mussels–think old-fashioned New England fare with lots of spice and coconut!

Coconut is a Konkan staple but there are plenty of dishes without this rich ingredient. While coconut, tamarind and dried red chillies form the base for most 'masolu', Konkani for spice paste, the coconut is sometimes used sparingly, less for flavour and more as a thickening agent or as a garnish.

## SPICES AND MASALAS
The basic masolu, like a mother sauce, is adapted to prepare different dishes: add sautéed onions for ambat, fried garlic for a koddel, curried beans with pumpkin and coriander seeds for amti or for a Puneri dal with peanuts and curry leaves.

Most vegetarian Konkani food employs fewer spices than you'd think. Many dishes are tempered with asafoetida and one additional spice, such as cumin, black mustard or curry leaves. It is unusual to find a Konkani dish with whole garam masala, a combination of five or six woody spices, as a base.

## COOKING TECHNIQUES

The flavour of Konkani food is also derived from techniques exclusive to the region: pan-roasting and deep-frying coconut, the use of fresh coconut oil, smoking turmeric, grinding seeds and lentils into spice mixes and the copious use of nuts and a number of souring agents like bilimbi, kokum and amboda. Ghee is commonly used in Konkan cooking while heavy cream and yogurt are not. Yogurt is found in the odd kadi or taak and as a condiment in chutneys but is infrequently the base for a dish, a common practice in Mughlai cooking. Idlis and dosas are mostly associated with South Indian food but Konkani cuisine also includes numerous crêpes, called 'polés', and idlis called sandans made with fruit and lentil batters.

Smoking and slow-roasting seafood and vegetables is another Konkan speciality. Since the tandoor is not a local feature, as it is in Punjab, eggplant and pumpkins are slow-roasted over open flames. Mackerel and sardines are roasted on cast-iron tawas. Dhuvan, a smoking apparatus, is layered with hot coals, soaked in coconut oil. The food is placed over the coals, sealed and left to absorb the smoke.

Steaming and wrapping foods in leaves is a popular Konkani technique: fish wrapped in banana leaves, shrimp in taro leaves and sweet rice pancakes in turmeric leaves. Dumplings are made in a modak patr, a perforated, metal steamer while a sanna patr steams sanna, a type of toddy rice cake.

## REGIONAL INFLUENCES

Konkan food is also inspired by the cuisines and produce of its constituent states, particularly Maharashtra. Maharashtra has six administrative regions: Konkan, Pune, Nagpur, Nashik, Aurangabad and Amravati. Amravati and Nagpur are also called Vidharba in local politics. The cuisine of Vidharba and Khandesh in eastern Maharashtra, bordering Madhya Pradesh has Muslim and North Indian influences. The city of Gondia, or Rice City, fed year round by the Wainganga river, produces long-grained, non-basmati rice and manufactures flattened rice or pohé that is consumed all over the Konkan.

Vidharban cuisine, called Varhadi has specialities like varhadi rassa, a spicy, non-vegetarian curry. Gram and peanut flour, yogurt, poppy seeds and dried millet are used to thicken curries and fresh coconut is replaced by desiccated coconut. Dagadphool, or stone flower, a kind of dry lichen, and garam masala are used in non-vegetarian dishes, mostly country chicken and goat meat. Vada bhaat, a yogurt curry served with rice and lentils, spicy Saoji curries and millet papads, garlic khitchdi, patodi, a steamed pancake and khanolé, sweet red pumpkin fritters, are typical Varhadi cuisine.

Kolhapur in Pune region is well-known for taambda (red) rassa, and pandhra (white) rassa, soups made with chicken or mutton stock, served with flatbreads.

Pune, an iconic city, once ruled by the legendary Peshwas, is Maharashtra's cultural and academic nerve centre. Though Pune is not strictly a part of the Konkan, communities have imbibed aspects of Pune's cuisine by virtue of religious obligation.

Ceremonial food is prepared without garlic and onions but unlike orthodox Jains of neighbouring Gujarat, root vegetables are acceptable for Konkan vegetarians. Garlic and onions in Puneri food are replaced with asafoetida, curry leaves and black mustard. Popular Puneri dishes are koshimbri, which are raw, seasoned salads made with chopped gherkins and tubers. Varan, amti and pitla are preparations of cooked chickpea, split yellow pigeon peas and red lentils. Missal pao, patal potato bhaji topped with crunchy chiwda and yogurt accompanied by buns, and pohé, spicy parched rice, are signature dishes. Pune's dry-fruit milkshake, Mastani, named after Peshwa Baji Rao's Queen Mastani, a plethora of lonchés (pickles), ladoos like rawa, dink (gum), and wadis, (cutlets of cilantro and cabbage) can keep you busy for months. Ghee is used copiously and tastes favour sweet and sour, less sweet than Gujarat's cuisine but more so than Goan or Mangalorean food.

Solapur, a Hindu pilgrimage spot is part of Pune region. Its cuisine borrows from Andhra and Karnataka. South Indian style podis or powdered spices, are sprinkled over ghee rice. Jowar millet breads are eaten with lasnachi chutney, a powder of dried red chillies, garlic and crushed peanuts. Breads stuffed with jaggery and groundnuts, and lapsi, cooked cracked wheat with jaggery are local favourites. Annapurna, goddess of food, a reincarnation of Parvati, is worshipped here and restaurants are named after her.

Aurangabad, named after Mughal emperor Aurangzeb, also called Marathawada, is famous for the Buddhist caves of Ajanta and Ellora. This region is heavily influenced by Maratha and Mughlai cuisine. Konkan dishes have been reinvented using northern ingredients like dry fruits, poppy seeds, garam masala, cream and paneer. Orange phirni, flavoured rice pudding, and chand ka tukda, deep-fried bread soaked in thickened milk, are served everywhere.

Southern Maharashtra cultivates vegetables, fruit, dairy products and sugarcane. After the sugarcane has been harvested the production of jaggery begins. You will see huge, open fires burning into the night. The sugarcane juice is boiled and thickened to make a crumbly, amber molasses, used all over India. Roasted corn (hurda), chickpea curry and fried peanut garlic chutney are local treats.

Konkan cuisine has many variations, some of which are Karwari, from my hometown of Karwar, Malvani from southern Konkan, Gomaantak from Goa and Udupi from Mangalorean, Uttar and Dakshin Kanara from Karnataka. Konkan food, though distinguished by its seafood has a huge selection of vegetarian and vegan food because the use of coconut precludes the need for cream and milk.

Malvan is a city and region in Sindhudurg, the southernmost part of the Konkan, bordering Goa. Malvani food, also called Sindhudurgi, shares similarities with Goan food on account of their proximity. Goa has two cuisines: Goan, the unique cooking of the Catholics, and Gomantak, the cuisine of Hindu Goans.

Malvani food employs banana in many forms. A pancake called kelphoolachi bhaji made with banana flowers, kelyache panchamrut, a rich banana cream, ghavan or rice pancakes with jaggery, dhondas or cucumber pancakes, khaproli, a pancake soaked in sweet syrup and the most well-known, Malvani malpuas, a sweet, deep-fried, eggless flour pancake, are staples of Malvani cuisine. Malvani food is more heavily spiced than the cuisine of Karwar or Pune. A sol kadi made with coconut milk is seasoned lightly with asafoetida and mustard seeds in Karwar and Pune but in the Malvan a paste of black peppercorns, cumin and garlic is stirred into the milk. Malvani vadé, crusty fried finger millet breads served with chicken curry, peppery pheasant and quail are signature dishes. Khatkhaté is a Gomantak stew of five root vegetables, beans, coconut and cashews made for Ganesha Chaturti.

Goan Catholic food is mostly non-vegetarian. Instead of coconut milk many curries are thickened with tomatoes. Pork is predominant in Goan food, where it is a part of most signature dishes like sorpotel and vindaloo, both rich stews of meat, vinegar and tomatoes. Bebinca, a rich, layered dessert and yeast-leavened buns are Goan specialities. Hindu Goan food includes seafood and mutton but excludes pork and beef.

The Saraswats of Karnataka who speak Kannada, have a natural give and take of culinary tradition with other Kannadiga communities. Bisebelebhat, a delicious risotto of lentils and rice is a signature dish from Karnataka but it is also eaten by Konkani speakers.

## KARWAR

Karwar, in Uttara Kanara, Karnataka, is a port, once frequented by Arabs, Dutch, Portuguese and British. The establishment of a nuclear power plant has cut off access to parts of the beach. My last visit was in April 2010, and I am happy to report the water is still blue and the sands of Devgarh Island still golden. Tourism is limited and domestic. Karwar has a ramshackle charm: quaint streets, sloppy shops and easy-going people. A mid-day meal of crusty fried fish and curry is always followed by a siesta.

Karwar has a diverse population; Goud Saraswats like my family, Konkan Marathas who are landowners, a large fishing community of Kharvis and Gambits, tribals like the Goulis, nomadic herders and the Vokkaliga or Goudas, who fled Portuguese Goa and came to live in Karwar's foothills. Karwari Christians or Caanarite Christians are Roman Catholics, originally from Goa and Mysore.

Karwari food is cooked in fresh coconut oil. Roasted and powdered turmeric gives Karwari curries an ochre tint and smoky flavour, distinct from Goan and Malvan curries. Garlic and ginger is an Indian staple but in Karwari cuisine garlic is absent in many signature dishes like yellow pomfret curry, dabdab, a vegetable stew and sukké tisrya or coconut clams. A technique which, I'm convinced gives Karwari curries an original taste, employs the same ingredients in two different ways, in the same dish. So green chilli and ginger are ground to a paste and also julienned and sautéed separately, then stirred into the coconut milk.

Dry-roasting coconut or browning it in oil is a particular Konkan technique. In North Indian cooking, onions are ground and sautéed with garlic, ginger and tomatoes until they release starch, necessary to thicken curries. For Konkan food onions are lightly sautéed and thickened with coconut and rice flour.

Most masalas are toasted spices ground together with coconut and stirred into coconut milk. They do not require a 'bhoona' –a Muslim technique where spice mixes, meat or onions are sautéed in oil slowly, to release flavour and colour.

## THE HOLY COCONUT

Coconuts, indigenous to India, are abundantly available. Botanically, a coconut is not a nut but like olives and mango, a drupe, a kind of fruit with a fleshy, edible endosperm.

There are two types of Konkan coconuts and many varieties –the drinking or water coconuts called 'paaniwalla', green and large, weighing about 1.5 to 2 kilos or more and the cooking variety: brown, fibrous and smaller, about 750 grams. They are the same fruit but picked and processed at different stages of growth. Dried coconut is called copra and is generally used to extract coconut oil. Fresh white coconut meat is used to extract coconut milk and ground up to make chutneys and grated as a garnish for raw salads and cooked vegetables.

Desserts like patoli, a rice and coconut pancake steamed in turmeric leaves, and payas, a rice pudding, are combinations of coconut milk, sugarcane juice and rice. Madgane, a creamy pudding is made with Bengal gram, coconut and rice to celebrate Gudi Padwa, the Hindu New Year.

My family in Mumbai celebrates the New Year as Gudi Padwa. Konkanis call it Samsara Padvo. It generally falls in the months of March and April when the cold has gone and the earth is reborn, at the end of the kharif crop. The farmers then prepare the soil for the summer harvest or Zaid. A gudi or pot, with a stick under it, is dressed in a bright orange sari with flowers and is placed on the right side of the front door. Some families use a coconut instead of pottery. This effigy signifies many things: the victory of Maratha forces, the flag of Brahma and the welcome return of Lord Rama to Ayodhya. We make shrikhand puri at home while our family in Goa cooks sweet potato kheer and the Punekars serve a thali with jackfruit and chickpea stew. It is also traditional to chew neem leaves with jaggery or coconut meat.

So revered is the coconut in the Konkan that Konkani women worship Gauri, also known as the Goddess Dakshinaya, in the form of a coconut. She is the first consort of Lord Shiva. Married women pray to her to grant their husbands a long life. This is also called Gauri Tritaya or Vaayna Pooja. Vaayna in Sanskrit means deity. The coconuts represent Gauri and are dressed up as faces of the goddess. Eleven coconuts are washed in turmeric water; chalk is used to draw eyes, kohl to enhance the eyes and kumkum or vermilion is applied between the eyes in the same way a married woman applies it to her forehead or in the parting of her hair. Black threads and red beads resembling the mangalsutra of a married woman are wrapped around the coconuts. The coconuts are placed on a bed of rice before a deity or photographic image of the goddess. Lamps and flowers adorn the coconuts and suitable rites and rituals are performed. Patoli and pohé are served as prasad or holy offering to the coconuts and later, as a meal to guests. The coconuts are then distributed to the eldest, married women in the household who place them with their Kuladevtas or family gods. The black threads are also distributed and tied to each woman's mangalsutra. Ganesh Puja, Gudi Padwa and Diwali are celebrated by most Hindus, Vaayna Puja is restricted to more observant Konkan families and the rituals may differ a great deal.

Coconuts are an important part of the Konkan economy as every part of this drupe can be used to make natural, organic products from face creams and body scrubs to coir mats from coconut fibres and brooms from the leaves. In my Grandma's kitchen the hollow, brown shells of used coconuts were re-used in innovative ways. Coconut shells used as a cup are called dhav in Marathi. A hole, in a shape as per the recipe, was made and it was used to pour batter for making deep-fried gram flour spirals called kodboles and sweet saffrony jalebis from refined flour. Wax was poured into the shells to turn them into candles which were used when the electricity went out. In the hot summers a large pot of water was left near Grandpa's gate for thirsty passersby and the shells were used as drinking cups. The fibre off the shell was also used as a scouring pad.

A variety of cash crops grow abundantly in the Konkan: coconuts, sugarcane, mangoes, cashew and rice. The Konkan region produces a low-yield, non-basmati, unpolished rice called ambé mor, or mango rice because it has the fragrance of the ripe fruit and kolam, a short-grained variety grown mostly in the neighbouring state of Gujarat. The production of ambé mor is sadly, dwindling because farmers prefer to grow basmati hybrids for the international market.

The Konkan displays its food with as much gusto as its gods. Diwali inspires a variety of mouth-watering preparations like

Karanji*, chakli*, kodbali*, phenori*, shankarpali*, chiroti*, shev*, chivda* and ladoos. Puran poli, a sweet, slow-roasted chapatti stuffed with cooked channa dal and jaggery is served warm with clarified butter or a bowl of cold milk. Two kinds of dumplings called modak are prepared exclusively for Ganesh Chaturti - ukhdiche or olé, a moist, steamed dumpling, stuffed with coconut and almonds, and eaten warm, and a dry variety made from thickened milk.

Strained, whipped yogurt with saffron, called shrikhand is served cold with hot, puffy puris. Boondiché ladoos, crunchy balls of deep-fried gram flour pearls are a culinary feat.

Fishing is an important natural resource of the Konkan. A huge variety of edible fish are caught through the year. Many are well-known all over the country like pomfret and rawas but others like kudgeri*, lepas*, negli*, murdusha and shetkal are eaten locally. Fishing in the Konkan is freshwater, estuary, creek and deep sea and age-old techniques exist alongside new ones. Khadans* or bamboo mats are used to divert fish into cylindrical fish traps called 'bhot'. Long line, bag and rapan nets are employed to catch small fish. A bamboo basket called kirkinda is used to store trapped fish. The fishing season starts in September with an offering of coconuts to the sea in a ritual called Narali Poornima. It ends in May before the monsoons.

In the Konkan it is always the man who does the groceries, especially the purchase of fish. Haggling with fisherwomen is normal practice and the price of pomfret one gets is a matter of pride for the patriarch, something he will boast about to his guests.

I can still see my grandfather return home from the Saturday market, his white Ambassador chock-full of vegetables and

* See Glossary for all asterisked terms.

fish stuffed into woven straw and cloth bags. He left early and was home before breakfast. The fish had to be cleaned and refrigerated immediately and select varieties like clams and gaboli (fish roe) had to be cooked and eaten the same afternoon so Grandma woke early on Saturdays to cut onions and grind spices. We sat on the floor with big bowls of water and brass thalis and peeled hundreds of prawns, washed clams, scrubbed mussels and coated steaks of pomfret and surmai with turmeric and salt before refrigerating them.

You can imagine, Saturday lunch was a knockout. Two or three kinds of fish fry; paplet, the most expensive fish, cheaper but equally tasty fish like bangda, Spanish mackerel, tarala, small sardines and jhinga fry with medium prawns. Kolmi, tiny shrimp were used to make pickles like balchao. We also ate crispy semolina-encrusted fish roe with fresh lime juice, tisrya sukké, dried coconut clams, fried kalva or oysters, rockfish, and my favourite for its sweet flavour, nagli, an estuary fish, also called ladyfish. All this had to be accompanied by vegetarian food for my great-grandmother. Thick, hot varan, chilled sol kadi, dahi bhaat, phulkas with melted ghee and then dessert. We could have slept till Sunday morning, except that Saturday dinner was also too good to miss!

Dried and smoked fish are eaten during the monsoon. Dried bombil curry, dried prawn balchao pickle and smoked mackerel are popular.

## FRUITS AND BEANS IN THE KONKAN

Bitter vegetables, leaves and gourds appear very commonly in Konkan cuisine. Karela or bitter gourd, bitter guwar, a type of cluster bean, ambat chukka or green sorrel is cooked with complementary flavours like coconut and red chilli. Shravani maat, a variety of amaranthus, available in flaming red or dark green is sautéed with onions and garlic. Aambadé, also called sour spinach, with narrower, coarse leaves is Indian Roselle. It is added to lentils to make palak ambat and moong ambat. Highly alkaline leafy vegetables are also cooked as 'alé bhaji' –in milk or curd, to neutralize oxalates. Mayalu or Malabar spinach is a vine with thick leaves that are battered and deep-fried. In Konkani the leaf is called vaali and is stir-fried with onions.

Konkanis eat a mind-boggling number of beans. Hyacinth beans called vaal* are cooked with wild spinach and in thick coconut curries. A type of fava bean, generally called broad beans are cooked in a thick yogurt and garam masala and served with bhakri. Sprouted green moong is so delicious when turned into a sweet and sour moogachi amti or a stir-fried salad with cashews and onions, it doesn't feel like the health food your nutritionist suggested. Cowpea varieties like black-eyed pea, called chowli are turned into stews, yard beans or eeiril in Konkani are sautéed with dried apricots. A Konkan speciality, shevya ché shenga in Marathi and mashinga in Konkani, is a nutritious, green, pod about twelve inches long, from the drumstick tree. It is cut and stewed into amti. String beans also called farasbi in Marathi, are made into usals with onions and cashews. I've found it an excellent accompaniment to roast chicken or poached fish.

Kulith or horse gram, generally used as cattle feed is popular in the Konkan, where it is roasted to make thick pitla, a paste-like curry and the beans are soaked and stir-fried. Jaggery, black and red rock salt for seasoning, local vegetables like meaty breadfruit, cashew nuts, jackfruit, field, runner and long beans like papdi, ghewda and val, give Konkani cuisine its unique character.

The Konkan grows a vast selection of exotic fruits. Papanas or pumelo, a type of citrus, green and larger than the 'breakfast grapefruit' but less bitter is cut open and sprinkled with spices and jaggery. Pomegranates, called dalimb in Marathi grow in northern India but are popular in the Konkan because Lord Ganesha was partial to them. Ananas or pineapple, papayas and a variety of bananas like rajeli, a king-size plantain, mutheli and velchi or dwarf, cardamom-scented bananas come from Thane in northern Konkan. Ripe bananas are the most commonly eaten fruit on the Konkan coast. Jalgaon in Maharashtra is the country's largest producer of bananas.

The Alphonso mango, native to India, is the Konkan's jewel. Named after the Portuguese King Alphonso who loved them, the word alphonso is pronounced 'hapoos' by locals. Unlike other mangoes, its outer skin is paper-thin and the flesh similar to an avocado, smooth and without fibre.

Devgad and Ratnagiri grow the best Alphonsos. Other local varieties are mankurad, pairi, mulgoa, totapuri or parrot head and chausa from Haryana. These cheaper mangoes are used for cooking while the expensive Alphonso is consumed as a fruit, on its own or with sweetened whipped cream. Sitaphal, mistakenly called custard apple is in fact sugar-apple from the same species, Annona. Sugar-apples are ripened and the soft, creamy flesh is stirred into ice creams, kheers and milkshakes.

Jackfruit or fanas in Marathi and ponos in Konkani, is found all over South-east Asia. It is the largest known fruit, can weigh more than forty pounds and is filled with fleshy seeds. An acquired taste, it is a nutritious and cheap summer fruit. The kappa jackfruit has soft seeds, best eaten fresh with a little honey or as a lightly seasoned salad while the baraka is juicy and used in summer drinks, pancakes and stuffed flatbreads. The jackfruit seed is used to thicken curries.

Early summer is also the month for cashew. Cashew belongs to the same family as mango but the cashew apple fruit, which looks like an inverted heart is not as tasty. The nuts however are roasted and spiced as snacks, added to sautéed vegetables and curries like usals, ambats and rassas, ground up and used as thickening agents in Xacuti, crushed and added to various desserts like steamed dumplings and kaju vadi, a marzipan-type candy.

The cashew apple is used in Goa to make feni, a strong-smelling liquor. We harvested several kilos of cashews in our Belgaum garden. The thick skin has to be broken and peeled off the white nut. The skin is acidic (used to make dental products) and oiling one's hands or wearing surgical gloves is recommended.

Chibud melons, an orange, striped melon, sometimes confused with Korean melon, are turned into stir-fried vegetables or sweetened for dessert.

My all-time favourite is breadfruit, called neer fanas* or videshi fanas in Karwar. The size of a Rugby football, this fruit has a green skin much like a jackfruit but is considerably smaller. It has proven very difficult to find in Mumbai, which is a pity because its meaty texture makes it a perfect substitute for fried fish and it is a cheap source of carbohydrate. Grandma coated chunky breadfruit slices with turmeric, cayenne and semolina and pan-fried it as a side dish for masala bhaat or curd rice. Konkanis also make patal and sukké bhaji with neer fanas. The latex from neer fanas is used to waterproof boats.

Jamun also called kala jamun* and jambhul is known as the fruit of the gods among Hindus, since it is believed Lord Rama subsisted on it during his fourteen year exile. Jamun can be eaten raw, pickled and made into jams. Its leaves are used to decorate a wedding pandal.

In the summer we enjoyed chilled 'baby coconuts', called tadgola or targulé in Konkani, the pitless jelly-like fruits of the Asian Palmyra tree. About two inches in diameter, they are filled with a sweet liquid that tastes like coconut water and are covered in a thin skin that must be peeled carefully, otherwise the juice leaks. The peeled fruit is chilled and then popped into one's mouth like a pani puri. The palm shoot of this tree is also cut to release a mildly sweet liquid called neer that is fermented to make tadi*.

## SOURING AGENTS

Souring agents like tamarind and sour tomatoes, yogurt and vinegar are important in Konkan cooking as they complement the sweetness of coconut and the saltiness of nuts. Ambadé, not to be confused with aambadé leaves are hog plums, also a drupe from the cashew family. When raw, they are used as souring agents, and as sweeteners when ripe. Kokum* sol, known as the queen of fruits by botanists is the dried, salted, red fruit of mangosteen. It adds tartness to sol kadi, kokum saar (a summer drink) and fish gravies. The fresh fruit is velvet smooth to eat, white on the inside and a royal purple on the outside. Unlike tamarind, kokum, despite multiple uses, has remained obscure. Kokum butter is an excellent substitute for animal fat, cod liver oil, even ghee and a remedy for cracked heels. Vatamba*, the fruit of the gamboge tree, also called false mangosteen and bilimbi*, the fruit of the sorrel tree, a small green cucumber, are used to sour curries, make pickles and beverages. Fresh green curry leaves from the citrus family, called godelimb or kadipatta are used abundantly.

Konkan food draws its complexity from different masalas or spice mixes. These spice mixes can be dry or wet, cooked or raw. They often derive their names from their colours: goda or sweet masala, lal or red, pandhra or white and kaala or black masala. Phodni, base and top tempering, are commonly used to spice dishes. Whole spices are thrown into hot oil and tempered to release flavour. Phodni at the start of the cooking process, is called base and when tempered spices are poured or stirred into a prepared dish it's a top temper. The spices used maybe similar but the taste differs.

## UNCOMMON HERBS, ROOTS AND SPICES

There are four dried spices in Konkan cooking that are rarely used elsewhere in India. Teppal or trifal not to be confused with the herbal remedy, triphool is a variety of Zanthoxylum, a herb bush from the citrus family. It varies from Sichuan pepper which belongs to the same genus but comes from a different species. Like pepper, teppal can be used fresh or dried, and has a unique, zingy flavour that distinguishes Gomantak curries from Goan ones. Dagadphool, also called kalapasi is, as mentioned above, a kind of dried lichen and nagkesar, a pungent, clove-like herb, are used in goda masala, a complex, spice mix applied to Maharashtrian vegetarian dishes. Marathi moggu, a variety of dried caper resembling a clove, is used in Chettinad and Udupi food. Dried Kashmiri chillies are frequently used in Konkan cooking, but the Karnataka chilli, byadgi, is preferred, because it is less pungent and produces excellent colour when ground. Gol mirch, a small round, red chilli is also used for tempers.

Turmeric, a rhizome from the ginger family is paramount in Konkan cooking for flavour and colour. Sangli, Maharashtra is an important centre of production. Halad, Marathi for the yellow powder, is processed by drying and grinding this root.

As in other parts of India, it is common for guests to drop by unannounced. So it was important for Grandma to have recipes at hand that required inexpensive ingredients with a long shelf life and did not need much cooking time. Her kitchen was always well-stocked with Konkan basics. Short -grained and long-grained rice, toor, split black gram and moong lentils, whole-wheat flour, semolina, parched rice, peanuts, ghee, black mustard seeds, cumin, curry leaf plants, asafoetida, onions, green chilli and lime bushes and jaggery. With these long-lasting ingredients she could prepare at least two dozen dishes for breakfast, lunch and dinner, including favourites like pohé, uppama, masalé bhaat, varan, flatbreads and fritters.

Various trail mixes, like deep fried rice chiwda, pretzels like mudukku and chakli, were prepared every month and stashed in tin jars. Potatoes were boiled, peanuts crushed and onions chopped in advance, to rustle up sabudana wadé, kothimbri vadé, and thalipeet at a moment's notice. Cool treats like malai kulfi, mango ice cream and poached fruit were served on hot days.

From our Konkan journey through these pages, it's not hard to deduce that I have hundreds of family recipes. These were not easy to catalogue. The earliest were written meticulously in multiple languages by my great-grandmother with a quill pen, on paper so yellowed and fragile, it was difficult to turn the pages without them crumbling to dust. I found that in form, these recipes bore a remarkable similarity to those from medieval Europe; succinct and general. A traditional Konkan recipe would call for a fistful (mushti) of rice flour, a pinch (chimoot) of turmeric and a palmful of ghee. It was expected that all women knew what do with these things, so further elaboration was unnecessary. The recipes after the Second World War, penned by my grandmothers in English with 'fountain pens', see a significant change; exact measurements in pounds and ounces and smaller quantities for nuclear families. New time-saving gadgets like mixer-grinders replaced traditional methods and the influence of British and American cookbooks is apparent.

If we are to preserve and pass down to future generations the multitude of sub-cuisines in this country, before they disappear forever in the 'multi-cuisinization', of Indian food, we need an approach that is well-defined and consistent.

The French have a reverence for technique and the Americans question everything. I saw this at play during classes at the French Culinary Institute in New York and in Paris at Le Cordon Bleu. Bread-baking begins with a study of gluten and yeast. Detailed histories of madeleines and tarte tatins are part of the teaching process. One look at *Larrouse Gastronomique*, the Bible of French cooking, reveals a culinary glossary that is longer than our list of gods and goddesses. There is a name for everything, a science for every spice and every recipe is recorded in grams and minutes, not by 'andaza' or word of mouth. Undoubtedly, the spontaneous nature of Indian cooking and the assertion of instinct are irreplaceable in a Konkan kitchen for the inimitable style and common sense they bring to the table.

In *A Sense for Spice* I attempt to embody some of these ideas. The glossary is  more than the sum of words you will find in the book but also contains names of ingredients and esoteric techniques you will only come across on a road trip through the Malvan or in traditional Konkani homes.

## GADGETS, MEASURES AND TOOLS

I found myself replacing my grandmothers' 'fry the onions in oil', with 'sauté the onions', a term that more correctly describes its equivalent in Marathi, 'paret', to stir and cook in small quantities of oil. The term 'cup' is used loosely in Indian cooking. A tandla mané, Konkani for a 12-oz brass or wooden rice measure, is no longer seen in modern Konkani homes. So when a recipe calls for a cup, it could be any cup a cook can get his hands on, as small as a 4 oz chai glass or a 10 oz coffee mug. I have converted to grams where possible and used American cup and spoon measures.

A Konkan kitchen has all the staples of an Indian kitchen: a griddle or tawa, a pressure cooker, a kadai or wok for deep-frying, a flat zara or perforated ladle for frying puris and a deep zara for frying fritters and food that needs to be fished out of a large kadai of oil. Flat-tipped tongs for turning flatbreads, a chimta or pakad, a levered tong used instead of a glove to lift hot vessels, a rolling pin called latné and a board for rolling called polpat. The Gujarati latné or velan is long and narrow because theplas and khakras have to be rolled thin. The Punjabi belan is stout as Punjabi parathas are stuffed and need a heavier pin. The Marathi belan is slightly thinner than a Punjabi one and shorter than the Gujarati pin. It can be used to roll phulkas and chapattis. The Gujarati velan is better suited for puris.

A 'tope' or cooking pot is a shape one doesn't find easily in American kitchens but a Konkan kitchen will have them in many sizes. A rimmed, deep, round pot with straight sides and a one-inch overhang, but no handles, it is used to boil milk, cook rice and lentils. Smaller ones are used to make tea. Topes are always sold with a matching lid.

Large earthen pots called ghagars have spouts for pouring water and milk. If they are made of copper and brass they are used for cooking and are called ghadgas. A dome-shaped copper pot lined with aluminum, now stainless steel, for sautéing is called dheg. A wood-fuelled fireplace or a stove is called chul or segdi though strictly speaking the latter generally refers to a coal-fired stove. Barani, meaning jars, are ceramic or stainless steel. Metal baranis usually carry milk or other fluids and have a lid and a large handle. The ceramic ones are used to store non-perishables and pickled foods. Before milk was sold in plastic bags the milkmen came to our home and measured milk, using an upturned ladle, into a metal barani.

An ulthane or kaltha, a long flat ladle is used for turning flatbreads on a tava while a curved, oval ladle called oyeralé is used for serving boiled rice. Sieves come in different sizes and calibres. Tea is strained with a galni, a small sieve with a handle, flour is sifted in a large chalani and rice and wheat is cleaned in a bamboo winnow called soop. A parat is a large metal plate with a two-inch rim used to knead dough.

## KONKANI THALI

A traditional Konkani meal is often eaten in a thali or taat – a large metal plate. But thalis in India come in different shapes. A Marathi taat is round but has a slightly elevated middle and an oblique rim. A taat is accompanied by little bowls, vatis, in Marathi, or katoris in Hindi. These are used for gravy dishes and desserts. It is standard to have toop or ghee handy in a small pot and a coconut-shaped pitcher also called matki or lota, for water.

A Konkan taat meal characteristically consists of rice, bread, a gravy or curry dish, lentils, dry cooked vegetables, condiments like raw salad, chutneys, pickles, papads and yogurt relishes followed by dessert. A typical Konkan lunch or dinner thali or taat meal usually starts with flatbreads like poli, puri or bhakri accompanied by one or more sukké or patal bhajis, a koshimbri, chutney, pickles and vadé or papad and solachi kadi or taak, served as a digestive. This is usually followed by a second course of lentils, a varan, amti or rassa with rice and more bread. Dried spice and lentil powders like methkoot* or milgai* are served with piping hot rice and spoonfuls of ghee or curd rice. A sweet like gulab jamun is served as a finale.

Every region has variations and every family, preferences. In some communities dessert is eaten before the main course. In my family, shrikhand is served with the main course followed by another dessert like puran poli at the end of the meal. Our family cuisine was a mix of Pune food from my father's side and Karwari from my mother's. Karwari meals always include a fish curry and a variety of fried fish, always served as a second course.

# MEASURES

1 cup = 8 fluid oz = 237 ml

4 cups = 1 quart = .95 litres

1 gram = 28 ozs

1 pound = 454 grams

1 kg = 2.2 pounds

1 tablespoon = 3 teaspoons

# MENUS

The meals or thalis described below are made for special occasions such as weddings and religious holidays, when several women get together and prepare an elaborate dining experience. You can select items from the menus according to your taste and the time you have available.

Choose one gravy and one dry dish with rice or flatbreads to start with and then embellish with your favourites like a fritter, a chutney, papads and a dessert

### TRADITIONAL VEGETARIAN MARATHI THALI MENU

**CONDIMENTS, SALADS AND APPETIZERS:**
**Kothimbri Vadi:** Fresh coriander cakes or batata kaap–potato fritters.
**Vaangi Lonché:** Aubergine pickle or green corriander chutney.
**Kakdi or Gaajar Koshimbri:** Cucumber or carrot salad with mustard seeds.

**BREADS AND ACCOMPANIMENTS:** Bhakri, millet flat bread with Doun laat jhunka–sautéed gram flour paste with spices or aamras–mango compote with purya or phulkas with ghee.

**VEGETABLES:** Cauliflower rassa–cauliflower with peas and tomatoes or matki chi usal–stir-fried green moong beans or valache birde–hyacinth beans in a thick gravy.

**RICE:** Amti Bhaat–pulverized toor with tamarind or varan –thick toor dal with ghee and cumin or masalé bhaat–spiced rice with onions or vangi bhaat.

**DESSERT:** Basundi or aamrus or shrikhand.

**TRADITIONAL VEGETARIAN KONKANI THALI**
**APPETIZERS/CONDIMENTS/SALADS:** Biscuit Aambodé–fuffy deep
fried lentil fritters with coriander chutney or papads.
Karela koshimebri–bitter gourd salad

**BREADS:** Paan polé–fluffy rice dosa with white butter and
methkoot or chapattis.

**RICE:** Dalithoi (toor with garlic) or kolombyo (a sambhar -style
dal) with boiled rice or bisebelebath–risotto of rice
and sambhar.

**VEGETABLES AND BEANS**
Chana sukké (dry garbanzo beans) or farasbi upkari (sautéed
green beans) or duddé randaayi or tori ghashi–snake gourd in
a coconut sauce.

**DESSERT:** Sitaphal rabdi or karanji

**TRADITIONAL KARWARI SARASWAT**
**NON VEGETARIAN THALI**
**STARTERS, SALADS, CONDIMENTS**
• Kandé bhajjis (onions fritters) or masalo mirsangé
(stuffed Goa chillies)
• Kakdi chi koshimbri or chowli koshimbri
• White or red Karwari coconut chutney

**BREADS:** Malvani vadé with chicken xacuti gravy or phulkas
with ghee.

**VEGETABLES AND BEANS:** Cauliflower or moong dabdab
• **DRY SEAFOOD:** Teesri sukké or pomfret stuffed with
green chutney

- **NON VEGETARIAN CURRIES:** Chicken xacuti or shaguti
- Karwari prawn curry with white rice

**LENTILS AND RICE:** Varan
- Dahi bhaat with papads
- Sol kadi

**DESSERT:** Sheera or langda mango ice cream

**GOAN/ MALVANI FISH THALI**
Prawns fry or tisri vadé
Methi surmai with chapattis
Ambotik and boiled white rice
Bebinca or rawa sheera

**COOKING TIPS**
Forearmed is forewarned, my mother says. And it's particularly true in a kitchen. Before you cook these recipes I suggest some advance preparation.

If you can, use freshly-grated coconut and good quality coconut milk. Avoid coconut powders and desiccated coconut. In India, vegetable vendors will break open the coconut for you at the market but you can also do this yourself by smashing the coconut on a concrete floor or with a heavy object like a khalbatta. Diagrams are available on the internet.

If you plan to use fresh coconut milk, remember it reacts to heat much faster than tinned milk. Fresh coconut milk is thinner than commercial coconut milk but its flavour is superior. Overheating fresh coconut milk will cause it to release coconut oil, which ruins a good curry. In Konkan recipes most of the cooking is done before the coconut is added to a curry or a sukké.

Always grate coconut before you grind it. It grinds smoother and faster. Over-grinding fresh coconut can also force out its oils. Sugar in India is coarse and should be powdered.

Konkan food unless specified, is best eaten the same day. Most recipes do not need to marinate.

Konkan cuisine doesn't use basmati in the same way Mughlai cuisine does. The texture and flavour of local short and long-grained rice like ambé mor and kolam will surprise you and add to your enjoyment of seafood curries. Jasmine rice also works well with seafood curries. Brown rice is a healthy option.

Use fresh, green curry leaves off a stalk and green coriander with small leaves, the larger the leaf, the soapier the flavour. Wherever possible include the stalks of vegetables like cauliflower, cabbage and cilantro in your recipe. They are packed with flavour.

Look for small, bright green chillies, locals call them lavang, after clove, on account of their small size (1-1½in) and punchy flavour. Kashmiri and byadgi red, dried chillies vary in length with an average length of 2 inches. If you live in the Konkan, visit local farmers' markets like Vasai and Dadar in Mumbai where farmers sell you the freshest seasonal produce. Even markets in Grant Road and Colaba are better than buying your veggies in a supermarket.

If you have the stomach for it and can get up at the crack of dawn, visit a fresh fish market. Sassoon Docks at 5 a.m. will reveal to you varieties of seafood beyond the pomfret and prawns you usually find in restaurants. Or walk down to Baga Beach in Goa at 7 a.m. when the fishermen bring in fresh catch.

There is some cookware that is very useful in Konkan cooking: A small quart-size anodized or enamelled cast-iron kadai, a 10 to 12-inch cast-iron tawa or griddle, tongs, a small, 8 to 10 -inch rolling pin, a flat, round slotted spoon and a cup-like tempering spoon.

A kadai can be substituted with a wok. But woks are larger and not so good for deep-frying small batches of bhajjis or papads. Buy lightweight tongs with flat slightly rounded tips so they don't puncture phulkas or parathas when you flip them. A tempering spoon with a solid, heat-resistant handle and a base on which the spoon can rest when the spices are cooling is indispensible. A flat pancake griddle or a large cast - iron saucepan can effectively replace a tawa. I prefer not to use non-stick griddles for Konkan cooking.

A masalé daan or thaan or dabba is a spice box. I prefer it in stainless steel with little lids over each compartment, which prevent spices from spilling about, and a larger lid over the top. Stainless steel is odour- break- water-proof and will help to keep you organized and your spices fresh. A Konkani masala dabba will always contain mori, black mustard seeds, hing or asafoetida, jeera or whole cumin, dhane or whole coriander seeds, halad or turmeric powder and lal mirchi bukki or red chilli powder and whole red chillies. Cloves, black peppercorns, velchi or green cardamom, tejpatta or dried bay leaves and cinnamon are used less frequently.

Avoid pre-ground, packaged cumin and coriander powders like the plague. A small, cheap coffee-bean grinder is perfect for grinding small batches of dry, whole spices. Since the spices are not sautéed after they are added to the dish, freshly-roasted and ground spices make a big difference to the final product.

Use fresh, peeled ginger root when a recipe calls for julienned or chopped ginger.

Grams are a unit of mass (or weight) while a tablespoon is a unit of volume. Therefore, it depends entirely on what you are measuring because density varies. I have tried to use grams where possible and an American cup (237 ml) for liquids like oil, milk and water. I would recommend using a standard American measuring kit of cups, a teaspoon and tablespoon.

Olive and sesame oils and animal fats are not suitable cooking mediums for Konkan food. Use corn, coconut, saffola, vegetable, soy oil, ghee or a good quality margarine. Coconut oil considered a tropical oil was rejected in the United States for many years because it is high in saturated fats. Ironically these tropical oils were replaced with hydrogenated oils which contain deadly trans fats. So tropical oils are back on shelves and if the smell of coconut oil is odious to you can now find 'deodorized' versions.

Several factors affect cooking time. Higher altitude (over 2000 feet) requires a longer cooking time. The strength of your flame, the type of pot you use, for instance copper-clad pots heat up and cool down quickly while cast-iron pots heat slowly but retain heat for longer periods. Cooking in covered pots and using a pressure cooker significantly reduces cooking time. Adjust accordingly.

Author outside ancestral home in Karwar

Ajoba and Nani at their housewarming in Belgaum

# THE
# **ADMIRAL'S**
# WIFE

Grandpa reappeared on a misty Sunday afternoon. He walked quietly into the driveway as if returning from a soireé, not a war. He slipped unseen past a gaggle of ayahs shelling peas on the lawn. The blossoming bougainvilleas and plush saffron mangoes met with his approval. The parrots hovering about his guavas did not. He strolled through a velvet tunnel of frangipani, stopping only to admire his roses.

Grandpa surveyed the expansive lawn of his government house. The grass was emerald green and morning rain still trembled upon its blades. He crouched forward and grazed a palm slowly over the blades. He smiled with quiet pleasure at their evenness. The gardener had not slackened during his long absence.

Grandpa's return might have gone unnoticed had it not been for his neighbour's dog Moti, who came charging out of the house, barking madly at the Admiral's homecoming.

The Indo-Pakistan war began in 1971 and the Admiral was stationed in a secret location. The Admiral – Ajoba, Marathi for Grandpa to us - had been away for six months. There were no reports on the radio, no telephone calls from the administration, and no postcards from the front. Most nights in New Delhi, where the Admiral's family was posted at the time, were spent in utter darkness. Save for the click of knitting needles, interrupted only by the sound of fighter bombers and wailing sirens, and the smells of roasted wheat bread emanating from basement shelters, not a leaf or twig stirred out of place.

The women and children spent the nights making bandages for soldiers and the days turning fresh ginger over hot coals, to prepare a rich candy with jaggery and cinnamon, a spice that helped preserve the nourishing treat as it travelled to the eastern and western frontiers, hundreds of miles away.

The Admiral came home that Sunday in December 1971, threw off his snow-white shoes and swung his enemy-scarred leg over his grandfather's teak chaise. He took in a deep breath of rainy, winter air, rubbed his palms over his belly and said to his wife, 'Aaah! This weather calls for fried fish.'

All happy and momentous occasions in our household were marked by food and festivity. Daddy's birthday called for coconut-roasted clams, my birthday meant home-made marmalade from crimson Nagpur oranges, and our grandparents' thirty-fifth wedding anniversary resulted in a five-course meal of such devastating flavour, we spent the entire weekend walking, very slowly. There is no doubt about it: we are a food family. We live to eat. The fact that we had trounced the enemy, resulted in a feast of tremendous proportions. Four cooks, three stewards, and five maids supervised by Grandma, cooked over hot stoves to prepare a meal friends and family ate off banana leaves. Though we ate many meals at the table, a custom adopted from British rulers, on a truly important day, we ate seated cross-legged on a stone floor, as if closeness to the earth was a reminder of our humble roots.

During our summer vacations, after Grandpa's retirement, this victory continued to be celebrated, more moderately, now that there was only Grandma to do the cooking without the battalion of government cooks.

And on every visit my cousins, sister and I, begged Grandpa to show us his wounded leg. The white scar of the injury sustained in the Second World War, when our men were sent out to fight for the Queen, still shone against his leathery skin, dried by sun and salty sea air, and we stood around it awestruck as if it was a monument of national importance. When we were teenagers, we gave him foot massages and the wound came up for closer scrutiny. The skin around it stayed soft and the shrapnel, he joked, was still floating around in his blood.

When I was three years old, Grandpa retired from the Indian Navy and moved out of his beautiful house on Akbar Road in New Delhi, where he had shared a garden wall with Indira Gandhi. Grandpa would have liked to retire in Mumbai but a civil servant's pension cannot afford such luxuries. My grandparents built a small sunny bungalow in Belgaum, a landlocked army training base in western India. A surprising choice for a man of the sea. He lived there with his wife and mother-in-law, the only naval officer in the entire town, until the day he died.

My great-grandmother, whom I called Panji, was cuddly and
pudgy-cheeked. Her lap, encased in well-worn cotton saris
scented with lime soap, was the most comforting place to rest
my head. We had so much in common; she dribbled as much as
I did and lost most of her teeth at the same time I did. Only mine
grew back and she was left with dentures, bobbing up and down
in a glass of water at night. Armed with a magnifying glass and
a fly swat she read us stories from the Mahabharata after lunch.
I'd fall asleep to the sound of her voice, telling me tales of
beautiful apsaras, gallant kings and my childhood hero, Tipu
the crow.

Every summer my sister and I and our ayah Hajrat Bi boarded
a dinky mini bus from Mumbai to Belgaum. The conductor tied
our bags to the roof with jute rope and before we set off, Mummy
reminded us 'Beta, have you done your sushus? The bus won't
stop for at least six hours.'

We ran to the station toilet, held our noses to the stench,
squatted and did our business. When I was sixteen, I finally
plucked up the courage to tell Mummy she had to stop
interrogating us about our toilet habits in public.

Over the years bus travel became more sophisticated and we
could watch Bollywood videos during the journey. Most times
the sound was bad, the pirated print awful and the bus shook so
much, you could barely focus on the screen. But we loved those
bus trips. We sang songs, ate all the goodies Mummy packed
us and drank hot, cardamom chai from enamel flasks. We laid
out bedding in the aisles and stretched our toes into someone's
hair. It was a tight squeeze but we loved the snug feeling of being
surrounded by people. You may be surprised but we slept very
well, woken sometimes by a bad bump in the road or a nudge
from someone who wanted the bus to stop, so they could relieve
themselves in the bushes.

As the bus ploughed further into rural India, away from the smog and congestion of Mumbai, the urban sprawl disappeared and villages with kitchen fires that burned into the night came into view. The smell of cut grass, the musk of cow dung and the earthy fragrance of roasted millet bread filled the air. There was abysmal poverty in these places but somehow it was made less brutal by large expanses of open land and green fields of sugarcane and rice than the blinding, almost unnatural squalor of slums and open sewers in Mumbai.

The last hour was always the most difficult because we could scarcely contain our excitement to see Grandpa. The bus rolled in, coughing up a trail of dust and when I looked out of the window, there he was, in his muslin shirt that swelled up like a balloon in the breeze, waving from his white Ambassador car. In the fifteen years he came to the station, he was never late and he always wore one of three shirts, a tortoise brown, a white checked and a dull green.

When we were children, it never occurred to us how frugally he lived because our plates were always filled with food, our beds warm and our hearts so happy.

When he died, my mother had the sad task of emptying his cupboards so they could give away his things to a charity. She told me how it pained her to watch corrupt politicians and businessmen plunder this country while a man who served his nation for forty years, lived so modestly.

Though grandfather was not a rich man, what he had he shared generously. His home was more like a guest house – it was always bursting with visitors and friends. When he died, Grandma showed me his guest book.

It was filled with messages from hundreds of people who had passed through his home. And a recurring comment they made was how well they slept, how peacefully the night passed in Grandpa's house.

Grandpa was a man of punctilious habit. He always woke at dawn, turned on his whiney radio at five-thirty, slumped down on his creaky armchair and smacked his legs thunderously with sesame oil. He drank his tea off a saucer so loudly that I woke not to the sound of chirping birds but slurping lips. Then out came his cane and on went his squeaky, white canvas shoes and off he went for a long walk. When he returned, he changed into his gardening boots and pottered about the orchard, digging for potatoes and picking guavas for Grandma's jelly-making.

When I was old enough to toddle into Grandma's kitchen, I was given my own polpat, a miniature version of a rolling pin and board made from wood. Grandma gave me leftover bits of dough to play with.

I rolled many chapattis but it was not until I was eleven, that I was able to create a flawlessly round and even piece of bread. Until then, the dough took the shape of several countries. 'Sweden?' Nani teased. 'Or is it America? Your mother was six when she rolled a perfect chapatti.' My mother is a cook of diabolical skill and I can't compete.

I think I first fell in love with India and its food in Grandma's kitchen. It was a magical place. Fantastical. It opened every day with the first light of dawn. Sounds came in cozy, familiar sequences. I lay in bed, half-awakened by the whispers of Grandma's Chanderi sari and the sweet fragrance of her jasmine hair oil; by keys clunking and the kitchen door opening with a quiet creak; by the tinkle of cups and saucers, the gurgle of milk, the slurring of drunken tea leaves against a sieve. Cooking started in earnest only after the sacred ritual of tea. The house resounded with the jangle of bangles on Grandma's arms as she flitted from one pot to another, soothing, coaxing, and nudging nature's bounty into its proper place.

On the cold stone floors lay crates of scandalously red pomegranates and bursting jackfruit. Here, woody spices were ground, sprinkled and massaged into onion pastes to create curries so aromatic, birds sang. On the dinky portable two-burner gas stove, lethargic pieces of dough came to life, puffed up with pride, and melted happily on my tongue.

Clumps of pasty cream became golden rivers of ghee, placid vegetables were suited with coconut and booted with curry leaves, and ominous bitter gourd was tamed into delicious submission, with lashings of jaggery and turmeric. Armies of unshelled peanuts were miraculously turned into crispy, chilie glazed snacks, scores of oranges found themselves transformed into saffron-coloured marmalades, and hordes of mangoes surrendered themselves to sweet and sour pickles, cumin-flavoured curries and sugary summer drinks.

Grandma's kitchen faced westwards. A cool place, dappled with soft sunlight streaming in through a curtain of banana trees. Its deep, rustic wooden cabinets were chock-full of treasures that were often forgotten for months, even years. These included bottles of bubbly wine distilled from Nasik grapes, dried shrimp pickles made for eating the previous spring, tin boxes of almond candy, prepared for Grandma's annoying aunt who came and almost never left, peppery papadams rolled out for a wedding in 1982 that never happened, (village gossip said, the bride ran off with her chauffeur), and dry-fruit cakes, soaking in rum for Mr D'Souza's annual Christmas party.

When we unearthed such treats, we had to ask permission to consume them. Often, we received an indulgent 'go ahead`, and enjoyed them at the dining table with everyone, but sometimes, the answer was a definite, 'No - it's for next month' or 'No, that's for Mrs Kumble's luncheon.'

So, to our infinite disappointment, we didn't get to eat them, at least not at the dining table, but clandestinely, in the wee hours of the night or during the family's afternoon naps. Often the findings, contained within a drum or a heavy glass jar, were too large to move out of the kitchen, so the cousins took turns bringing bits and pieces into the bedroom. On days when Grandma was out at a party or busy in the garden, we went in threes; two climbed into the vast cupboards and ate to their hearts' content while a third stood guard. If an adult was seen in the area, the watchman had a vigorous bout of coughing. One summer, Cousin Vimal found himself a jar of plums soaked in brandy. He didn't share them with us. He tottered about so alarmingly after this dessert that we locked him in the kennel until he'd slept it off.

Grandma always said the gift of cooking made and unmade her. The Admiral's wife, as she was later known, was a tall, soft-spoken woman with luminescent skin and silky tresses. She looked so ethereal, it was hard to imagine her bent over a hot, steaming pot. But Grandma was a fabulous cook. She cooked and cooked and we ate and ate.

She was born the second daughter of an affluent family in Dharwad, a town in the southern state of Karnataka. Dharwad is equidistant from Pune and Bangalore. Since the days of the Hoysala dynasty who ruled the region between the tenth and the fourteenth centuries, it has been an important stop for travellers between the Western Ghats and the eastern plains. A liberal cultural hub in Karnataka, the region has produced some of India's most celebrated writers and musicians, amongst them Pandit Bhimsen Joshi, Gangadhar Gadgil and G.A. Kulkarni. It is referred to as 'college town' by locals for its numerous educational institutions and is home to the prestigious Karnataka University. A confluence of many languages–Marathi, Kannada and Konkani–Dharwad is an interesting mix of traditional Marathi homes, colonial buildings and post-Independence architecture as well as a varied cuisine.

Grandma's father, a thriving barrister travelled as far as New Delhi to present cases. Grandma earned her undergraduate degree in psychology; such higher education for women was unusual in India at the time. Grandma wanted to study further, to research mental illness, but fate had planned otherwise. Like other women of her generation, she had to learn how to cook and clean. This was her resume for the marriage market, the same way a man would use a college degree. 'Mool ani chool', my grandmother says in Marathi. 'Procreating and sautéing is a woman's lot.'

She excelled as a cook to please her father and younger brother, who loved spicy curries and coconut desserts. As a reward for her labours in the kitchen, her father gifted her books, tennis lessons and even allowed her to travel with her sister to cities outside their town, unaccompanied.  Tongues wagged at the liberties Barrister Sabnis' daughters were given. But the Barrister didn't bother with local gossip and petty jealousies. He had a handsome, strapping son, two talented daughters and a beautiful wife. He was a voracious reader of European literature and donated books to the university library in the hope that new ways of thinking would make their way into Dharwad.

The Sabnis bungalow in Dharwad was built to conform to Vaastu, the Indian science of architecture, in the old Marathi style called Mhadiche ghar or a house with two floors. It

had low doors, a flat tile roof, a huge winding porch, and a
large central courtyard, and was surrounded by an orchard.
There were two wells, one for the family and the other for
the house help and a smaller bungalow behind the main
house for the widows of the family. Dressed in maroon,
they were supposed to have their heads shaven and walk
barefoot. In ancient Hindu tradition, widows had to eat
separately and their diet consisted of plain food in small
quantities. It was argued that keeping widows ugly, underfed
and uncomfortable would make them less attractive to
men and less likely to have the energy to think too much.
Barrister Sabnis did not enforce these rules except when he
had visitors. The family ate together and consumed the same
food. The widows came in and out of the kitchen and did not
shave their heads. The Barrister insisted they be able to read
and write and shared his books and newspapers with all the
women in the family. Tradition does not allow widows to be
present at weddings or births as their presence is considered
inauspicious. The Barrister pushed his limits with this taboo
as well, by inviting them to stand by the doors as spectators.
The cold war he waged with the town's more orthodox
came at a more modest price for him than it might have
for someone less affluent, high caste and astute. Barrister
Sabnis donated generously to the local Shiva temple and to
the town's schools and hosted delicious dinners cooked by my
Grandma. He worked tirelessly for the Red Cross, earning him
favour with India's white establishment.

Admiration for Grandma's culinary skills spread far and
people came with marriage proposals from different parts of
the country. She was kept busy cooking for guests, charities,
and the steady stream of relatives visiting through the year.
Cooking was not an easy responsibility. Water had to be
drawn from the well in heavy pots and carried to the kitchen.
Wood had to be chopped, coal smoked and cast-iron, copper
and silver utensils polished and mended. Whole spices and

lentil batters were ground by hand using heavy stone pestles called ragdo. Vegetables and fruits were harvested from the garden, cleaned and sorted by the women of the house. Refrigeration was not an option so every ingredient had to be processed for immediate consumption or in a manner suitable for preservation.

When Grandma turned fourteen her life's routine was put in motion by her mother. Grandma woke at 5 a.m. every morning and spent two hours in the kitchen preparing breakfast and lunch with her mother. Then accompanied by female friends and a watchman, she walked sixty minutes to school dressed in a cotton sari, a light cardigan and canvas shoes. She returned home at noon, served the men lunch and worked again in the kitchen till seven.

The Barrister did not keep fixed hours, so the women of the house stayed awake, late into the night or early into the mornings to cook and serve him. When Grandma married a young naval officer, the routine changed but didn't get any easier. Meals were served every day at precisely the same time. Morning tea at six, breakfast at eight, elevenses, lunch at one p.m., tea at four, drinks at seven and dinner at eight. The grandfather clock was set to gong at each of these times. Grandma would wake with a start, jump out of bed and head straight into the kitchen. At night she was always the last to fall asleep. After the kitchen was cleaned, the leftovers put away neatly in little stainless-steel boxes and the tea cups arranged for breakfast she went to bed with a toothpick. She would rehearse the next day's menu aloud, as she picked her teeth. If they were hosting guests at a party and the menu was complex she worked through several toothpicks, tossing them into the dustbin beside her, her movements becoming more frenetic as she mauled her gums. The thoughts pursued her even in her sleep and she talked aloud, mumbling and dreaming through the day's routine.

Throughout their married life, in the dozen homes they lived in, the old grandfather clock, wound and oiled regularly by Grandpa announced the routine and pace of my grandmother's life. When he died she gave the clock to my mother. It now sits in the passageway in my mother's house, unwound and defeated. My sister and I look at it sometimes and remember the great meals and the great burdens borne by women like my grandmother and generations before hers that allowed their men to make such successes of their lives. We thank God we no longer have to jump to the sound of a gong.

Grandma's younger brother Babu never set foot in the kitchen. He rode a bicycle to university and went where he pleased and returned at all hours, to freshly-made beds, hot meals and head massages from his mother. Grandma loved her brother and never felt even a twinge of jealousy. He was kind and charming. Girls made friends with Grandma in the hope they might meet him or be invited to the house for tea. Babu brought his sisters flowers for their hair, new saris, and took them to the talkies. There is a black and white picture of Babu, tall, all of sixteen, dressed in cricket whites, on her dressing table. I looked at it often as a child, mesmerized by the handsome face that stared out from the frame.

It was the last photograph of him. He died a few months before his seventeenth birthday, of typhoid. His death was agonizingly slow and it killed with him his father and mother. Grandma says that she has never again believed in God. Even when she speaks of him, seventy years after his death, tears well up in her eyes. Sometimes I think she lost a son and not a brother.

'Happiness is like sand between your palms,' Grandma said to me when my father died. 'But the sun that sets must rise again. This is the wheel of karma.'

A few years later, Grandma married and moved away to another city. From being known as the Barrister's daughter she would be known for the rest of her life as the Admiral's wife. Grandma and Grandpa had been childhood friends, as had their parents who lived in Dharwad. They came, as did thirteen generations of my family tree, from the same community. Every summer when school was out, the kids in the neighbourhood gathered to play in Grandpa's father's orchard. Grandpa was a bully and Grandma didn't like him. He tied her pigtails to various objects: chairs, railings, tree branches, even a cow's tail. Eventually they tied the knot. But of course, it was a very correct 'arranged' marriage. Arranged by the two of them.

Grandma never travelled to the United States, nor did she become a world famous psychologist, but what Destiny took from her, she gave to us. The food she cooked and the love she spread filled many a grandchild's heart with happiness, and made many a family gathering a memory to cherish forever.

\*\*\*

Both my grandmas made outstanding ladoos. My paternal grandmother's besan and dink* (gum) were crunchy, sweet and salty and my maternal grandmother's rawa and shredded coconut and saffron were rich and satisfying. In Belgaum we also made two kinds of papads: black pepper and cumin. In Grandma's kitchen, making ladoos was always an indoor activity while papads were rolled outdoors. For the ladoos, fine semolina or chick pea flour was roasted in large kadais (woks) and then drenched in ghee, sugar and milk. Raisins were added to the scalding, sticky mixture. It took skill to mould them into perfect little balls and Grandma and Hajrat Bi juggled valiantly, to subdue the heat and fury of the spitting semolina. Finally, the rolled balls were set on

* See Glossary for all asterisked terms.

brass plates in pyramid formation and allowed to cool off. Dink ladoos are made with freshly-grated coconut, almonds, sunth (sun-dried ginger), jaggery, saffron, and one unique ingredient, crunchy pieces of gum from the sap of the babul tree. These ladoos, at once sweet and salty, nutty and chewy, are my favourite.

Grandma also made coconut pak, a close cousin of the ladoo. The technique involved is somewhat similar to the process of preparing English boiled sweets. The sugary syrup is cooked until it is boiling and sticky. The extent of its stickiness is judged by testing it with a fork. The consistency of the sugar was either one taar or two taar. Taar in Marathi are the strings of a percussion instrument, like the sitar or sarod. Grandma tested the elasticity of the sugar by inserting a fork into the syrup and gently pulling it out of the pot. If it pulled one string it was suitable for soft candy and if it pulled two strands it would make for a chewy texture.

A true patriot, everything in Grandpa's home was made in India. The only exception he made was his Black Dog whisky. And as a man who took his hospitality very seriously, it was taboo to eat at restaurants when we were visiting. Onions and potatoes were planted every year, ginger and cilantro grew wild in the backyard, and every conceivable tropical fruit could be found in our garden. To grow what you eat is a life-changing experience. Every year new papayas and bananas appeared on trees that were decapitated after the season. Perky, wild strawberries popped up all over the mulched patch north of the house and green chillies dangled wantonly from their bushes. We had 'fruit salad days' in the summer. We walked around the garden picking fruit at will, guavas, pomegranates and chikoos. We washed them by the tap near the garden swing where we sat and demolished them one by one, the pips jettisoned back to the earth they had come from.

Karwar fish market

Karwar Bay

Dried surmai

Early catch, Baga beach, Goa

Grandpa at the annual banana competition

Grandparents' house in Belgaum

Author in Karwar

Dagadphool or stoneflower

Dhania or coriander seeds

Marathi moggu

Mori or black mustard seeds

Hing or powdered asafoetida

Lavang or cloves

Haldi or turmeric

Breadfruit or neer fanas

Drumsticks or shevya cha shengya

Hog plums or aambadé

Author shopping in Karwar spice market

Bedgi or
byadgi chillies

Kashmiri
dried chillies

Gol
mirch

Jaiphal
or nutmeg

Javitri
or mace

Inside a Konkan kitchen: Ulthane and oyerale spoons with bharnee, taat etc

Local deities in a Karwar home

Most cooking basics such as chutneys, jams, roasted spices, and ghee were also prepared at home. Making ghee was an elaborate process. Cream was spooned meticulously from the top of boiling milk and saved in a glass jar until it was sour enough to make ghee and white butter. Grandma churned the cream with a ridged wooden spoon, to separate the water from the fat. The result was a creamy, frothy, white butter, she served at breakfast. I spread it on home-made brioche or on sliced white bread that came from Swami's local bakery, wrapped in sheets of Kannada newspapers. I drizzled it with treacle and could tear through as many as three sandwiches in a single sitting.

The first year of their marriage, Grandpa was stationed in Karachi, the farthest the Admiral's wife had ever been from home. Grandma loved Karachi, then still a part of India. Some of her best curries were learned from Muslim neighbours. She often speaks about their life there and sometimes while reading news from Kashmir she wonders about old friends. Grandpa travelled extensively for his work and brought back recipe books and ingredients that supplemented Grandma's culinary range. Good cocoa was used to make brownies; Parmesan went into minestrone soup and gelatin into mousse.

Grandma didn't travel with her husband unless they were moving to a new post, which was always within India. Her first trip outside the country was in 1988 at the age of fifty-six when she went to England to visit her eldest daughter. 'I did armchair travelling,' Grandma says. This involved sitting down for an hour every day, with a cup of tea and reading *The Illustrated Weekly*, a magazine similar to *Good Housekeeping*, the embodiment of good taste for an Indian housewife. It arrived every month filled with recipes for European desserts and entrées, photographs of exotic countries, advertisements for cosmetics and crystal, cut-out patterns for dress-making, photos of beauty queens and delicious movie gossip. Grandma read every one of them from cover to cover until the day the magazine went out of circulation. All the paper that came into my grandparents' home, newspapers, cardboard, toothpaste and cake boxes had to be sold or used to line drawers and cupboards, make strips for lighting lamps and stoves, or as wrapping to ripen fruit from the garden. Grandpa exempted Grandma's magazines from this monthly cast-off.

\*\*\*

Though Grandma made delicious apple pie, chocolate soufflé and cheese omelettes, her forte was Karwari food, the cooking of our community. Karwar and Dharwad are sometimes called twin cities because their communities and culture have a lot in common, even though they are quite distant. Karwar is a small seaside town, a two-hour drive from Goa, while Dharwad, south-east of Belgaum lies, as mentioned earlier, between Pune and Bangalore. Due to its proximity to the sea, Karwari cuisine is dominated by fresh fish, coconut, peanuts, curry leaves, rice, and coriander.

Karwari, Konkani and Malvani foods are all west coast cuisines, fundamentally similar, but different enough for the locals to spend afternoons arguing about which one is the best. Western and southern cooking employ many similar ingredients but the techniques are different. Idlis, dosas and appams, breads made from rice, are South Indian fare while vades, puris and tawa bhakri (pan-roasted millet flour bread) are eaten in the west. A southern Indian fish curry tastes very different from a Karwari one; though both have onions, coriander and coconut, the latter is usually spiced with cloves and pepper as well. In Konkan cuisine a coconut curry is never tempered with spices, a technique used in Kerala cuisine. If a coconut-based dish is tempered, onions are omitted. A mixed vegetable, dab dab, for instance is prepared

with a temper of mustard or cumin for a religious occasion.
On other days the temper is supplemented with chopped onion.

At Grandpa's we ate off taats, large plates with an inward
turning rim, arranged on the dining table, with water
tumblers, a little ghee pot, a flat oval ladle, especially
designed for serving rice, a pickle holder and carefully
labelled bottles of powdered methkoot and lasnachi chutney.

Methkoot is made by roasting and grinding five different
grains and pulses, fenugreek leaves, salt, chillie powder,
and several spices. Warm basmati rice is softened between
fingertips, and doused with spoonfuls of ghee. Methkoot is
then massaged into the rice.

Lasnachi chutney is a deep orange, coarse and spicy powder
made from dried and roasted garlic and crushed red chillies.
It is served as a condiment with breads and yogurt.

Every meal began with phulkas or rotis, and ended with rice
and lentils. My younger sister adored phulkas. But instead of
dipping them in curry, she enjoyed soaking them in water.
She'd take a hot piece of phulka and dunk it into her glass
of water and eat it with incredulous delight. This culinary
choice persisted until she was eleven. It embarrassed my
mother no end when she appeared at social gatherings with
a phulka in one hand, a glass of water in the other while we
feasted on elaborate pilafs and desserts.

We always ate Indian food with our hands. It was only when
I moved to the United States that I realized how curious and
difficult non-Indians find this process. Grandpa made sure
that as we ate, our palms always remained clean. 'Only use
your fingertips,' he would say. It was for this reason we never
placed napkins on the table–we didn't need them. The food
went straight from the plate to the mouth, barely touching

the lips. My sister was left-handed; something that concerned Grandpa, who considered it pernicious to eat with the same hand you washed yourself with after answering nature's call (another revered Indian custom that is considered odd in the West!).  He spent hours training her to eat with her right hand. On the days we ate non-Indian food, we used forks and knives. 'Elbows off the table,' Grandpa said. 'And the knife and fork must always be placed together in the centre of the plate when you finish.'

We even had round soup spoons. 'Ladle the soup from the side closest to you towards the other side and then sip from the corner, not from the tip,' he'd say. Even napkins had to be folded and placed neatly on the table after the last course. You might wonder that our meals were cause for great strain but we actually enjoyed the attention he gave us, and the food was so good we would have survived any dictum, even sipping tea standing on our heads!

Grandpa grew up in the British Raj, where Indians were treated as second-class citizens in their own country. It was not uncommon to find signs that read, 'Dogs and Indians not allowed' outside British establishments in India. Grandpa said to us once, 'You must learn to speak English, eat crumpets and play cricket better then the English.'

But he also ensured that we learnt Sanskrit from the holy texts just in case in his own words, 'all this Western culture corrupted us'.

\*\*\*

Coconut and mango were staples in Grandma's cooking. She used them to prepare stuffed eggplants, curried sprouts, green beans with cashews, and diced cucumbers with crushed peanuts.

In the summer we always had a surfeit of mangoes because Grandpa grew them in his garden. He had ten mango trees and in a good year they bore more than 150 mangoes each. So many that Grandma sent basketfuls to neighbours and relatives. If you haven't eaten an Alphonso mango you have not lived. There is no mango in the world, (I've tried a majority) that surpasses the magnificence of the King Alphonso. Grandpa disagreed vociferously. 'Langda is the world's best mango. It may not have the perfect shape of an Alphonso but it's the sweetest of them all.'

I suspect a different reason for this dissenting opinion. Despite his best efforts and to his supreme embarrassment, Alphonsos fared miserably in Grandpa's garden. Langda, on the other hand, thrived.

Grandpa touted without a shred of modesty that anything that grew in his backyard was better than commercial produce. I must admit, in some cases, he was right. He grew the most luscious seedless, Indian papayas–he told us they were called 'disco papitas' because when halved, they were bright, bleeding orange, like traffic lights in the rain!

Grandpa harvested velvety sitaphal, bursting with flesh, and ruby litchies. Grandma's repertoire of fruit-based desserts and entrées was remarkable. Her stewed guavas with cinnamon and nutmeg, sticky apple jams, and mango coconut curry, were lip-smacking good. Bananas and plantains are harvested throughout the year. Grandpa often decapitated the tree to accelerate its growth and fruit production. We had two kinds in our garden: the regular, large, yellow bananas also called Nendra and the tiny, Indian speciality–Velchi or cardamom bananas that tasted, for some mysterious reason like the spice they were named after. Grandpa sliced the colossal clusters off the tree and hung them from the ceiling fan in the veranda. They swung heavily and happily in the breeze and we stood beneath them, waiting for the fruit to ripen and fall into our eager hands. Grandma let us eat the first few dozen and then left the rest to blacken. These she peeled, mashed and caramelized with cardamom and ghee to make a sticky, sweet halwa.

Breakfast was always a special meal. If Grandma was in a good mood she made thalipeet.  A delicious bread that both South Indians and Konkanis claim as their own, thalipeet is made from rice, wheat and jowar flour. The three flours are kneaded into dough with chopped onions, spices and cilantro, then rolled out and cooked on a tawa or griddle, over a large, fresh plantain leaf with generous amounts of ghee. As the dough cooks it separates from the leaf, which is then peeled off. The flaky bread is eaten hot off the griddle with white butter and garlic chutney.

On Sunday mornings Grandma made dosas, rice crépes stuffed with turmeric potatoes. This preparation was elaborate and arduous. In the 1980s we didn't have electric grinders. The rice, mixed with urad dal (white split pea), had to be soaked in water overnight and ground to a fine paste by hand with a heavy, four-foot long stone pestle in a granite mortar. As Grandma's was the only home in the neighbourhood with such a contraption the other women cooks, led by Hajrat Bi, gathered over a weekend to help prepare this delicacy. They took turns, sifting, grinding and scraping the lentils. Every two hours they took a chai break, sipping the steaming brew from saucers and massaging their aching arms and legs. Hajrat Bi, who ate betel leaves all day long, sat on the floor and helped macerate the batter. Once the dosa batter was done the women divided it amongst themselves. They took it home and fermented the paste overnight. The following day, Sunday, it was spooned over sizzling hot iron griddles and spun in concentric circles to make crisp, round crépes. They were slapped with fiery red chutney and stuffed with turmeric potatoes.

Grandma prepared coconut chutney to accompany the
dosa, unlike any I have ever eaten. It was thick, red and
piquant. This chutney tasted great smeared inside toasted
sandwiches, with sliced cucumber and cheese, and when
added to thick yogurt, made a delicious dip for sliced
vegetables, fritters and pan-fried whole wheat breads.
Two months before the monsoons commenced their annual
trip through Belgaum, in early July, Grandma began her
papad-making. Unlike ladoos, papads have to be made
outdoors. As crisp as glass, as smooth as marble, piled one
on top of the other, the papad is an architectural wonder.

In the north and west of India, papads are made of lentils
like toor, masur, or gram, while in the south, they are called
papadams, and are often made with dried rice or split Bengal
gram. Rice papadams are best deep-fried.

On a dry, cloudless day, coir mats and huge dome-shaped
baskets made from straw were laid out on the mud floors of
the garden and held down by small rocks. A variety of spices,
fresh red chillies and fruits were strewn across them so they
could dehydrate in the sun. Red chillies, garlic, and bay leaves
were dried and used through the year. Dried raw mangoes
were grated and used to spice curries, ginger was powdered
to make chai masala, desiccated coconut and parched rice
was added to chiwda, and dried bananas were deep-fried to
make chips.

To make papads, the lentils were washed, dried in the sun,
powdered into paste and mixed with water to make a soft
dough. The women gathered in the early hours of the morning
over a period of six days and worked from dawn to dusk,
sifting, grinding, and rolling. They sat cross-legged, saris
drawn over knees, tongues wagging, hands never resting. The
papad dough was spiced with Tellicherry pepper, dried garlic
and cumin, then rolled out into paper-thin circles. These were

slapped onto the straw baskets, covered with sheets of muslin and left to harden. This took two or three days depending on the weather. The dried papads were then stored in large brass tins to be roasted or fried through the year. The dogs helped keep away hungry crows and pecking sparrows and my sister and I served refreshing limewater and tea to the battalion of papad rollers.

It was, of course, a matter of great misfortune if it rained. Grandma and Hajrat Bi ran helter-skelter, hastily collecting the half-dried papads and flying chillies in their sari pallus.

Every now and then, we'd also visit Grandma in the cooler months. Belgaum, being landlocked, had warm days and very cool December evenings.  When it rained, the temperature could fall to 12 degrees centigrade. There were also occasions when we'd have a hailstorm.  The hailstones, some the size of cherries, fell with loud smacks on our glass windows. My sister and I ran around the garden like dervishes, holding out steel bowls  to the sky, waiting for the ice to crash land.  Then we'd charge back into the house and pop them into our mouths like cold, crunchy candy. Grandpa disliked such weather because hailstones damaged young fruit. After such a storm it was not unusual to find dozens of dented mangoes and guavas lying about the garden.

\*\*\*

Electricity and water were always in short supply in Belgaum. It was not unusual to have only a few hours of hot water in the mornings and power in the evenings. On cooler, drier days if we had a power cut Grandpa lit a charcoal segdi (stove) on the front porch. We sat by it roasting peanuts and warming our toes. The moths gathered around the kerosene lamps and the sound of crickets and toads filled the air. In the distance you could hear the tinkling bells of cows and water buffaloes returning home from their grazing. There were always fireflies buzzing around the orchard. We'd scoop these wonders into little glasses, cover the tops quickly, and place them on our bedside tables, where they'd twinkle through the night. Dawn in Belgaum was as enchanting as dusk. I loved walking barefoot in the garden. The fading moon, hanging like a melon in the yard, and the grasshoppers making funny noises with their hind legs was so soothing, I'd often fall asleep on the porch until Brandy, our beloved mutt, licked my face awake.

Brandy was a stray and sick puppy when Hajrat Bi found him. She smuggled him into the house with Grandma's consent, but didn't dare tell Grandpa. Hajrat Bi nursed him back to health in the outhouse where she lived. When Grandpa discovered this little bundle he roared so loudly, the frightened pup peed all over his slippers.

For some unfathomable reason, this incident was the beginning of a deeply loving relationship. Brandy, as Grandpa named him, after the two pegs he drank every evening, became very attached to each other.

Commercial dog food was uncommon in India in the early 80s. Dogs ate leftover scraps; rice, bones and bread.  But since everyone in the family had special meals cooked for them, we felt Brandy deserved one too. Grandma collected pieces of chicken, bacon and mutton and boiled them with lentils, whole wheat and millet flour to make cookie dough. It was an exciting but difficult event for Brandy who'd sit outside the kitchen, drooling. As children we couldn't bear to see him like this. We'd walk by him and when no one was looking, drop a biscuit or a piece of dough close to his nose. Thirty years later I still cook meals for my dogs in the United States and here in Mumbai.

When Grandpa died, Brandy went just a little mad. He'd run around the house in a frenzy, looking everywhere for his master: the bedroom, the bathroom, the garage; he'd sniff his master's slippers, his robe, before finally falling down beside them in a futile heap. Sometimes we'd find him sitting by Grandpa's armchair, wailing.

A year later he died, on Grandpa's first death anniversary. Grandma found his beautiful white body under the guava tree in the front yard, where she had him buried. I returned the following summer to a very quiet house and discovered that Brandy was gone forever. I was terribly angry with Grandma. 'Why didn't you tell me, why', I kept asking. I felt I'd lost my dearest friend. I wept for hours. I wished I could have seen him one last time. Nobody understood how much I loved him. How he slept by my bedside and made me feel safe and happy. Brandy was never leashed and came and went from the house as he pleased. When my sister and I walked two miles to the local library, Brandy followed us. As he wasn't allowed inside he sat by the gate, sometimes an hour or two until we came out with our books. Then he escorted us home. When I was upset he came to me and licked my tears as if to say, 'Don't cry, I love you.'

\*\*\*

Grandpa's dislike of urban life explained his rural choices but I never understood why he didn't move back to Karwar, the home of our ancestors, where the family had its 100-year-old house.

He explained that Karwar was still a village, and he'd have nothing to do all day except fish and drink toddy. That didn't sound too bad to me! Belgaum, he felt was more 'developed', had a more tolerable water shortage problem, fewer blackouts and was close enough to Karwar to make frequent visits.

Our visits to our ancestral home were always opportunities to eat both estuary (the Kali river flows into the Arabian sea) and salt water fish: huge, lime-flavoured jumbo shrimp, turmeric-dipped pomfret (which tastes a bit like trout), and colossal mussels prepared with fresh coconut from our own trees and served on banana leaves with mounds of steamy rice.

Visits to Naganath, a Shiva temple in Karwar were planned as picnics. Devotees leave offerings of sugar and rice near the anthills. The ants are revered for their industry and are believed to be loyal servants of the King Cobra, a snake with mystical powers.

The old house we stayed in during those brief visits had innumerable rooms, most of which were never used, except every four years when the entire clan gathered for a family reunion. These reunions were wonderful, filled with laughter or occasional weeping when a relative narrated his misfortune, and many memorable meals.

Our family get-togethers comprised of two kinds of people: relatives (R) and not really relatives (NRR). The former consisted of those related by blood, however distant the common ancestor may have been, and the latter consisted of close friends, friends of close friends, friends of those related conjugally and so on. This differentiation was never, and is never, made verbally in an Indian household. So everyone, for the duration of the holiday, was a Mama, Tao, Tai, Maushi, Aka, Kaka and Atya. On one occasion, we counted forty-five such NRRs!

You could only tell the difference between Rs and NRRs in the disparate treatment of these two parties. Guests were treated better than family. The ancient Sanskrit shloka, 'Atithi Devo Bahv', (the guest is God) was taken very seriously. A guest or NRR would therefore be served before the family at a meal, and would be treated with more patience and indulgence than an errant son.

All these members came together under one umbrella, that of the patriarch of the family. The purpose of such gatherings, for us, when we were children, was to eat wonderful food, play hide-and-seek, be pampered with sweets and head massages by all the elders, and spend our time lolling in the orchard, reading comic books. Of course this was not the case for the adults. These gatherings were more than just fun. It gave them a chance to get to know new members, sort out family issues, help each other financially, and bond socially.

There were times when money was lent to a relative in trouble or a few strings were pulled to find someone a job. Often enough, it gave loved ones a chance to grieve together for the loss of a family member or to offer their congratulations and gifts to newlyweds, if they had missed the wedding.

It is true it takes all sorts to make this world. My Rs and NRRs who came together for these holidays were a loving, brilliant and, in some cases, utterly eccentric lot. I recall a Mama (NRR) who was kept away from all forms of public transport. This was because he had a tendency to randomly climb onto buses and trains that took him to unknown destinations. He would go missing, sometimes for weeks, and the police had to be called in to search for him. Sooner or later he was found, accidentally or because he called from another city or state, to say he didn't know how he got there. His wife lived in fear that someday he'd lose his memory long enough to forget he was married and take on a new wife.

Another, Kaki (NRR), loved collecting recipes from all her relatives during our holiday but refused to share any of her own. Grandma once said it was a good thing, because she was such a lousy cook.

A Tao (NRR), refused to drink anything unless it was a clear liquid. He strained everything: tea, coffee, lassi, lentils, even curries, several times before he consumed them. It was a very strange sight to see him sitting at the table with a dozen strainers and pots and pans while we ate our meals. When the women offered to cook him clear soups he was mortally offended. He said it would deprive him of the pleasures of their wonderful cooking.

A cousin (R) adopted stray animals, not for herself, but for other family members. So before you knew it you'd find yourself the guardian of a stray cow, maybe even two. During one vacation, I remember two dogs, a cat, a goat, and a buffalo sunning their bodies in our backyard as family elders looked on in dismay.

Our Karwar family home was, in one word, mammoth. A crumbling ruin of stone and brick with huge windows, archways, long corridors lined with rooms, and heavy wooden doors with crusty, cast-iron latches. From the windows hung cumbersome bamboo drapes that were rolled up in the morning to let in the sun and rolled down in the afternoon to make the room dark for pleasant naps. Huge glass lamps in many colours–peacock blue, verdant green and saffron yellow–hung from the impossibly high ceilings. Every night the women flung open the vast windows and put up the moth screens. The candles in the lamps were lit and they swung happily in the summer breeze to the tune of moths and chattering children. Aunts and older cousins took turns letting the lamps down from the ceiling before they lit them and drew them up again. Most walls were whitewashed, dotted with shabby but smiling photos of my ancestors. I always marvelled at their magnificent moustaches, starched caps and serpentine turbans.
The women wore luminous silk saris and nose-rings so pendulous they looked like harnesses for a camel race. What I admired so much about those pictures was the extent of their embrace. They encapsulated huge families

drawn tightly together, as one would imagine matchsticks in a box. They were all crammed into one, tiny frame and into an even tinier moment, made possible by the quick flash of a bulb so that a century later we might remember them and all the good they stood for.  Not a single member, however distantly related, was ever left out or forgotten. When I sit down with some of these photos, it takes an hour for Grandma to identify the sixty-odd people in a single frame; who they were, what they did, and the memorable tidbits about their lives.

The photography session always caused a flutter in the family. Aunties took out their best saris and jewellery, the men had the barber come in to give them a shave, and the dhobi came in to steam and iron their turbans and starch their black caps. The courtyard teemed with such excitement you would think we were all going to a wedding.

Nai Golé was the family barber. His father and grandfathers had shaved, cut, twirled, and shaped our ancestors' moustaches. Dressed in a dhottar, a muslin garment wrapped around and then between his legs, and a long shirt, he would arrive at the house at seven in the morning on his bicycle to which, was strapped a big brass box. Nai always came to the house after his prayers at the temple, his head anointed with vermilion powder. When he arrived, he left his slippers and cycle at the door and went to the kitchen for his breakfast. Nai Golé was respected in our family. Grandpa thought of him as an artist as skilled in his trade as our family jeweller or tailor or sari weaver. It was understood that Grandma was to put him in a good mood before he began work on Grandpa's precious hair.

Nai Golé's moods had a devastating effect on his work. I remember on one occasion my cousin Arun let the air out of his cycle tyres. Nai Golé massacred three family moustaches and gave an uncle what looked like a receding hairline. But on good days he worked magic on the men. Moustaches glistened, hair bristled with alertness and muscles and nerves were massaged into quivering, ecstatic, mounds of jelly. Treatment from Nai Golé demanded an early morning nap–it was not humanly possible to do anything else. The way to Nai Golé's heart was through his stomach. He loved Grandma's cumin-flavoured aambodés accompanied by sweet-and-sour coconut chutney, finished off with steaming mint-flavoured chai. After a hearty breakfast he rubbed his stomach, expelled a few appreciative burps, and then began work. We loved watching Nai in action. He took his shirt off, under which he wore a vest, and said a small prayer to the photo of Goddess Parvati pasted on his mirror. He oiled his body from head to toe, as if he were a wrestler waiting to jump into the ring, making loud, slapping sounds as he slathered oil on his arms and legs. Like his father, he was a small, bald, burly man with hands as large as his feet. His most prominent feature was his perfectly round paunch. Cousin Arun said Nai looked like he had swallowed a football.

His brass box contained the tools of his trade: razors in all sizes, shiny blades, sponges, creams, lotions, tweezers, long metal ear buds and many other interesting and daunting instruments. Nai Golé didn't just cut and shape hair. He gave his customers a veritable facial, massage and most importantly, the town's latest gossip. And, if you were a favoured client, a few pearls of wisdom in the form of Marathi metaphors. His scissors made little clicking noises and he worked with immense speed. He always sang when he was working. Fortunately for his clients he had a wonderful voice–rich, deep and tuneful. Like many artists, he didn't like suggestions. He cut hair the way he thought best.

The dhobi was also invited to the house for the photo sessions. Again, his family had been close to ours for several generations. Dhobi Mangal Malekar drove a bullock cart to work. A cycle would have been too small for his gargantuan

iron steamers, sacks of coal and ironing boards. Mangal
Malekar loved his bullocks, Ramu and Shyamu, like a father
loves his children. Bullocks he said were unappreciated
animals. With a sturdy and stoic demeanour, a black velvet
coat and a deep, guttural cry, they merit much more respect
and attention. It was said that when Ramu fell sick, Mangal
carried him on a sled strapped to his shoulders for a distance
of ten miles, in the rain, to the local doctor. When the
local doctor told him he didn't know how to treat animals,
Malekar threatened to run an extra hot iron over him if he
didn't cure his bullock.  It was not unusual for townsfolk to
be intimidated by this laundry man; at six–foot-two he was
at least four inches taller than the tallest man in Karwar. But
for all his legendary aggression he was a gentle giant when
it came to animals and children. He loved coming to our
home for the photo sessions. It gave him an opportunity to do
some of his favourite things: treating Ramu and Shyamu to
sugarcane which Grandma kept ready, playing ball with the
children, and most of all, baiting and taunting Nai Golé. Our
barber may have been a temperamental artist who wreaked
havoc with his appliances, but he was no match for Mangal
Malekar. The mention of his name made Nai Golé wince.
He became extremely nervous, which meant, again, that
he was unable to focus on his work. On one occasion when
their paths crossed in our home, Nai became so upset he
abandoned my uncle's shave and left him with half a beard.

It was therefore a necessary logistical exercise to make
sure their paths did not cross on these days. Granny called
the barber to the house four hours before Mangal Malekar
and most often, Nai Golé had finished his work before his
nemesis came through the door

Our home in Karwar was beautiful in a shabby, comfortable
way. The floors of the mansion were resplendent with mosaic
tiles that twinkled in the dark like a starry sky. As children,

we slept on the floor, on warm, soft cotton-stuffed mattresses while the grown-ups slept in beds, so colossal they could have easily squeezed a dozen eight-year-olds in their fluffy depths. The beds resembled dinosaurs, with huge wooden legs and creaky four-posters curving towards the ceiling. They were draped with white mosquito nets that fluttered around their ankles at night, keeping creepy crawlies at bay. Like the beds, the cupboards were also carved from rich, long-grained, chocolaty wood, with enamel work and bevelled mirrors. They made the perfect hiding place when we played chor-police and hide-and-seek. Graceful and solid, so lovingly carved, they looked like wise old men watching us grow up and make our way in the world. If I'd had my way, I'd have put them into our family photographs. A big one next to Grandpa and a small one beside me.

Sometimes, on a particularly quiet night when we lay snuggled in bed, we heard little sounds coming from them: a squeak, a tiny shudder, a sigh.

'Is there a ghost inside Grandma?' my sister asked.

'No ghosts in this house. They were so frightened of your grandfather they all ran away. The cupboards are talking to each other,' Grandma explained. 'They are trees after all. With life still in them.'

'What do they talk about, Nani?'

'About the forests they come from. During the monsoons they are happier being here in the house where it is dry, but in the summer they prefer to be out on the hill tops enjoying the warmth and cool breeze.'

The house was originally built with two kitchens, one strictly vegetarian and the other non-vegetarian where eggs and fish were permitted. But after the passing of our more orthodox ancestors the vegetarian one was turned into a stable for cows. The kitchen was on the first floor and opened into a large open courtyard, a form of architecture that enabled joint families to gather in the courtyard, and even sleep there on particularly warm nights.

The courtyard functioned as a conduit for exchanges, gossip, and communication between the myriad rooms that lined it on all four sides. It also facilitated the easy transportation of hot, steaming food from the kitchen, onto our plates and into our hungry mouths.

In all Indian joint families there is a feeding hierarchy. In ours, the head of the family, the patriarch, my grandfather, sat in the centre. On his left sat the men from the paternal side of the family and on his right the maternal. So if you were Grandma's cousin you sat on the right and the older you were the closer you got to be to my grandfather. Might I add that in this hierarchy, the women typically ate after the men but in my family, it tended to be less enforced. My grandfather was a progressive man. Before every meal he made the obligatory gesture of inviting the women to eat with him. Grandma, a very practical woman always refused because it was impossible to serve thirty-five men and feed oneself at the same time. The patriarch, being in the centre, was always served first, and it was untraditional for anyone to get up and leave until he had finished eating. Two mats were laid out for each person. A thin coir mat to eat on and a low square wooden stool called a chowpat or chowrang, to sit on.  On special occasions, a large, silver taat about fifteen inches in diameter was laid out on the coir. On its shiny surface were placed four vatis, or tiny cups, later to be filled with gravy-based dishes. The chowrang was adorned with rangoli, religious drawings made with coloured powder. Incense sticks were lit and waved about the room and freshly-plucked flowers were placed on every taat.

On regular days, freshly-cut banana leaves were washed with a combination of lime juice and tamarind and used instead. Since everyone ate with their hands there was no need for cutlery. Every male member who sat down to eat was also furnished with a tumbler for drinking water, and a small bowl of saffron water. Between every course he could dip his fingers in this water so the flavours of the previous dish would not interfere with what followed. The patriarch was the only one who never poured his own water. The youngest daughter-in-law stood by to refill his cup.

The men mostly wore long-sleeved shirts and dhottars. Headgear and slippers were forbidden during meals. First a lota, a washing basin and a towel was passed outward from the centre to the single file of men so hands could be washed and faces rinsed. Then the youngest woman in the household (you had to be over thirteen to qualify for the job) began by serving the patriarch two chutneys: one coconut and the other a lime or vegetable pickle. Then the other women in the family, in ascending order of age, served him the remaining dishes. First came the fritters, or anything deep-fried, followed by the non-vegetarian dishes—fish, lamb or chicken. The vegetarian dishes were also served in a particular order. The gravies, lentils and curries came first, followed by the dry vegetable preparations and finally, the breads. On an average day there were at least five entrées, four side dishes and four condiments on the menu.

First, Grandpa took a little water from his silver tumbler and sprinkled it around his plate, offering thanks to God for the food. Then he ate a single morsel from his plate. It was the signal that the rest of the party could now be served. The women stood in single file, carrying hot and heavy pots with ladles, tongs and spoons, moving as quickly as they could so the food was not cold by the time everyone had been served.

Finally everyone would eat. A woman's job was to refill a plate before the guest asked for more. So the women made several trips to and from the kitchen, reheating, refilling, and passing around freshly-made hot breads. It was not uncommon for them to be sweating profusely from this activity, wiping their brows with the ends of their saris. When I turned thirteen I was instructed in their ways. I was surprised how difficult this was. To bend my knees whilst carrying heavy pots and serve people exact quantities of gravy and rice without spilling any of it was hard enough but to do it wearing a sari was hell! During this meal, Grandma sat on a wooden stool, fanning herself with a bamboo fan. Her years of serving and cleaning up were done, and it was her place to supervise the cooking and administer the meals. The only task she undertook was serving the rice. When Grandpa had finished with his bread, a pot of hot rice was brought out and Grandma served him from it. Only then were the younger members in the family permitted to begin the rice course.

As you can imagine, these occasions took much energy and planning especially during family get-togethers. On one Sunday, I counted ninety-one family members – twenty-three men were served a complete meal, in this fashion, in four separate sittings.

After the men had retired for their afternoon naps, the women finished their meals and retired to the common room. One must not forget that the children were fed before the men, and supervising twenty-five boys and girls was no easy task. I recall the moans and groans the women uttered in Marathi as they got down on the floor and rested their aching backs. Sometimes they would warm wooden rolling pins over a fire and ask the children to run them over their sore backs.

As children, if our family reunions coincided with Ganesh Chaturti, it was culinary utopia. Lord Ganesh, the son of Shiva the Destroyer, is among the most loved of Hindu gods revered as the Remover of Obstacles.

The celebration of Ganesh Chaturti can last two weeks for some families. Huge deities of the god are worshipped, and then finally, sunk in the ocean with pomp and ceremony. Lord Ganesh has two passions: food and food. The rotund god, whose image has become a universal art form, is presented with fruits, modaks and milk baths during the holiday. Grandma made the most wonderful modaks, steamed rice dumplings stuffed with coconut, saffron and almonds. These delights are served warm, with a delicious shira, cardamom-flavoured semolina and a light usal of baby peas seasoned with cumin.

The Ganesh arti, or prayer, is fairly long, and until it's done no one is permitted to eat. The food must first be offered to Lord Ganesh, who will bless it, after which it is ready for mortal consumption.

How we envied him as children, this dimpled, smiling God, seated or supine, depending on the artist who had fashioned him from clay, surrounded by luscious bananas, mounds of dry fruits, the choicest modaks and shira. To be Ganesh for a day was better than being king.

An aunt recounted a story (I'm sure it's been embellished but that's what makes it so much fun). During one such celebration in Karwar. an NRR whom the children were instructed to call Kaka came to stay for Ganpati puja. He spent most of his time bragging about his success in the sporting arena. He described himself as a champion cyclist, a keen wrestler, and even went so far as to tell us that had he taken his swimming seriously, he would have won an Olympic medal. The family listened to this spiel while he stuffed his face with ladoos and mithais my grand-aunts served him, commenting on how the desserts in his hometown were so much better.

Every year the family especially ordered the deity of Ganesh. For this occasion, it was eight feet tall and ten feet wide. Lord Ganesh had been moulded and cast on a huge mud pedestal.

He sat there, happily, in the middle of our courtyard, covered in silken robes, garlands of flowers, and mountains of food. The arti was a huge event with as many as two hundred people in attendance. By the time the day of visarjan or immersion arrived, the children had all become so attached to this benevolent figure that some of them became distraught at the thought of his imminent departure.

A truck pulled up at the front gates of the house and several members of the family lifted the mammoth statue and loaded it onto the vehicle. Whilst family members were straining under the weight of this task, Kaka tried to look busy  by belting orders at everyone. Finally everyone got into the truck and left for the river Kalinadi, about an hour away, where Lord Ganesh would be set afloat. The deity would drift for a few miles and then sink.

The submersion was a crowded and difficult affair as many other families had gathered to do the same with their gods. After it was over, the family got into the truck to start for home. At this point, they noticed Kaka was missing. They assumed he must have either not left with them, or gone off on his own to enjoy the festivities.

When the group returned home they discovered he wasn't there either. After an hour or so the family began to worry and went back to look for him. It turned out that Kaka, after a huge lunch, had fallen asleep in the truck, on the pedestal, under Lord Ganesh's robes! Unseen by anyone, they had submerged him, along with the clay god. When they arrived at the banks of the river they found him hanging on to Lord Ganesh for dear life as he floated away towards the sea. It turned out that our freestyle champion was terrified of water!

My Grandpa enjoyed many such family reunions before he died at sixty-nine. He left the world as quietly as he had returned from war. He was sitting in his armchair, his faithful dog Brandy at his feet, having a drink with his doctor when the clock struck seven and a tiny vessel in his brain imploded. He entered peacefully into the cycle of karma or hopefully was liberated from it. For three days in protest of his passing and in her anger and despair at being abandoned by her only devotion, my grandmother flouted every rule he had ever set in their home. She drank tea at lunch, she showered in the evenings and ate eggs and toast for dinner. She imagined the Admiral smacking his baton in angry disbelief as he looked down from heaven. 'Well you shouldn't have left me,' she'd say, looking upwards.

I didn't get to say goodbye to my grandfather, to the man who thought I made the best masala scrambled eggs in the world. I would have loved to spoil him with my cooking, had he lived longer.

As children we never realized how fortunate we were to grow up with plenty to eat, in a privileged world where we were not discriminated against on account of our caste or class. But in India, for millions of people food is a prized commodity and dignity, a rare object. There are still kitchens where Indians are denied entry because of their caste, schools where 'untouchable' children may not eat with the rest and colonies of widows, half starved and forgotten.

The year Grandpa died, my grandmother decided she would never cook again. I began, at this time, to cook with greater purpose. I think I had a subliminal need to preserve family traditions, so many of which have their roots in our kitchen. With time many of these traditions have changed, some are gone forever like lamps set afloat in the sea, never to return. But I am trying to make new ones and also keeping some of the old ones alive, whether I'm in my kitchen in New York or Mumbai, Boston or Belgaum. And I am glad to say that many of our new customs are better than the ones of yore because they respect not just the food we cook but also the human being who eats it, irrespective of his position in society.

# BRIGHT
# AND EARLY
# **BREAKFAST**

Breakfast was always at 8.30 a.m. and always at the dining table. Forks, knives and serviettes for a king's breakfast or a taat with vatis for an Indian one. We never ate cereal; porridge never touched our lips; and we'd never heard of skimmed milk. Instead, it was an entirely home-cooked meal; in Grandpa's words, a 'zabardast' or vigorous start to the day.

Several dishes such as pohé or beaten rice and thalipeet or multi-grain flatbread, were also prepared as tea time snacks. They were however, never served for lunch. Even today, when I order pohé for a quick lunch from the Zunka Bhakar stall below my apartment building, I smile, knowing Grandpa would not approve.

# DOUBLE ROTI UPAMA

## COOKED BREAD SALAD
### 4 SERVINGS

*Like panzanella and bread and butter pudding, this is a great way to use day-old bread.*

### INGREDIENTS
360-400 gms 2-day-old bread
¾ cup finely chopped red or white onions
1 tsp turmeric powder
1 tsp or more cayenne pepper powder or red chilli powder
1 tsp salt or to taste
1 tsp sugar or to taste

### TEMPERING
4 tbsp vegetable oil
½ tsp black mustard seeds
1 tsp husked, split black gram or urad dal
A pinch of asafoetida powder
3-4 green chillies, 1½"- 2" long, chopped
12 fresh curry leaves, torn

### GARNISH
1 tbsp fresh; or frozen, defrosted, unsweetened coconut
Juice of 1 lime
1 tbsp finely chopped fresh coriander leaves

### METHOD
Slice off and discard the crusts and cut the bread into ½" cubes.

Heat the oil for the tempering in a kadhai or wok on high heat. Add the tempering spices and sauté for 30-60 seconds.

Reduce heat to medium and add onions. When they turn light brown, add the bread pieces. Sprinkle in the spice powders, salt and sugar and toss well. Add 2-3 tbsp of water.

Cover and cook on low heat for 5 minutes.

Uncover, stir and cook for another 5-7 minutes, till the bread turns golden and crisp at the edges.

Garnish with coconut, lime juice and coriander leaves.

Serve warm with tea or coffee.

# BASMATI PULAO WITH BUTTERED EGGS AND FRIED ONIONS

## 6 SERVINGS

*This dish may sound strange but it's so addictive and so easy to make you'll want it all the time. We ate this on mornings after a dinner party because there was always basmati pulao left over. Grandma made a mountain of rice on each plate with a well in the centre, plopped a crisp, fried egg into it and topped it off with paper-thin, fried onions.*

### INGREDIENTS
2 cups basmati rice
4 tbsp butter, ghee or vegetable oil
1" stick cinnamon
4 black peppercorns
3 cloves
1 dried bay leaf
½ tsp salt or to taste
6 tbsp butter, ghee or vegetable oil
6 eggs or more
red chilli powder to taste
salt to taste

### TO SERVE
1 cup thinly sliced and deep-fried onions

## METHOD
### Pulao
Wash the rice and soak it in water for 2 hours. Drain and dry completely using clean kitchen towels.

Heat the butter, ghee or oil in a large pan on medium heat. Add the whole spices and sauté for 1 minute.

Remove the whole spices with a slotted spoon and discard.

Gently stir the dried rice into the hot spiced butter, ghee or oil for about 1 minute.

Add 4 cups of boiling water and the salt. Stir gently. Cover and cook for about 6 minutes on medium heat, till tender and fluffy.

Switch off the heat and let the pulao rest for 10-12 minutes. Fluff up with a fork.

### Eggs
In a very hot skillet melt 1 tbsp of butter, ghee or oil. Fry one egg till its edges are crisp. Sprinkle chilli powder and salt over the yolk. Repeat with remaining eggs.

### TO SERVE
Place a cup of pulao on each plate. Make a well in the centre.

Put an egg in the well and top generously with fried onions.

# BUTTER AND POTATO TASTY TOASTS

## 2 SERVINGS

*A tasty toast is an Indian-style panini, except it's cooked on the stove top in a cast iron sandwich press. You can also use an electric sandwich maker. Nothing beats the combination of boiled potatoes and salty butter. Indian butter is salted but if you use unsalted butter you can either use a saltier cheese or season the potatoes separately.*

### INGREDIENTS

2 tbsp unsalted butter + more for cooking
4 slices sandwich bread, crusts removed
2 tbsp grated salted, mild, white Cheddar cheese (optional)
1-2 green chillies, 1½"-2" long, finely chopped
1 small brown potato, boiled, peeled, cut in ¼" rounds
salt to taste

### METHOD

Butter the bread slices on one side.

Place a slice in the sandwich maker, buttered side down.

Spread half the cheese (if used) and the green chillies over the bread.

Cover with half the potato and dot with some butter and salt lightly; use less salt if the cheese is heavily salted.

Top with another slice of bread, buttered side up. Press together and toast on low heat, till golden brown; or follow the instructions for the sandwich maker.

Cut in half and serve warm.

Repeat for the second sandwich.

# VIMALA TAI'S CHILLI SCRAMBLED EGGS

## 8 SERVINGS

### INGREDIENTS

8 eggs
4 green chillies,
1½"-2" long, slit
½ cup cream or malai
from the top of boiled milk
¼ tsp salt
2 tbsp butter,
preferably unsalted

*These eggs are simply delicious with griddled bread like gutli pao.*

*My paternal grandmother told me that the best way to get creamy scrambled eggs is to first stir the eggs in a hot pan with the heat off, then stir them again on low heat.*

### METHOD

Whisk the eggs, cream and salt together in a bowl, till smooth.

Melt the butter in a large skillet on medium heat. Add the green chillies and sauté, till the butter begins to brown.

Turn the heat off and stir in the eggs. Stir vigorously to prevent them from sticking to the bottom of the skillet. Scrape the sides with your spatula.

Turn the heat on to low and continue stirring, till you have the desired consistency.

Taste for salt. Serve immediately.

# POLÉ
## Crêpes

Pan-fried crêpes called dosai in Kerala are called polo and dosa
in the Konkan region, where they are popular fare. In Marathi, a
wadi can also mean a small pan-fried pancake, such as a besan
wadi or a varhadi patoli made with gram flour or besan.

Karnataka, not Tamil Nadu, is arguably the dosa's birthplace
and it is made with a variety of whole grains, rice and pulses
— chickpea, horse gram and moong — and also with semolina
and pithiya or pre-ground flour mixes. Polé in the Konkan can
be made with more exotic ingredients such as watermelon rind,
jackfruit and tapioca.

Most dosas or polé involve natural fermentation and some have
a leavening agent like toddy, yeast or baking soda but a wadi
doesn't. Dosas are consumed for lunch, breakfast and as a snack,
though some, like the Konkani doddak, made with beaten rice
and creamed semolina is strictly breakfast fare, while surnoli,
a spongy pancake made with maggé or orange cucumber,
sweetened with jaggery and yogurt, is always served as a snack.

Dosas are largely egg-less crêpes in different sizes and can be
crisp and lacy, or thick and soft; extremely large, like the paper
dosa or small like a Kerala lentil dosai. Some, like the Kerala
muthai, use whipped eggs in their batter; and Kerala appams or
hoppers are served with meat curries. But in the Konkan, they
are traditionally pure vegetarian fare.

Benné dosa made with white butter, soyi polo with tender
coconut and sanna polo, made with lentils and rice are

specialities of the Konkan region. Kemunda polo is made with the inner white rind of a watermelon and kuwepitta polo with arrowroot flour. Paan polo is the Konkan's most unique dosa with a crisp exterior and a soft interior studded with pores.

Ramdan is a Konkani polo that requires each dosa to be individually seasoned as it cooks, while for most other polé, the tempered spices are stirred into the batter. Idli batters are often converted into polo batter by adding spices and chopped vegetables.

In Konkan homes, polé are served with a variety of condiments, butter, ghee, coconut or coriander chutney, jaggery, treacle, honey, choon, a dried spice mix like lasnachi chutney, an Andhra podi like gunpowder or a liquid saar.

In Tamil Nadu, further south, sautéed potato and sambhar serve as accompaniments with white coconut chutney.

Dosas are stuffed with vegetables, the batter is mixed with purées and spices and in the case of the Karnataka Mysore dosa, a spice paste is slathered over the crêpe as it cooks.

Dosa recipes may appear simple, some call for only rice, water and salt but don't be fooled, they require tremendous skill and experience. Each recipe has variations in technique, fermentation time and slightly different methods of spreading, frying and folding. Some batters are poured into the centre of the frying pan and spread outwards with a ladle, some are thick and are cooked like an American pancake, others like ramdan are made in a kadhai or wok, while some like surnoli are cooked on one side only. Salt is added at different stages, some batters call for salt during the fermentation process, to inhibit the production of gluten, while others contain no salt and are served with salted butter.

Dosas require a sturdy grinder or food processor capable of grinding grains to fine powders and batters. I recommend non-stick pans to beginners because a dosa tawa or cast iron griddle requires more skill and needs more oil.

# PAAN POLÉ
## Rice Crêpes

**MAKES 6-7
6" ROUND CREPES**

### INGREDIENTS
1 cup inexpensive medium
grain rice, washed and soaked
in water overnight
2 tbsp fresh grated coconut,
ground to a paste (optional)
½ tsp salt
vegetable oil as required

*These delicate crepes are folded into a triangle
to resemble a betel nut leaf preparation called
paan and are very popular fare in Konkan homes.
Serve this with methkoot and white butter or with
xacuti, koddel, ghashi or any gravy dish. If you
have never made polé or dosas before, opt for a
good quality non-stick pan instead of a traditional
cast-iron griddle. Can be made ahead and warmed
in a covered dish in the microwave.*

### METHOD
Wash the soaking rice and drain completely.
Pulse and grind to a powder in a  food processor
for 3-4 minutes.

Add water 2 tbsp at a time to create a thick,
smooth, grain-free batter. Add up to 2 cups
of water.

Cover and ferment overnight in an oversized
bowl, in a cool and dry place.

Grind coconut to a smooth paste. Stir coconut
and salt into fermented, puffy batter with a
whisk. Add more water if required to create a
batter the consistency of whole milk.

Heat a 7"-8" wide non-stick pan on high heat.
Add ½ tsp cooking oil. Take the pan off the heat
with your left hand and pour ½ cup of batter
into it.

Swivel it around quickly to spread it evenly
and thinly across the pan. The batter will sizzle
and bubble.

Cook till the top is dry and the bottom is crisp
and very lightly browned. If your crepé is too
thick you will need to flip it and cook it on both
sides, otherwise fold it over into a triangle twice
and serve warm.

Repeat with remaining batter.

# HARA BHARA OMELETTE
## Omelette Stuffed with Green Herbs

**4 SERVINGS**

### INGREDIENTS

4 small green tomatoes
2 long (about 4"-5") Goa green chillies or jalapenos
2 tsp finely chopped fresh dill leaves or sepu
1 tbsp chopped fresh coriander leaves
2 green onion bulbs, finely sliced in rings
juice of 1 lime
½ tsp salt + extra
¼ tsp turmeric powder
¼ cup fresh, hung yogurt or Mexican crema, whipped
4-8 tsp butter or vegetable oil
8 eggs, whisked

### METHOD

Char the green tomatoes and the long chillies on an open fire using tongs. When cool scrape the charred skin off the green tomatoes.

Chop and mix the peeled tomatoes and chillies with their charred skin.

Add the fresh herbs, green onions, lime juice and salt. Cover and refrigerate for 6 hours or overnight.

Remove, keep covered and let it reach room temperature in the morning or whenever you feel like an omelette.

Put a small skillet on high heat. When hot, switch off the heat and add the turmeric powder. Let the turmeric powder and pan cool. Stir in the hung yogurt.

Put an omelette pan on low heat. Add 2 tsp of butter or oil.

Whisk 2 eggs with a pinch of salt and pour it into the pan. Swirl to spread as evenly as possible.

When the omelette is cooked, spread a few spoons of the herbs and some hung yogurt on to it. Fold and slide on to a plate.

Serve hot with pieces of fresh kadak pao, baguette or Portuguese buns. Enjwaaaay!

# IDLI
# Steamed Rice
# and Lentil Cakes

One of my French teachers at cooking school once told me, 'Never mess with ze baguette.'

Well you don't mess with the idli either, monsieur. A grainy idli will be jettisoned with the same contempt and rage by a south Indian as a soggy baguette by a Frenchman.

Idlis are an institution in coastal southern India. Every state specialises in different shapes and flavours — flat, round, stuffed, buttered, spiced, idli fry, button, kanchipuram, tatté and many more.

Since part of the Konkan stretches into Karnataka, the idli is integral to Konkan cuisine. Idlis in the Konkan come in varying shapes. Undiyo or dumplings are made from idli batter; the dough is shaped like a ball with a small hole in the centre and pressure-cooked. Some, like kotté, are steamed in turmeric and jackfruit leaves that give them a delicate fruity flavour.

Sanna idli is prepared in Karnataka and Goa by adding toddy, fermented palm sap, to the rice batter. Yeast is used as a substitute. Sanna idlis are smoother and spongier than Madras idlis with a white, shiny appearance and a mildly tangy flavour. They are round, but unlike other idlis, these are uniformly thick like a round brick and are cooked in a special steamer with deep pockets like flan cups.

Sandan is possibly the most popular idli in the Konkan made with various grains, horse gram, semolina and dried green peas. Sandan was traditionally prepared in an atti, a huge metal pot with small compartments called gindals that were lined with muslin cloth, leaves or ghee to lubricate the batter as it steamed.

You will need a good, heavy-duty grinder to make a smooth, grain-free batter and a steamer, pressure cooker with a suitable stand for the batter or an idli cooker. I use cream of rice or idli rava instead of raw rice because it is easier to grind and requires less fermentation.

# MASALA SANDAN
## Semolina Cakes with Cashewnut, Tamarind and Ghee

### MAKES 6-7 SANDAN
### 3"- 4" ROUND

*These are scrumptious. Serve them warm with a dollop of ghee and white Karwar chutney.*

### INGREDIENTS

1 cup rice semolina or rava/sooji
1 cup husked, split black gram or urad dal
¼ tsp baking soda
2 tbsp grated fresh; or frozen, defrosted, unsweetened coconut
2 green chillies, 1"- 1½" long, finely chopped
2 tbsp finely chopped red or white onion
2 tsp finely chopped fresh coriander leaves
½ tsp tamarind paste
ghee for serving

### TEMPERING

2 tbsp ghee
2 dried red Kashmiri chillies, stalks removed, torn to pieces
½ tsp husked, split Bengal gram or chana dal
10-12 cashewnut pieces, unsalted, raw

### METHOD

Wash the semolina and urad dal separately and soak each in 1 cup of water for 2 hours.

Drain the rice and urad dal. Wash and drain again.

Grind together for about 10 minutes to make a smooth paste. Gradually add up to 1 cup of water and stir periodically, to facilitate the grinding. Stir in baking soda. Ferment in a large, covered bowl overnight.

Heat the ghee for tempering in a small skillet and sauté the red chillies and gram, till golden. Add the cashewnuts and switch off the heat. Reserve.

Stir the tempered ingridents and remaining ingredients except the ghee, into the batter.

Pour into 3"- 4" round idli containers and steam for 20-22 minutes on low to medium heat, till fluffy and cooked through

Serve hot with ghee.

# POHÉ
# Parched
# /Beaten Rice

Pohé, phove or beaten or parched white rice is made both sweet and savoury and is possibly the Konkan's most commonly consumed dish.

Sweet pohé in our family was prepared for Janmashtami, Lord Krishna's birthday. The parched rice was mixed in coconut milk and jaggery. Extra-thin parched rice, also called nylon rice, does not need as much active cooking as thick-cut parched rice, so several raw pohé recipes call for a fine cut of pohé, which is either soaked or washed in water or another liquid to cook it. Salted Karwari pohé is made by smoking extra-thin parched rice with a hot coal and coconut oil. We also make a dahi pohé, where thin parched rice is soaked and stirred into thick curd, with coconut and green chillies.

For religious holidays in the Konkan, pohé is prepared without onions. Phodniché or tempered kandé pohé is cooked by frying spices in hot oil and actively cooking the parched rice in the spiced oil. Conservative, arranged marriages in the Konkan are colloquially referred to as 'kandé pohé' ceremonies. The prospective bride offers the spiced rice to her future in-laws who eat it, not only as a token of hospitality but also to judge her cooking skills!

# PHODNICHÉ KANDÉ POHÉ

## Parched Rice with Caramelised Onions

### 6 SERVINGS

### INGREDIENTS

2 cups raw, thick-cut parched rice or pohé
¼ cup finely chopped red or white onions
2 small cooking potatoes, peeled, diced into ½" cubes, soaked in water
1 tsp cayenne pepper powder or red chilli powder
½ tsp turmeric powder
¼ cup unsalted, roasted peanuts (optional)
¼ cup cooked green peas (optional)
1½ tsp kitchen salt or to taste
1 tsp grated jaggery or sugar or to taste

### TEMPERING

¼ cup vegetable oil
¾ tsp black mustard seeds
a pinch of asafoetida powder
2 green chillies, 1½"- 2" long, finely chopped
8-10 fresh curry leaves, torn

### OPTIONAL GARNISHES

Juice of a ¼ lime
2 tbsp chopped fresh coriander leaves
2 tbsp grated fresh; or frozen, defrosted, unsweetened coconut

### METHOD

Wash the rice quickly in running water. Then drain for 30 minutes in the colander. The rice will soften and puff up.

Put the oil for the tempering in a large kadhai, wok or pan on high heat. When hot, add the tempering spices.

When the spices begin to splutter, sauté the onions, till translucent.

Add the drained potatoes and spice powders and continue to cook for 3-4 minutes, till the potatoes soften and onions caramelise. Add ½-1 cup of water to prevent burning. Cook till the potatoes are tender and dry.

Add the drained rice, turmeric powder, peanuts, green peas (if used), salt and jaggery or sugar and stir well.

Reduce heat to low, sprinkle 3-4 tbsp of water and cover. Sprinkle 2 tbsp of cold water over the lid also. Cook for 6-10 minutes. Stir periodically and add a little water if required.

The rice should be soft, light and fluffy. If not, add more water a little at a time, and continue cooking. Switch off the heat.

Stir in lime juice, coriander leaves and coconut, as you like.

Taste and add more salt or sweetener.

# MASALA PANEER ON GRILLED BREAD

## 10 SERVINGS

*This masala paneer can also be used to make tasty toasts, canapés and cocktail samosé; or serve it on Melba toast as an appetiser.*

### INGREDIENTS

5 square breakfast rolls, gutli pao or Portuguese rolls
Butter to spread on rolls
2 tbsp vegetable oil
¼ tsp turmeric powder
½ cup finely chopped red onions
2 green bird chillies, finely chopped
½" fresh ginger root, peeled, finely grated
1¼ cups crumbled, fresh paneer
1 tbsp tomato paste or ketchup
1 tbsp chopped fresh coriander leaves
¼ tsp cayenne pepper powder or red chilli powder
½ tsp lemon or lime juice
salt to taste

### METHOD

Slice the bread rolls in half so that you have 2 flat surfaces. Spread the butter on both sides of the pieces.

Put the rolls under a medium hot grill, till crisp and golden.

Heat the oil in small skillet. Add the turmeric powder, onions, chillies and ginger. Sauté for about 2 minutes on high heat, stirring continuously.

Reduce heat and add the crumbled paneer. Mix well.

Stir in the tomato paste or ketchup, coriander leaves, cayenne pepper powder and lemon or lime juice.

Add salt to taste.

Spread over the buttered and grilled rolls and serve.

# NIZAMI EGG PARATHA WITH VINEGAR ONIONS

### MAKES 6 PARATHAS
### 6" WIDE

*Simply delicious! Inspired by the culinary genius of the Nizami chefs of Golconda and Bijapur, a few hours drive from the Konkan coast near Karnataka, this is a fabulous egg roll. Good for breakfast, lunch and dinner. If making the patrel dough is too time-consuming you can substitute with partially cooked frozen parathas. Malaysian parathas and rotis in frozen sections are also a good option.*

### INGREDIENTS
### Vinegar onions
2 tbsp white vinegar
1 cup very finely chopped red or white onions

### Egg paratha
patrel paratha dough prepared the previous night with 2 cups of wholewheat flour
ghee or vegetable oil as required
wholewheat flour or atta for dusting
6 large eggs, separated
1 tsp salt or to taste
4-6 green chillies, 1½"- 2" long, finely chopped
4 tbsp finely chopped fresh coriander leaves

## METHOD

Stir the vinegar into the onions and set aside at room temperature.

Divide the patrel dough into 6 balls. Rub each ball very lightly with a little ghee or oil.

Dust a clean, flat surface lightly with flour and roll each ball into a ¼" thick, round paratha about 5" -6" wide.

Rub the surface of the paratha with ¼ tsp of ghee or oil and knead it again into a ball. Then roll again into a 5" round paratha. Repeat with the remaining dough.

Place the parathas next to each other on a large tray. Keep them covered with a damp, clean cloth. Whisk the egg whites to stiff peaks in a large bowl. Gently blend in the whisked yolks, salt, green chillies and coriander leaves. Reserve.

Put a flat, cast iron griddle, non-stick pan or tawa on low heat. If you are confident heat two griddles side by side.

Place a paratha on the warm but not hot surface and cook both sides slowly, pressing down on the bread gently with a flat spatula or clean cloth to ensure even and slow cooking. Don't blister the bread. When both sides are lightly cooked and a little puffy, but not brown, pour about 2½-3 tbsp of the egg mix along one side, very slowly, spreading as evenly as possible.

Let it cook slowly, till the eggs firm up. Spread a little ghee or oil around the paratha so it melts and slips below the surface of the bread. Raise heat to high and cook for 30 seconds.

Turn the paratha and cook, till the egg is well done. Spread ¼ tsp of ghee or oil over the top of the paratha. Slide or lift the paratha off the griddle and put it on paper towels, with the egg side down. Let it cool for about 2 minutes. Turn the paratha over, spread 1 tsp of vinegar onions over the eggs and gently roll the paratha.

# SEVIAN UPAMA
## Rice Vermicelli Pilaf

*In Indian groceries you will find two varieties of vermicelli noodles — light brown, roasted wheat vermicelli, often called sevian and a similar thin, but white vermicelli made with rice.*

**4-5 SERVINGS**

### INGREDIENTS

1 tbsp + 4 tbsp vegetable oil
1 tsp salt or to taste
1 cup finely chopped white onions
½ cup shelled fresh green peas
½ cup finely diced or julienned carrots
8-10 green beans, sliced into 3 diagonal strips
1 packet (200 gms) commercial rice vermicelli broken into 4"- 5" pieces
juice of 1 small lime
¾ tsp sugar

### TEMPERING

6 tbsp vegetable oil
1 tsp black mustard seeds
a pinch of asafoetida powder
6 green chillies, 1½"-2" long, finely chopped
12-14 fresh curry leaves, torn

### GARNISH

¾ cup grated fresh; or frozen, defrosted, unsweetened coconut
10-12 unsalted cashewnuts, coarsely broken and fried or toasted
3 tbsp fresh coriander leaves, finely chopped

### METHOD

Add 1 tbsp oil and 1 tsp salt to 2 litres of water. Cover and set to boil on high heat.

While the water boils, heat the oil for the tempering in a kadhai or wok. Add the tempering spices and sauté for 30-60 seconds on high heat.

Add the onions and sauté for 2-3 minutes, till translucent.

Add the green peas, carrots and beans and cook on low heat, till the vegetables are tender. Sprinkle with water if required and stir occasionally to prevent burning.

When the water-oil mixture comes to a boil, switch off the heat and immediately add the vermicelli. Stir well with tongs or a pasta tool and cover tightly for 4-5 minutes.

Drain the vermicelli completely and add it to the cooked vegetables.

Toss to coat the vermicelli evenly with spices and vegetables. Cook on low heat for 4-5 minutes longer, tossing periodically. Switch off the heat.

Toss with lime juice and sugar. Taste and stir in salt.

Mix in the garnish ingredients and serve warm.

# THALIPEETH
## Multigrain, Roasted, Spiced Flatbread

**MAKES 6 THALIPEETH
5" ROUND**

*This delicious flatbread is made all over the western coast of India, but especially in Karnataka. A combination of jowar (sorghum) or bajra (pearl millet), rice and semolina, it has a wonderful texture and tastes delicious with white butter and peanut coconut chutney. Millet flours can be found at any Indian grocery stores.*

*Some recipes require gram flour but I find it makes the thalipeeth too dense. The dough is flattened on to pieces of banana leaf. These come in uneven sizes so you may need to adjust the number you need. Always buy an extra leaf, in case you accidentally tear one.*

*Thalipeeth can be prepared large, but I find it's easier to manage a 5"- 6" disc of dough on smaller pieces of banana leaf. Use a flat griddle or non-stick pan if you don't have a tawa and always cook it on low heat.*

*This recipe calls for rice semolina but you can also use durum or wheat semolina.*

**INGREDIENTS**

2 cups rice flour
1 cup pearl millet or bajra flour; or sorghum or jowar flour
5 tbsp fine rice semolina or rava/sooji
1 tsp salt or to taste
½ cup milk + 1½ cups water
1 tsp sugar
2 tbsp melted ghee, margarine or vegetable oil + more for cooking
2 green banana leaves in good shape, about 18" long
200-250 gms white onions, finely chopped
4 green chillies, 1½"- 2" long, finely chopped
½ cup finely chopped fresh coriander leaves
1 tsp powdered, roasted cumin seeds

**METHOD**

Stir the flours, semolina and salt together in a large mixing bowl

Warm the milk with 1½ cups of water, the sugar and 2 tbsp of ghee, margarine or oil in a pan.

Using your fingertips mix the warm liquid into the mixed flours to form a soft dough. Cover and let it rest for 30 minutes in a cool place.

Wash and wipe the banana leaves very gently. Use a pair of sharp scissors to cut 6 rough squares about 7"- 8" along both edges of the thick stem. The leaves should be smaller than your griddle.

Turn the ridged end of each leaf over so that the smoother side faces upwards. Place them one on top of the other. Reserve.

Knead the onions, green chillies, coriander leaves and cumin powder into the dough.

Divide the dough into 6 equal-sized balls.

Spread a banana leaf piece on a dry, clean surface. Brush with a little ghee or oil.

Flatten a piece of dough in the centre of the banana leaf. With your fingertips and palm press downwards and outwards to form a thin, round, flat bread about ⅓" thick. Use a fork to lightly dot the bread with holes.

Put a smooth griddle or large skillet on low heat. Pick up the dough with the banana leaf and invert it on to the griddle, so that the leaf is on top.

After 2 minutes of cooking, when the bread is beginning to harden, the steam will separate the leaf from the dough and you can peel it off quite easily.

Cook both sides slowly, till light brown. Spoon ghee on both sides and cook till it turns a golden brown.

Serve immediately with white butter and peanut coconut chutney or plain yogurt.

# UPEETH
## Buttery Semolina with Green Peas

### 4-6 SERVINGS

### INGREDIENTS
2 tsp salt or to taste
1 tsp sugar
½ cup cooked, drained green peas (optional)
¾ cup finely chopped red or white onions
2 cups medium coarse semolina or rava/sooji
juice of ½ a lime

### TEMPERING
6 tbsp ghee or vegetable oil
½ tsp black mustard seeds
½ tsp cumin seeds
a pinch of asafoetida powder
1 tsp husked, split black gram or urad dal
10 fresh curry leaves, torn
3-4 green chillies, 1½"- 2" long, finely chopped
1" fresh ginger root, peeled, julienned

### GARNISH
2 tsp grated fresh; or frozen, defrosted, unsweetened coconut
½ cup store-bought fine gram flour strings or sev
2 tbsp finely chopped fresh coriander leaves
3 tbsp unsalted, cashewnut pieces, fried or toasted

*This is a delicious, comforting dish prepared across India. In Karnataka it is called upeeth, in the Konkan, usli, and is served with coconut chutney. In the north, it is upma, served with yogurt; and in Tamil Nadu, uppamma is creamy and moist and served plain. Upeeth is also made with rice and wheat vermicelli, day-old bread and corn. Our family version is crumbly semolina, topped with fried sev. For a little colour and a dose of vitamins add cooked green peas to it.*

### METHOD
Bring 3 cups of water to a boil in a pan with the salt and sugar. If you need to boil the green peas, add them to the water.

Sauté the semolina in a dry pan for 4-5 minutes, till golden not brown. In the meanwhile, put the ghee or oil in a large kadhai or heavy-bottomed pan on high heat. (Semolina doubles in volume when cooked in hot water, so you need an oversized pan.)

When the oil is hot, add the mustard seeds, cumin seeds, asafoetida powder and urad dal.

When they begin to splutter, after 60-90 seconds, add the curry leaves, green chillies and ginger.

Add the onions and sauté, till they soften; do not brown them.

Reduce heat to medium and add the semolina.

Add the boiling water and peas (if used) to the semolina. Stir vigorously. The semolina will boil and spit and slowly begin to solidify. Keep stirring to prevent lumps.

Reduce heat and continue to stir, till the semolina has a crumbly texture and all the water has evaporated. Stir in lime juice.

Taste for salt, garnish and serve warm.

# VATANA BATATA RASSA
## Stewed Green Peas and Potatoes

**4-6 SERVINGS**

*This delicious and nutritious dish can be served for breakfast, lunch or dinner. If fresh green peas are not available buy dried green peas or sukké vatané, soak them overnight and then parboil them. You can replace the roasted whole spices with goda masala or kumta masala for a change.*

## INGREDIENTS
### Spice paste
2 tsp + 3 tsp ghee or vegetable oil
1 tsp coriander seeds
1 tsp cumin seeds
1 tsp white poppy seeds or khuskhus
¼ tsp caraway seeds or shahi jeera
3 cloves
4 black peppercorns
1" cinnamon stick
1" dried bay leaf
1 dried star anise or chakra magi, seeds removed
4-5 dried red Kashmiri chillies
100-125 gms white onions, finely sliced
½" fresh ginger root, peeled, coarsely chopped
5 cloves garlic, coarsely chopped
100 gms shredded fresh; or frozen, defrosted, unsweetened coconut

### Vegetables
1 tbsp ghee or vegetable oil
¾ cup white onion, quartered
500 gms (about 3 cups) fresh, shelled green peas, parboiled
200-250 gms potatoes, cut into small ½" pieces
2 tsp salt or to taste
juice of ½ a lime

### GARNISH
2 tbsp finely chopped fresh coriander leaves (optional)

## METHOD
Put 2 tsp of ghee or oil for the spice paste in a skillet on low heat. When hot add the whole spices and roast them, tossing all the while, till fragrant and hot. Drain with a slotted spoon and reserve.

Add 3 tsp of ghee or oil to the same skillet and sauté the sliced onions, ginger and garlic on medium heat for 4-5 minutes, till light brown.

Add the coconut and sauté for about 6 minutes longer, stirring periodically, till fragrant and barely golden.

Remove from heat, cool and grind the coconut-onion mix with the whole spices to make a smooth paste. Sprinkle in a few tbsp of water if required. Reserve.

Add 1 tbsp of ghee or oil to the same skillet and sauté the quartered onions for 2-3 minutes, till golden but not brown.

Stir in the green peas, potatoes and 2 cups of water. Cook on high heat for about 4 minutes, till the vegetables are nearly tender.

Add the spice paste and 1 cup of water. Reduce heat to medium and simmer for about 10 minutes, stirring occasionally, till the vegetables are tender and the curry has thickened.

Remove from heat and ladle into a serving bowl. Stir in the lime juice and salt and taste. Sprinkle coriander leaves on top (if used) and serve warm with pao or flatbreads.

# APPETISERS AND SNACKS

Konkan culture is curiously formal and informal. Informal, because guests drop by unannounced or with little notice, bring innumerable friends with them and expect to be entertained formally.

Tea culture in the Konkan is elaborate and many important rituals such as arranged marriages, inaugurations of offices and homes, welcoming new neighbours are followed by beverages and snacks. The term tannek mana in Konkani refers to recipes that are suitable for both tea and breakfast. Pohé, uppama, thalipeet and bhajjis would be tannek mana.

Dabbé kaan is a general term for food that can be prepared and stored in brass and tin boxes for a while, like sweet coconut or semolina ladoos, and kodbolé and chakli, both deep-fried pastries. So it was important for Grandma to have recipes at hand that required ingredients that did not perish easily and cooked quickly. A variety of trail mixes such as spicy chiwda, prepared with parched rice, fried rice Indian pretzels like mudukku and chakli were prepared at the end of every month and stashed away in tin and glass jars. The kitchen was always well stocked with grated coconut, boiled potatoes and crushed peanuts to rustle up potato fritters with chutney, tapioca cutlets, kothimbri wadé and batata wadi.

Cool treats like malai kulfi, eggless mango ice cream, limbo pani and chilled, spiced poached fruit were served on very hot days.

# NON-VEGETARIAN
## Appetisers and Snacks

## VIMALA TAI'S ALU WADI
### Colocasia Leaves Stuffed with Tamarind, Caramelised Onions and Shrimp

**MAKES 4 ROLLS, ABOUT 6"X 3" FOR 12-14 SLICES**

*Alu wadi, also called patrado in the Konkan, patrel and patra by the Parsis and Gujaratis is a steamed and pan-fried roll made with colocasia leaves. These are dark green, large, thick leaves that resemble elephant's ears. Some people have an allergic reaction to the calcium oxalates in the leaf. They must be cooked, preferably by steaming, soaking in a warm tea bath or stewing in milk to leach out the oxalates. Popular all over western India, it is prepared vegetarian by the Parsis, Jains and Gujaratis. My paternal grandmother's Saraswat version however, was knock your socks off, chock full of shrimp. This sweet, spicy, soft and crisp appetiser is a crowd pleaser and a talking point no matter which country you serve it in.*

*It is the most difficult recipe in this book. Make it when you are not in a rush and invite a friend to help.*

*Buy colocasia leaves fresh from your grocer. Use leaves that span about 8" long and 6" wide once the stalk has been cut off. If you get a bunch of leaves with varied sizes start the assembly with the largest on the outside and lay the smallest one inside.*

## INGREDIENTS

24 fresh colocasia or
arbi/patrel leaves,
8" x 6" without rips
4 tbsp vegetable oil + more for frying
1 cup small shrimp,
shelled and cleaned
(size: 80-90 shrimp/kg)
sealing paste made with ½ cup gram
flour or besan and ½ cup water
6 pieces of kitchen twine,
each 9" long

### Spice paste

2 dried red Kashmiri chillies,
stalks and seeds removed
3 green chillies,
1½"- 2" long, finely chopped
6 fenugreek seeds
4 cloves
6 black peppercorns
3" cinnamon stick
1 tsp coriander seeds
4 cloves garlic
2" fresh ginger root, peeled

### Filling

1½ cups gram flour or besan
½ cup rice flour
½ cup wholewheat flour or atta
1 tsp grated jaggery or
powdered sugar
1 tsp turmeric powder
3 tbsp tamarind paste
1 small ripe, yellow banana, peeled
(use 1 velchi or ½ a regular banana)
1 tsp salt or to taste

### TO SERVE

2 limes or lemons, cut into wedges

## METHOD

Wash the colocasia leaves and cut off the stalks. Using a small sharp kitchen knife, slice off and flatten the thick veins of the leaves without damaging them. Wipe the leaves and pat dry with a clean kitchen towel.

Create 4 sets of 6 leaves each. Start by distributing the largest leaves then move on to the smaller ones.

Combine the spice paste ingredients and grind to a fine consistency. Add 1-2 tbsp of water as required, to facilitate the grinding.

Put 4 tbsp of oil in a small skillet on low heat. When hot, sauté the spice paste for 3-4 minutes, stirring continuously. Remove and cool.

Return the sautéed spice paste to the grinder and add the filling ingredients with 2 cups of water. Grind again to make a smooth paste.

Start with 1 set of leaves. Spread the largest leaf on a dry surface, with the stalk end closest to you. Spread 1½ tbsp of filling all over the leaf using your fingers or a pastry brush. The leaf should continue to be visible. Imagine you are applying a balm to the leaf.

Place another leaf over it and repeat the process, till you have layered 6 leaves.

For the last 2 leaves, spread 1 tbsp of shrimp over each leaf with the filling.

As you would with a burrito or kathi roll, turn the two vertical ends inwards and then roll slowly and tightly, upwards, starting with the end closest to you. Roll as tightly as possible.

Use kitchen string to tie the roll at both ends and in the centre. Tie firmly but not too tight as this will cause the roll to tear. Secure the open end with a little gram flour paste.

Repeat with the remaining leaves to make 3 more rolls. Place the rolls in a steamer, water bath or pressure cooker as soon as they are ready and cook for 15 minutes. Keep them covered with thin muslin cloth, so they steam slowly and do not get wet.

Remove the rolls from the steamer and let them cool completely. Refrigerate overnight on an open tray.

Place a roll on a clean, dry cutting surface. Using a sharp knife, slice the roll into 1" thick slices. Repeat with the remaining rolls.

Pour 1" of oil into a non-stick pan and put it on medium heat. When hot, fry 1 slice on both sides, till golden brown. Test to ensure the filling and leaf are cooked through. Drain in a sieve or over paper towels.

Repeat with the remaining slices.

Serve warm with lime or lemon wedges.

# RED MASALA CHICKEN

### 6-8 SERVINGS

*These bite-sized appetisers are not originally Konkani but are nevertheless very popular in the Konkan. Delicious with a cold beer. You can substitute the kacharia, a wild sour berry found in Rajasthan, with raw papaya and dried mango powder or amchoor. Kacharia acts as a tenderiser.*

## INGREDIENTS

600 gms boneless, skinned chicken
vegetable oil for frying

## MARINADE

50-70 gms white or red onion,
finely chopped
2" fresh ginger root, peeled
7 cloves garlic
2 tbsp Malvani garam masala
or kumta masala
or good quality garam masala
4 dried kacharias or a tsp of
kacharia powder (see note)
3 tbsp full-cream milk, plain yogurt
2 tsp vegetable oil
2 tsp salt or to taste

## BATTER

2 cups gram flour or besan
1 tsp salt or to taste
2 tsp cayenne pepper powder
¼ tsp red food colouring or
tandoori colour
a pinch of baking soda or sodium
bicarbonate

## TO SERVE

6-8 lime wedges

## METHOD

Wash the chicken, pat dry and cut into 1" cubes.

Grind the ginger, garlic, spice powder of choice and the kacharia to a smooth paste.

Combine the paste with the remaining marinade ingredients and rub into the chicken. Cover and refrigerate for about 6 hours or overnight.

Remove the chicken from the refrigerator and bring to room temperature.

Combine the batter ingredients in a bowl and mix well.

Pour 2" of oil into a small kadhai or skillet and put it on medium heat. When hot, but not smoking, press 1 piece of chicken into the dry batter to coat thickly on all sides. Test-fry it in hot oil, till golden brown and fully cooked.

Repeat with the remaining pieces. Drain on paper towels and serve warm with lime wedges on the side.

*Note*: Substitute 2 tsp grated raw papaya + ½ tsp dried mango powder or amchoor for the kacharia.

# CHOW CHOW CHICKEN CHAMUNCHA
## Chicken Pastries

**MAKES 12-14 PIECES**

*This triangular snack known worldwide as samosa is called chamuca or chamuncha in Goa and are generally non-vegetarian. Unlike Punjabi samosa, made with a thick crusty refined wheat flour pastry, these are made with samosa patti, a thick phyllo-type dough sold in stores as strips. They are much easier to work with because they are thicker than Greek phyllo. My paternal grandmother made two delicious versions with spiced chicken and seafood filling.*

*Chow chow, which is the minced chicken filling, was also made as an entrée for a quick Sunday dinner with phulkas.*

*If you get a samosa patti that's a different length, don't worry, just cut them to size with a pair of scissors.*

*These can be rolled, filled and frozen in an airtight container for several days. Line each layer of chamunchas with plastic or butter paper. They can be fried frozen as well.*

### INGREDIENTS
2 tbsp vegetable oil + more for frying
¼ cup finely chopped white onions
¼ tbsp ginger paste
1 tbsp finely chopped garlic
3-4 green chillies, 1½"- 2" long, chopped
1½ tbsp tomato paste or ketchup
½ tbsp garam masala powder
1 cup chicken mince
1 tbsp chopped fresh coriander leaves or parsley
juice of ½ a lime
salt to taste
12-13 samosa patti, 6"- 8" long and 1½"- 2½" wide
thick sealing paste made with refined flour or maida and water

### METHOD
Put 2 tbsp of oil in a small pan on medium heat. When hot, sauté the onions, ginger, garlic and green chillies for about 2 minutes, till soft and fragrant.

Add the tomato paste or ketchup, garam masala powder and chicken and sauté, till the chicken is completely cooked and dry.
Add coriander leaves, lime juice and salt to taste.

Cool completely.

**TO ASSEMBLE**
Open the packet of samosa patti. Remove one patti
and place it on a dry surface. Cover the others with
a clean damp cloth.

Place ½-1 tbsp of filling at one end of the rectangular
strip. Adjust this to the exact size and width of the
patti.

Hold the tip of the same corner and fold over to form
a triangle. The filling must not spill out. Keep folding
in opposite directions going from right to left, each
time making sure to keep the folds tight and the
filling intact. Use a pastry brush to dab the ends of
the patti with the sealing paste and seal the ends of
the triangle.

Place on a tray and cover.

You can also layer the samosas with wax paper and
freeze them in an airtight container for a month.
Defrost for 20 minutes then deep-fry.

**TO FRY**
Pour 2" of oil in a small kadhai or wok on medium
heat. When hot, fry 4-6 samosas at a time, till
golden brown.

Drain in a colander lined with paper towels.
Serve warm with mint chutney.

# KOLMI CHAMUNCHA
## Shrimp Pastries

**MAKES 12 PIECES**

### INGREDIENTS

2 tbsp vegetable oil
¼ cup finely chopped white onions
2-3 green chillies,
1½"- 2" long, finely chopped
½ tbsp peeled, finely chopped fresh ginger root
1 tbsp finely chopped garlic
1 cup small shrimp, shelled and cleaned (size: 80-90 shrimp/kg)
1 tbsp finely chopped fresh coriander leaves
¼ cup grated fresh; or frozen, defrosted, unsweetened coconut
¼ tsp coriander powder
1 tsp cayenne pepper powder
½ tsp tamarind paste
salt to taste
12 samosa patti,
7"- 8" long and 2"- 3" wide
vegetable oil for frying

### METHOD

Heat the oil in a small skillet. Sauté the onions and green chillies on medium heat, till soft.

Add the ginger and garlic and sauté for 1 minute.

Add the shrimp and cook, till they change colour and all water evaporates. Cool the mixture.

Add the remaining ingredients, except the patti and oil for frying. Mix well.

Assemble and fry the samosas as given for chow chow chicken chamuncha. Serve as is or with tomato sauce.

# KOLIWADA PRAWNS OR FISH

## 5-8 SERVINGS

*If truth be told, this is not a traditional Koli dish but I love it. It's easy and quick and always popular. If you decide to use fish, select one that's meaty and doesn't have small bones. Ghol, cod, pollack and rawas are good options. If you use prawns you can remove the tails if you don't want debris.*

### INGREDIENTS

15 medium-sized prawns (size: 30-40 prawns/kg) or 600 gms skinned fish fillets
vegetable oil for frying
1 cup rice flour

### BATTER

1 tsp cayenne pepper powder
2 tbsp garam masala powder
½ tsp carom seeds or ajwain
1 tbsp chopped fresh coriander leaves
1 tbsp ginger paste
1 tsp garlic paste
2 tsp salt or to taste
¼ tsp red food colouring or tandoori colour
juice of 1 lime

### TO SERVE

2 limes, cut into wedges

### METHOD

Shell the prawns, if used, and remove the tail if desired. Devein and wash well.

Cut the fish, if used, into 1" cubes. Wash well.

Pat the seafood dry with paper towels.

Mix all the batter ingredients in a bowl. Add the seafood and mix well to coat it evenly.

Taste and add more salt if required.

Pour 2" of oil into a small kadhai or wok and put it on high heat.

Coat and press each seafood piece generously and evenly in the rice flour.

Reduce heat to medium and fry 1 piece of seafood for 3-4 minutes, till golden and fully cooked. (Fish cubes will take longer to fry than prawns.)

Taste to test if the piece is cooked through.

Repeat with the remaining seafood.

Drain in a sieve lined with paper towels.

Serve warm with lime wedges on the side.

# PRAWNS SEMOLINA FRY

**4 SERVINGS**

*A classic Konkani dish, pronounced 'frawns phry' by locals, it allows you to enjoy the flavour of a good prawn. Serve as an appetiser or a side dish with lentils and plain, boiled, white rice.*

## INGREDIENTS

12 medium to large-sized prawns (size: 30-40 prawns/kg)
1 tsp turmeric powder
1 tsp cayenne pepper powder
1 tsp salt or to taste
1 cup fine semolina or rava/sooji
vegetable oil for frying

## METHOD

Shell the prawns and remove the tails. Devein and wash well. Drain thoroughly.

Combine the spice powders and salt in a small bowl. Sprinkle it over the prawns and toss to coat evenly.

Pour ½" of oil in a kadhai or wok and put it on high heat.

Dredge the prawns with semolina.

Reduce heat to medium and fry for 3-4 minutes, till golden brown and cooked through.

Drain on paper towels and serve with a squeeze of lime.

# TISRI WADÉ
## Small, Black Hard-Shelled Clam Fritters

**MAKES 17-20 FRITTERS**

*These are so unusual you have to try this dish at least once. It's New Orleans meets India. I serve these wadé as finger food without a sauce, just a squeeze of lime to highlight the flavour of the clams. Around 2½-3 kg of clams will give you about 1 cup of clam meat.*

### INGREDIENTS
1 cup freshly shelled and washed, raw clams or tisri
1½ tsp rice flour
1½ tbsp very finely chopped red or white onions
½ tsp salt or to taste
¼ cup fine semolina or rava/sooji
vegetable oil for frying

### Spice paste
½ cup finely grated fresh; or frozen, defrosted, unsweetened coconut
2 tsp Karwari sambhar powder or methkoot or use a commercial sambhar powder
½ tsp cayenne pepper powder or red chilli powder
⅛ tsp turmeric powder
½ tsp tamarind paste

### METHOD
Squeeze out all the liquid from the clams. Squeeze them several times. The liquid can be added to a fish curry or a seafood stock. Cover and reserve the drained clams in a sieve.

Grind the spice paste ingredients to a coarse consistency without any water or oil in a food processor.

Stir the clams into the spice paste with the rice flour and pulse just once to incorporate the clams and spices. Do not grind to a paste. The clams must not be whole but they must not be blitzed either.

Remove and transfer to a bowl. Mix in the onions and salt to form a loose dough.

Put the semolina on a plate.

Make small balls, about ¾" wide of the clam mix between your palms and pat each ball in the semolina. Flatten slightly between your palms, till the dough keeps its shape and holds together. Arrange on a plate.

Pour 1" of oil into a non-stick frying pan and put it on medium heat. When the oil is hot, but not smoking, fry the clam fritters till golden and crisp.

Drain on paper towels and serve warm with a crisp, dry, white wine, beer or limbo pani.

# VEGETARIAN
## Appetisers and Snacks

# Bhajji Fritters

Bhajjis, not to be confused with bhaji or stir-fried vegetables, are fritters in Marathi. They are prepared with vegetables, fruit, meat and seafood. In north India they are called pakoda or bhajia. They make excellent finger food and are best eaten straight from the frying pan, but they can be prepared 2 hours in advance and kept warm in an oven. Bhajjis are served as is with a variety of sauces, sandwiched between pao and sometimes served as a side dish in a thali meal. In the Konkan we prepare two types of bhajjis — olé and sukké. Olé bhajjis are vegetables or meat dipped in a batter, while sukké or dry bhajjis are vegetables mixed with dry flour and very little water or patted in semolina.

Here are a few tips for a crispy fritter: Heat your oil to 180°C and maintain a consistent heat. If you don't have a cooking thermometer, use the sizzle test — drop a little batter into the hot oil; if it sizzles and rises to the surface, the oil is ready. If you overheat the oil and it begins to smoke, cool it and discard. Use refined vegetable oils, such as saffola, sunflower and soy, with a high smoking point (220°C to 225°C).

Reducing the heat while frying the fritter, results in greasy and soppy bhajjis. Drain the fritters in a colander lined with paper towels and then lightly pat them with fresh paper towels to remove any excess oil. Always batter the vegetables just before you begin frying. Vegetables and fruits tend to release water if they sit too long in a salty batter.

# OLÉ BATATÉ BHAJJI
## Batter-Fried Potato Fritters

**4-6 SERVINGS**

### INGREDIENTS
250-300 gms brown potatoes
vegetable oil for frying

### BATTER
1 cup gram flour or besan
1 tsp cayenne pepper powder
½ tsp turmeric powder
1 cup club soda
1 tsp salt or to taste

### METHOD

Scrub the potatoes and peel them. Slice the potatoes lengthwise into ¼" slices and soak them in water for 1 hour.

Blend the batter ingredients in a bowl, to make a smooth, lump-free batter about as thick as a pancake batter. Add a little water, if required.

Drain the potatoes and pat dry with paper towels.

Pour 2" of oil into a small kadhai or wok on high heat.

Dip the potato slices in the batter, coating them evenly, and fry till golden brown.

Drain the fritters in a colander lined with paper towels.

Serve warm with tomato ketchup, tomato chutney or coconut chutney.

# SUKKÉ BATATÉ KACRYA
## Crisp Potato Fritters

**4-6 SERVINGS**

*A kacri, singular for kacrya is a finely sliced vegetable, rolled in semolina or rice flour and pan-fried. The vegetables are not as finely sliced as Japanese tempura because they are rolled in a dry ingredient and take longer to cook. If the vegetable is too thin it will fry to a dry crisp and if it's too thick it will burn the semolina or flour.*

## INGREDIENTS

250-300 gms finely sliced brown cooking potatoes (about ¼" thick)
1 tsp turmeric powder
1 tsp cayenne pepper powder
½ tsp salt or to taste
vegetable oil for pan-frying
1 cup fine semolina or rava/sooji

## METHOD

Wipe the potatoes and toss them with the spices and salt.

Pour ½" of oil into a wide skillet on medium heat. When hot, coat the potatoes with semolina and fry them on both sides, till golden and tender.

Drain and serve as is or with ketchup, Worcestershire sauce or coconut chutney.

# SUKKÉ VAANGI CHÉ KAAP
## Crisp Aubergine Fritters

*Kaap is finely sliced vegetables, such as breadfruit and aubergine that are salted and leached before frying.*

### 6 SERVINGS

### INGREDIENTS

1 large (about 800 gms), firm Indian or Italian purple aubergine or baingan
3 tsp + 1 tsp salt or to taste
1 cup fine semolina or rava/sooji
2 tsp cayenne pepper powder
1 tsp turmeric powder
vegetable oil for frying

### TO SERVE

6-8 lime wedges

### METHOD

Wash the aubergine and cut into ⅓" thick slices.

Toss the slices generously with 3 tsp of salt and place in a sieve or colander for 4-5 hours, to drain. Pat dry with paper towels or a clean kitchen cloth.

Combine the semolina with spice powders and 1 tsp of salt in a bowl.

Pour ½" of oil on to a large flat griddle or skillet on medium heat.

Dredge each aubergine slice in semolina on both sides and fry on medium heat, till golden brown and tender.

Drain on paper towels and serve warm with lime wedges.

Best served as a side dish with lentils and plain, boiled, white rice or curd rice.

# SUKKÉ KANDÉ BHAJJI
## Onion Fritters

**MAKES 12-14 FRITTERS**

### INGREDIENTS
500 gms onions,
sliced in paper-thin rings
1¼ cups gram flour or besan
¾ tbsp cumin seeds
½ tbsp coriander seeds
3-4 green chillies,
1½"- 2" long, finely chopped
3 tbsp fresh coriander leaves,
finely chopped
1 tsp cayenne pepper
or red chilli powder
1 tsp turmeric powder
1½ tsp salt or to taste
vegetable oil for frying

*These are my favourite bhajjis. I love the crunch of fried whole coriander and cumin seeds and the sweetness of onions. It's important not to make the batter soppy, just wet enough to hold the onions, spices and flour together. Use a mandolin or a very well sharpened knife to slice the onions as finely as possible. If your food processor has a blade attachment that can slice the onion finely in rings or half rings it will save you time. Do not shred or grate them. This bhajji can also be sandwiched in a bun or served with mint chutney .*

### METHOD
Toss all the ingredients, except the oil, in a large mixing bowl. Let it rest for 5 minutes. This will allow the flour to absorb the excess moisture from the onions and determine how much water the batter will need.

Meanwhile, pour 2" of oil into a small kadhai or wok on medium heat.

Slowly pour ¼-½ cup of water, at room temperature, into the onions and mix the batter with a fork. Keep adding water, till the onions and flour come together in a loose, sticky mass.

Drop a small piece of batter into the oil. If it sizzles and rises to the surface, the temperature is correct.

Using 2 tablespoons drop 2 tbsp of batter into the oil. Fry one first, till golden brown. Taste it for salt and make sure it is crisp and cooked through.

Repeat with remaining batter.

Drain in a colander lined with paper towels.

Serve warm with mint chutney or coconut chutney.

# MIRSANGÉ MASALO
## Stuffed Goan Chillies

### 6 SERVINGS

Mirsange is Konkani for chilli and can mean a red or green pepper but not a black peppercorn. Indians used Tellicherry black pepper and other varieties of black pepper before the genus Capsicum was introduced to the subcontinent by the Portuguese. The Konkan produces approximately 20 varieties of red peppers and more that 35 green ones. Several are close to extinction because wholesalers prefer farmers to grow a few hybrid varieties that people are familiar with, and which sell well. In Goa, villages specialise in growing green chilli varieties one cannot find elsewhere in the world. Like heirloom tomatoes, families have cultivated these species for generations. Among the green chillies, lambat mirsang (long chilli), patal salichi (thin-skinned chilli), pandra mirsang (white chilli) are names most Indians have never heard of. Villages like Moira, Pernem and Aldona grow rare and unique chillies whose flavour cannot be compensated by the common varieties, in the same way that the zing of a scotch bonnet in a jerk chicken cannot be replaced with a jalapeno.

The most commonly used red chillies in the Konkan are the dried, long Kashmiri ones. The Bedgi or Byadgi grown in Karnataka, is smaller and more withered looking. It produces a better colour but is less spicy. Sankeshwari grown in Maharashtra is also mildly spicy and is generally ground into cayenne pepper powder. In Goa, the black double Aldona, the short, dark red Timiti, the slender Tarvati, the potent green lavngi mirsang, jalgi mirsang, portugali, put-quepari, piment moida and piment malaget are other hybrids. The smaller potent red chillies are used to make local curries. East Indian masala, Rechado, Bafado, Cafreal, Xim Xim are all a combination of local vinegars and chillies. As children, we had a saying when a spicy vindaloo made us weep, 'Double Aldona, only rona' (if with Aldona you fry, baby you will cry).

Goan chilli is the generic term used for a 4-5 inch long, light green, sturdy and thick stuffing chilli, easily available in markets. These are served as condiments with curd rice or varan bhaat.

## INGREDIENTS

6 long Goan chillies or long green peppers, with stalks
1 tbsp fresh coriander leaves, chopped
paste of 1 heaped tbsp gram flour or besan and 2 tbsp water
3 tbsp vegetable oil
juice of ½ a lime

### Spice paste

1 tbsp grated fresh; or frozen, defrosted, unsweetened coconut
½ tsp roasted coriander seeds
¼ tsp turmeric powder
1" fresh ginger root, peeled, roughly chopped
½ tbsp grated jaggery
1 tsp salt or to taste

### GARNISH

a squeeze of lime juice
1 tsp chopped fresh coriander leaves

## METHOD

Wash the chillies and pat dry. Slit them lengthwise on one side to enable stuffing. Do not remove the stalks.

Gently scrape out the seeds, taking care not to tear the skin on the other side. Discard the seeds or use elsewhere.

Grind the spice paste ingredients to a fine consistency.

Stir in the coriander leaves.

Stuff this mixture into the chillies.

Gently apply the gram flour paste over the slits to seal them.

Put the oil in a 6"- 8" non-stick frying pan on medium heat. When hot but not smoking, reduce heat to low and arrange the stuffed chillies, slit end facing upwards in the oil.

Cook for 5 minutes. Then gently turn over and continue cooking till the entire external surface of the chilli is crisp and shiny.

Drain on paper towels.

Squeeze lime juice over them and garnish with coriander leaves.

# OLÉ GOBI BHAJJI
## Cauliflower Fritters

**MAKES 15-16 FRITTERS**

*These are unusual fritters, with a crisp skin and a soft interior. They taste great dunked in a yogurt curry or served with lentils and plain, boiled, white rice. Smaller florets fry faster and make better finger food.*

*The batter for this fritter must be thick and sticky so that it clings to the florets.*

### INGREDIENTS
18-20 (about 1 kg) cauliflower florets, 1"- 1¼" long and 1" wide
vegetable oil for frying

### BATTER
2 cups rice flour
2 tbsp fine semolina or rava/sooji
1 tsp garlic paste
1 tsp cumin powder
2 tsp cayenne pepper powder
2 tsp turmeric powder
2 tbsp peeled, grated fresh ginger root
¼ tsp baking soda
1 tsp salt or to taste

### METHOD
Combine the batter ingredients in a bowl and mix well.

Add the cauliflower florets and toss. Set aside for 15 minutes.

Meanwhile, pour 2" of oil into a small kadhai or wok on medium heat or a deep fryer at 180°C.

Slowly add up to ¾-1 cup of water at room temperature to the cauliflower, to form a thick pasty batter that clings to the florets. Mix together with your fingers or a spatula.

Sizzle test the oil for temperature: fry one fritter and taste for doneness and salt as given for sukké kandé bhaji.

Then repeat with the remaining batter.

Adolee or traditional slicer and grater with baby eggplants

Curd rice or dahi bhaat with vaangi lonché or aubergine pickle  231

Totapuri mango relish  232

Kakdi chi koshimbri or seasoned cucumber salad  140

Pomfret stuffed with green chutney  182

Mangalorean fish curry  190

Bangda fry

Karanji 145

Aam Panna 233

Kalvach dabdab or clams in a dry coconut gravy  186

Karwari curry with fish or prawns 190

Spinach chicken 196

Varan 157

Basundi with pistachio, saffron and almonds  236

Kothimbri vadé  130

Beetroot saar  138

# Wadi Fritters

Wadi, (wadé for plural) in Marathi, is possibly the most liberally used culinary term in the Konkan. This is because it can mean fritters, doughnuts, rolls, cutlets, candy and cookies.

They are cooked in different ways: steamed, pan-fried, deep-fried and boiled in syrup.

Bhajjis or fritters are not considered to be wadé even though they sometimes have the same ingredients. Wadé are served as appetisers, a side dish for lunch and for dessert. Surali wadi, a snack that resembles paparadelle, is made with gram flour or besan pasta, seasoned and rolled. Bhakar wadi is a crisp, deep-fried and spiced pastry that looks slightly like rugelach. Kopra and kaju wadé are candy-like desserts cut into diamond or square shapes and sprinkled with nutmeg or green cardamom. Mashed potatoes dipped in gram flour and deep-fried are called batata wadé, ground lentil fritters are called moong wadé, sweetened sesame are tilgul wadi. Alu wadi, rolled colocasia leaves and sabudana wadé, tapioca and potato fritters the list is endless. Savoury wadé are served with chutneys and dips, buns and yogurt. A wadi is also called ambodé in Konkani.
'Dole ahet ki wadé' is a phrase often used to scold a careless person; do you have eyes or fritters?

# KOTHIMBRI WADÉ
## Coriander Leaf Squares

**MAKES 9 WADÉ
2" SQUARE**

*These delicious coriander leaf and gram squares are typical Konkan fare, and can be served with tea, coffee or white wine. They make elegant finger food and if you're hunting for a vegan recipe look no further.*

*You can shallow-fry or bake them. Prepare them a few hours in advance, cover with foil and keep them warm in a slow oven. You can also add 2 tbsp of finely chopped fresh fenugreek leaves to the coriander leaves.*

### INGREDIENTS
1 tbsp vegetable oil + more for shallow-frying and brushing pans
1 tbsp gram flour or besan
¼ cup rice flour
1 large cooking potato, steamed, peeled and mashed (about 100 gms)
¼ tsp baking soda or sodium bicarbonate
¼ cup finely chopped white onions
2 tsp white sesame seeds or til (optional)
¾ cup coarsely crushed unsalted, roasted peanuts
3 cloves garlic, finely chopped
2 cups fresh coriander leaves and stalks, washed and very finely chopped
2-3 green chillies, 1½"- 2" long, finely chopped
1 tsp cayenne pepper powder
1½ tsp Malvani garam masala powder or any commercial garam masala
1 tsp sugar
½ tsp salt or to taste

### METHOD
Line a round 6"- 8" pressure cooker dish or an ovenproof baking dish about 6"x 6"x 2" with parchment or butter paper. Brush the paper lightly with oil on both sides. If you are going to bake the wadé, preheat the oven to 180°C.

Mix all the ingredients, except the oil for frying in a large mixing bowl. Add upto ¼ cup of water, a little at a time, to form a thick but spreadable dough. Only use as much water as is required to just bind the ingredients.

Taste and add more salt, if required.

Pour the mixture into the lined dish.

Steam for 15-17 minutes on low heat, till firmly set. The wadé will be slightly moist but completely set.

To bake it, cover the dish tightly with foil and sprinkle the foil with 1 tbsp of water.

Bake in the oven preheated for 35-40 minutes.

Remove the wadé and leave uncovered to cool to room temperature.

Cover and chill for 4-5 hours or overnight.

Remove from the refrigerator, and while still cool, cut into squares, wedges or diamond shapes, using a thin, sharp knife. Let the pieces reach room temperature. Pour 1" of oil into a large, shallow, non-stick pan. When the oil is warm, fry the squares on medium heat on both sides, till golden brown.

Drain on paper towels and serve immediately.

They are very flavourful served on their own, but you can also serve them with bataté dahi chutney.

# SABUDANA WADÉ
## Pearl Sago Fritters

**MAKES 12-14 FRITTERS**

*Sabudana or pearl sago, is produced from tapioca, a starch extracted from the cassava plant. It is also called tapioca and sold as flour or as pearls. The type of sago used in the Konkan is white and smaller than the tapioca used in Japan and parts of South East Asia. Sabudana khichdi, a stir-fry of sorts and sabudana cutlets are consumed by Hindus during religious fasts when cereals and grains are not permitted. These vegan, gluten-free fritters are soft and crunchy, salty, sweet and nourishing. I like to serve them as appetisers with a glass of limbu pani or a dry, crisp, white wine. I also serve these during Passover, the Jewish holiday when the observant abstains from grains or leavening agents.*

*I prefer to steam or bake my potatoes rather than boil them in water, because they absorb less liquid. The key to a crisp wadi is a dry dough.*

### INGREDIENTS
250 gms pearl sago or sabudana
500 gms medium-sized potatoes, boiled, peeled, mashed
200 gms coarsely crushed, unsalted, roasted peanuts
2-3 tbsp chopped fresh coriander leaves (optional)
10 fresh curry leaves, chopped
1½ tsp cumin seeds
a pinch of asafoetida powder
3-4 green chillies,
1½"- 2" long, finely chopped
2 tsp salt or to taste
1 tsp sugar
vegetable oil for deep-frying

### METHOD
Put the sago into an oversized bowl. Pour water at room temperature over the sago and then drain immediately. Return the sago to the bowl.

Pour fresh water at room temperature into the bowl again, to barely cover the sago.

Cover the bowl and set aside for 3-4 hours. The sago will absorb most of the water, puff up slightly and soften. But it must not be mushy. If the sago feels hard, toss it in a little more water and wait for 15 minutes.

Drain completely. Pat down lightly with paper towels to remove all traces of liquid.
Put the sago into a large bowl and add the remaining ingredients, except the oil.

Mix gently with your hands without mashing the sago seeds. Form the dough into 12-14, balls, 2" round. Flatten each ball slightly to form a flying saucer shaped cake or patty. The centre should not be too thick or the insides will not cook. Place them on a large plate and cover with a clean, dry cloth.

Pour 2" of oil into a kadhai or wok on high heat. When hot, test the oil by dropping in a wadi. If it sizzles and rises to the surface immediately, the oil is ready. Fry till golden, drain and taste for doneness.

Reduce heat to medium and fry 4 wadi at a time; more if you are confident. Keep the heat constant. Fry till golden and crisp.

Drain with a slotted spoon and place in a colander lined with paper towels. Serve warm with bataté dahi chutney or Karwari red coconut chutney or as is.

*Note*: These fritters cannot be baked or steamed or frozen because when potato is frozen and thawed, it releases water which makes the tapioca glutinous. But they can be shaped and refrigerated in an airtight container the night before, brought to room temperature and fried.

# BISCUIT AAMBODÉ
## Lentil Fritters with Ginger

**MAKES 10-12 FRITTERS
2" ROUND**

*This strange sounding fritter is the Konkan version of the south Indian doughnut-shaped wada, made with urad dal. Aambodé are easier to make because they are dropped into hot oil and don't require shaping. Served as a snack with tea instead of biscuits, they should be served straight out of the fryer. You can double the recipe and make the batter earlier, a few hours before your guests arrive, which will give you a chance to test it.*

*Appé, similar to aambodé, is a cross between a wada and a bhajji or fritter. Appé batter is spooned and fried in a pan called an appé kaili, resembling a Swedish Ebelskiver pancake mould.*

### INGREDIENTS
½ cup husked, split black gram or urad dal
1 tbsp grated fresh coconut, liquid squeezed out
4 fresh curry leaves, finely chopped
½ tsp fresh ginger root, peeled, finely chopped
2 green chillies, 1½"- 2" long, very finely chopped and rubbed with 1 tsp salt
salt to taste
vegetable oil for frying

### METHOD
Wash the dal and soak it in excess water for 3 hours. Rinse well and drain completely.

Grind the dal to a smooth paste for 10-15 minutes, turning the motor on and off, to scrape the insides with a spatula. Add 1-2 tbsp of water as required, to produce a thick, fluffy and creamy batter. Do not make the batter runny.

Stir in the coconut, curry leaves, ginger and green chillies.

Add salt to taste.

Pour 2"- 3" of oil into a small kadhai or wok on medium heat.

Drop 1½ tbsp of batter into the hot oil. If it sizzles and rises to the surface, the oil is ready.

Cook the first fritter till golden brown, drain, cool and taste to make sure the inside has cooked through; it should be spongy inside and crisp outside.

Using 2 tablespoons, drop about 1½ tbsp of batter in the rough shape of a ball into the hot oil, holding the spoon close to the oil as steadily as possible, as if piping a rosette.

Fry 4-5 fritters at a time, on medium heat, till golden on all sides. Drain completely and serve warm with Karwari red coconut chutney.

# SOUPS
# AND **SALADS**

Soups, consommés and salads in Konkan cooking are never eaten as a first course. Saar, saaru, kada, ukad and kadi are the soupy or brothy curries made with vegetables and lentils, sometimes thickened with rice flour, that are consumed as a condiment, beverage or after-dinner digestive. Traditionally, dishes like sol kadi and tamatar saar are poured over plain, boiled, white rice or sipped after or before the meal as a digestive, while salads are eaten with the main meal as condiments. Saaru pudi, is a ground masala a Konkani housewife would keep in stock in a running kitchen, made with spices like Guntur and Byadgi chillies, cumin and turmeric and added to various saars.

Kochimbri, palya, khis-khis are different salads prepared with uncooked and cooked vegetables, garnished with spices, onions and yogurt.

In a modern Indian family, the elaborate preparation of a full thali is a rare occurrence reserved for festive occasions, so the recipes below have been adapted for preparation as a complete first course.

# SOL KADI
## Kokum
## Coconut Soup

### 6 SERVINGS

*Sol is the sour, maroon, salted fruit of a plant from the mangosteen family. Also called amsul and kokum, its botanical name is* Garcinia indica. *This soupy curry derives it flavour from sol. It is a staple for Konkani families all over Maharashtra. My recipe is in the traditional Pune style, while the Malvanis stir black pepper, garlic and curry leaves into the coconut milk. Kokum curry can be served as a beverage before a meal to stimulate the appetite, during the meal with plain, boiled, white rice and varan or after the meal, again as a beverage to aid digestion. In our home it was always served cold but I do know some folks prefer it warm. This chilled soup is absolutely delicious and best served in a small glass or vati. Pour it over plain, boiled, white rice or eat it with varan bhaat or dalithoi.*

**INGREDIENTS**
8 soft, dried kokum fruit soaked in 1½ cups of hot water
400 ml coconut milk
salt to taste

**TEMPERING**
1 tbsp ghee or vegetable oil
1 tsp black mustard seeds
a pinch of asafoetida powder
10 fresh curry leaves, torn

**METHOD**
Heat the oil for tempering in a small pan or tempering spoon on high heat. Add the mustard first and sauté for 30 seconds, then curry leaves and asafoetida and sauté for about 1 minute on high heat, till they splutter and turn fragrant.

Pour the spices and oil over the soaking kokum fruit and its water. Stir well and press down on the fruit to release its juices.

Add coconut milk and stir well. Add more water for a thinner consistency if desired. The kokum will colour the coconut milk pink.

Add salt to taste.

Chill the sol kadi and serve it in a cup, vati or small glass, or with warm plain, boiled, white rice.

# TAMATAR SAAR
## Spiced Tomato Soup

**6 SERVINGS**

*Saaru is the Konkani term for the Marathi saar. This is the rasam of the Konkan. A beautiful flavourful broth bursting with goodness, it can be served as a soup or thin curry with masalé bhaat, curd rice or plain, boiled, white rice. You can cook the tomatoes without steaming and peeling them for a more chunky curry.*

## INGREDIENTS
### Spice powder
½ tsp black mustard seeds
½ tsp aniseed or chhoti saunf
½ tsp cumin seeds
4 fenugreek seeds
3 black peppercorns
3 dried red Kashmiri chillies, seeded

### Stock
1 kg plum tomatoes
1 tsp tamarind paste
4 green chillies, 1½"- 2" long, finely chopped
2 tbsp finely chopped red or white onion (optional)
1 tbsp peeled, julienned fresh ginger root
1-2 tsp sugar or jaggery
salt to taste

### TEMPERING
2 tsp vegetable oil
1 tsp black mustard seeds
1 tsp aniseed
10 fresh curry leaves , torn
a pinch of asafoetida powder

### GARNISH
2 tbsp chopped coriander leaves

## METHOD

Toast the spice powder ingredients in a dry skillet on medium heat. Cool and grind to a fine consistency. Reserve.

Steam the tomatoes, till the skin softens. Remove the skin, stem and as many seeds as you can without losing pulp. Mash the flesh to a coarse purée. If you don't want to steam the tomatoes, chop them coarsely.

Add the tamarind paste to the tomatoes. If using steamed tomatoes, add 1 cup of water; if using uncooked ones, add 2 cups. Stir well.

Put the oil for tempering in a medium-sized pan on high heat. When hot, add the tempering spices and sauté, till they splutter.

Add green chillies, onion (if used) and ginger and sauté for 1 minute, till translucent and soft.

Pour the contents of the pan over the tomatoes and stir together with the jaggery or sugar and the spice powder.

Taste and add salt and more tamarind or sugar or jaggery.

Simmer for 10-12 minutes if using steamed tomatoes, else for 20-25 minutes. If you prefer a thinner soup, add more water.

Garnish with coriander leaves and serve warm.

# BEETROOT SAAR
## Beetroot Soup

**5-6 SERVINGS**

*This rich, velvety beet soup is Konkan's goulash. It is traditionally thinned with water and eaten with plain, boiled, white rice. I like to drizzle it's ruby surface with a little sour cream or hung yogurt and garnish it with a sprig of coriander leaves.*

### INGREDIENTS
**Spice paste**
4 black peppercorns
1 tsp cumin seeds
3-4 fenugreek seeds
5 dried red Kashmiri chillies, stalks and seeds removed
3 tbsp grated fresh; or frozen, defrosted, unsweetened coconut
1 tsp tamarind paste

**Soup**
500 gms (7-8) red beetroots
1 tbsp ghee or vegetable oil
salt to taste

**TEMPERING**
5 tbsp ghee or vegetable oil
6 fresh curry leaves, torn
½ tsp cumin seeds
a pinch of asafoetida powder

**GARNISH**
6 tsp sour cream or hung yogurt
6 sprigs fresh coriander leaves

### METHOD
Toast the whole spices for the spice paste in a dry skillet for 2-3 minutes on high heat.

Cool and grind to a fine consistency with the coconut. Add the tamarind paste and grind again. Reserve.

Boil the beetroots, till tender and peel them.

Cut 2 beetroots into ¼" cubes and reserve for the garnish.

Chop the remaining beetroots coarsely and purée them. Transfer the purée to a large pan.

Add the ground spice paste and 2 cups of water and cook for 10 minutes on low heat.

Put the ghee or oil for tempering in a small skillet on high heat. When hot, add the tempering spices and sauté for 30 seconds.

Pour the contents of the pan into the beetroot purée and stir well.

Add salt to taste. Add more water for the desired consistency. I like it creamy but not too thick.

You can serve it hot or chilled. (Cover and chill.)

Ladle the soup into 5-6 cups or bowls. Garnish with the reserved beetroots, sour cream or yougurt and coriander sprigs.

# SALADS

## CHOWLI CHI KOCHIMBRI
### Black-Eyed Bean Salad

**4-5 SERVINGS**

*This is a quick, delicious and filling salad. Traditionally served as a condiment with plain, boiled, white rice and lentils, it's also terrific with toasted pita wedges or mashed and spread on a sliced baguette.*

### INGREDIENTS
juice of 1 lime
1 tbsp chopped garlic
3-4 green chillies,
1½"- 2" long, finely chopped
2 tsp golden honey
or grated jaggery
4 cups boiled black-eyed
beans, drained
1 cup finely chopped green
onion bulbs
4 tbsp finely chopped fresh
coriander leaves
salt to taste

### TEMPERING
½ cup vegetable oil
1 tsp cumin seeds

### METHOD
Heat the oil for tempering in a small skillet and sauté the cumin seeds for about 30 seconds. Switch off the heat and let the spiced oil cool.

Stir the lime juice, garlic, green chillies and honey or jaggery together in a large bowl.

Add the beans, green onions, coriander leaves and tempering and mix well. Add salt to taste.

Cover and refrigerate for 4-5 hours to allow the spices to infuse the beans.

Serve chilled.

# KAKDI CHI KOCHIMBRI
## Cucumber and Peanut Salad

### 6 SERVINGS

*This enduring Konkan recipe is a great way to eat cucumbers. Served as part of a meal in the Konkan, it also makes a healthy midday snack. Add yogurt, labaneh or sour cream to this and you have an Indian version of tsatsiki. I sometimes add finely chopped tomatoes and onions for a change.*

*Cucumbers, belonging to the gourd family, are native to India, where several varieties are available. Dosakai, the sambhar cucumber, a round yellow melon from Andhra Pradesh is used in pachadis, dals, and dosa batters, and are deep-fried and sautéed.*

*Kheera, a dark green, thick-skinned north Indian cucumber is consumed raw and also used to make kheer, halva and sautéed vegetables. The puneri, or Poona kheera, is typical to the Konkan and available everywhere. A light green, thin, bitter skin shields a crisp, juicy, mildly sweet flesh.*

**INGREDIENTS**

1 kg puneri or similar mild, tender, 6" long cucumbers
½ cup grated fresh; or frozen, defrosted, unsweetened coconut (optional)
1 tsp powdered sugar (more, if coconut is omitted)
Juice of 1 lime
½ cup or more crushed, unsalted peanuts
1 tsp salt or to taste

**TEMPERING**

3 tbsp ghee or vegetable oil
1¼ tsp black mustard seeds
a pinch of asafoetida powder
3-4 green chillies, 1½"- 2" long, finely chopped
10 fresh curry leaves, torn

**METHOD**

Peel the cucumbers and quarter them lengthwise. Gently scrape off any large seeds.

Dice the cucumbers into ¼" cubes.

Put the diced cucumbers in a colander or sieve placed over a bowl. Cover and refrigerate till ready to serve.

Remove the cucumbers from the refrigerator. Discard any water that may have accumulated in the bowl below the colander or sieve.

Toss the cucumbers with coconut and sugar.

Put the oil for tempering in a small skillet or tempering spoon on medium heat. When hot, add the tempering spices and cook for 30-60 seconds, till they splutter and turn fragrant.

Cool and pour the contents of the pan over the cucumbers. Toss well, till the cucumbers are coated with the tempering.

Add the lime juice and peanuts and toss again. Add salt to taste just before serving.

# KARLECHI KOCHIMBRI
## Crisp Bitter Gourd Salad

**2-3 SMALL SERVINGS**

*The crisp bitter gourd or karela is rounded off with sweet coconut, sour lime juice and a hint of chilli. It is traditionally served as a side dish and adds great texture and flavour to lentils and rice.*

### INGREDIENTS
600 gms (about 6) bitter gourds
2 tsp + 1- 2 tsp salt
vegetable oil for deep-frying
½ cup finely chopped red or white onions
2-3 green chillies, 1½"- 2" long, finely chopped and mixed with 1 tsp of salt
1 tbsp finely chopped fresh coriander leaves
2 tbsp grated fresh; or frozen, defrosted, unsweetened coconut
juice ½ lime
1-2 tsp grated jaggery or sugar

### METHOD
Wash and dry the gourds. Using a sharp knife cut off the tips. Slice and scrape off the spiny surface with a knife. Squeeze the gourds between your palms to release its bitter liquid.

Slice the gourds into fine rings about ¼" thick. Sprinkle with 2 tsp salt and leave to drain in a colander for 15 minutes. Squeeze out all the water.

Soak them in water for 5 minutes, drain and squeeze again.

Rinse in fresh water once more and squeeze out all the water and salt.

Spread out on a large plate to dry in a sunny place for about 4 hours.

Remove and discard the seeds. Pat the gourds dry with a clean kitchen towel or paper towels.

Pour 2" of oil in a kadhai, wok or deep pan on high heat. Fry the gourds, till crisp and golden. Drain in a sieve lined with paper towels, till they cool to room temperature.

Toss the fried, cooled gourd slices with the remaining ingredients.

Taste and add more salt and jaggery or sugar. Serve immediately.

# MAKECHI USAL
## Cold Corn and Green Bean Salad

### 4-5 SERVINGS

*This can be served as a cold salad or hot with flatbreads. Blanch the green beans and corn to help retain their texture and colour.*

### INGREDIENTS

500 gms golden corn kernels, blanched
200 gms tender French or green beans, blanched
3 tbsp ghee or vegetable oil
1 tsp cumin seeds
2-3 green chillies, 1½"- 2" long, finely chopped
½" fresh ginger root, peeled, julienned
½ cup finely chopped white onions
juice of 1 lime
salt to taste

### GARNISH

2 tbsp finely chopped fresh coriander leaves

### METHOD

Drain the corn and beans and reserve.

Heat the ghee or oil in a large kadhai or wok. Add the cumin seeds, followed by the green chillies, ginger and onions. Sauté for 1 minute on medium heat, till onions soften.

Add the corn and toss well. Cook for 1-2 minutes, till the corn is tender and some of the moisture has evaporated.

Add the green beans and toss again. Cook for another minute.

Switch off the heat and let the salad reach room temperature.

Add lime juice and salt to taste.

Garnish with coriander leaves, cover, refrigerate and serve chilled.

# FRIED COLOCASIA ROOT SALAD

**4-5 SERVINGS**

*This is sinfully good. Wash the colocasia, it's pretty dusty when you buy it. Boil it in hot water till it's tender but not mushy. When cool, peel it and discard the skin. Cover and refrigerate for up to 3 days if you plan to use them in batches. Slice just before frying and serve immediately.*

## INGREDIENTS

1 kg colocasia or arbi
vegetable oil for deep-frying
salt to taste

### Spice powder

1 tsp dried mango powder or amchoor
½ tsp powdered sugar
1 tsp cayenne pepper powder
or red chilli powder
½ tsp cumin powder
½ tsp coriander powder

## METHOD

Scrub the colocasia and boil, till tender but firm. Cool and peel. Slice into ½" thick discs.

Pour 2½" of oil into a small kadhai or wok on high heat. Fry the colocasia in batches, when the oil is hot but not smoking. Stir gently with a slotted spoon to ensure even cooking. Fry till golden. The root should be crisp on the outside and soft inside.

Drain in a sieve lined with paper towels.

Mix all the spice powder ingredients in a small bowl and sprinkle it over the fried colocasia. Toss to coat evenly. Add salt to taste and toss again.

Serve immediately as an appetiser or a side dish with a pulao or biryani.

# DALIMB KAKDI KOCHIMBRI
## Pomegranate and Cucumber Salad

### 6-8 SERVINGS

*This cold salad is terrific in the summer. You can slice the cucumbers in different shapes; I sometimes julienne them or scrape them into long strips with a zester. Traditionally, this salad is stirred together but I think it looks prettier layered in a small glass trifle bowl or a long platter. I can eat this salad as a meal but it's great with a spicy dish like vaangi bhaat or a biryani.*

### INGREDIENTS
500 gms puneri or similar mild, tender, 6" long cucumbers
1¼ kg (about 4) bright red sweet pomegranates
1 tsp salt or to taste
juice ½ a lime
2 tbsp finely chopped green onion bulbs
2 green chillies, 1½"- 2"long, finely chopped
1 cup cold, plain hung yogurt, whipped smooth with ½ cup cold water (see note)
½ tsp freshly ground black pepper
½ tsp powdered, freshly roasted cumin seeds

### GARNISH
1 tbsp finely chopped fresh mint leaves
1 tbsp finely chopped fresh coriander leaves (optional)
½ cup shelled, toasted walnut pieces

### METHOD
Peel the cucumbers and quarter them lengthwise. Gently scrape off any large seeds. Cut the cucumbers into 1" cubes.

Extract the seeds of the pomegranates, and reserve any liquid that may be released.

Combine the salt, lime juice, onions and green chillies in a bowl. Toss well and let it rest for 25 minutes.

Toss the cucumbers with half the onions and green chillies.

Layer the bottom of a small glass bowl or rectangular platter with the cucumbers.

Spoon the hung yogurt over the cucumbers.

Toss the pomegranate with the remaining onions and green chillies and spread over the yogurt.

Sprinkle with the ground spices.

Drizzle the reserved pomegranate juice on top.

Garnish with walnuts, mint and coriander leaves and serve cold within 2-3 hours.

*Note: About 4-5 cups of yogurt should give you 1 cup of hung yogurt. Refer to shrikhand receipe to make hung yogurt. You can also use labbaneh or plain low-fat yogurt.*

# KARANJIA
## Puffs or Empanadas Stuffed with Almonds, Poppy Seeds and Coconut

**MAKES ABOUT 15-16 RELISH**

### INGREDIENTS
**Coconut filling**

6 tbsp sliced almonds, or slivered
2 tbsp white poppy seeds or khus-khus
1½ cups grated fresh; or frozen, defrosted, unsweetened coconut 24 tbsp
¼ cup sugar, powdered in a grinder
½ tsp jaggery, crumbled
½ tsp powdered green cardamom seeds
8-10 saffron strands (optional)

**Karanjia dough**

3 cups refined flour or maida plus more for dusting
a pinch of salt
½ tsp plain yogurt
2 tbsp melted ghee or vegetable shortening
¾-1 cup plain whole milk or water, warmed
vegetable oil for frying

**Sealing paste**

2 tbsp refined flour mixed with 3 tbsp water

### METHOD
**Filling**

Toast the almonds and poppy seeds in a dry skillet for about 1 minute on medium heat.

Cool completely and stir in the remaining ingredients.

**Karanjias**

Combine all the ingredients, except the oil for frying, to form a soft, pliable dough. Add more flour and milk or water if required for a glossy and smooth dough.

Knead for about 2 minutes, cover and rest for 15 minutes.

Make 14-16 balls from the dough. Dust a little refined flour on a clean, dry surface and roll out the ball of dough into a 3"-3½" round circle. Fill the centre with about 2 tbsp of filling and flip one end over the other to form a half moon. Use a fork to press down the edges. With a brush seal the ends very lightly with paste to make sure they don't open up while frying.

Keep the puffs covered at all times with a clean and damp cloth to prevent drying.

Pour 2"- 3" of oil into a small kadhai or wok on high heat. Lower heat to medium, then fry 3-4 karanjias at a time, till golden brown.

Drain on paper towels and serve warm or at room temperature.

To store, place in an airtight container after they have cooled completely and refrigerate for up to one week.

**To reheat**

Remove the karanjias from the refrigerator and bring to room temperature.

Put them in an oven preheated to 150°C for 15 minutes.

# KURLICHI KOCHIMBRI
## Crab and Mango Salad

**4-6 SERVINGS**

*I love this salad because you can really enjoy the flavour of the crab. It's an expensive treat, but then treat yourself often!*

### INGREDIENTS

500-600 gms cooked
white crab meat
2 tbsp peeled, julienned
raw green mango or kaccha kayri
¼ cup finely chopped
green onion bulbs
3 green chillies,
1½"- 2" long, finely chopped and
mixed with 1 tsp salt
1 tbsp peeled, julienned
fresh ginger root
2 tbsp finely chopped
fresh coriander leaves
½ tsp powdered,
freshly roasted cumin seeds
½ tsp powdered,
freshly roasted coriander seeds
juice of ½-1 lime
½ tsp powdered sugar
salt to taste

### TEMPERING
1 tbsp vegetable oil
¼ tsp cumin seeds

### GARNISH
1½ tbsp unsalted, fried
or toasted cashewnuts

### METHOD

Toss all ingredients, except the salt, tempering and garnish, in a large bowl.

Put the oil in a pan on high heat. When hot sauté cummin seeds for 30 seconds

Cool the spiced oil and pour it over the salad.

Mix well and add salt to taste.

Chill for at least 1 hour and serve garnished with cashewnuts.

# BANGDA KISKIS
## Roasted Mackerel Salad

### 4 SERVINGS

*No, this isn't two roasted smooches but it's pretty hot and tasty if you like mackerel. Kiskis in Marathi is kismoré in Konkani and means shredded or pulled.*

*Mackerel is called bangda in western India and comes in smaller sizes comprising 8-9 pieces per kg and a larger size with around 5 pieces per kg. A dark, smoky fish with a mildly bitter aftertaste, it's inexpensive and available all through the year, sometimes during the monsoons as well.*

*I like to serve kiskis as an appetiser with hummus, toasted pita, even a cheese platter or fresh labbaneh and lavash. You can omit the coconut but replace its sweetness with a dash of grated jaggery or sugar. Traditionally, it is roasted over charcoal and served as a condiment with plain, boiled, white rice, yogurt and lentils.*

## INGREDIENTS

4 whole mackerels about 5"-7" long
juice of ½ a lime
½ tsp tamarind paste
3 green chillies, 1½"- 2" long, finely chopped
½ cup finely chopped white onions
4 tbsp vegetable oil
1 tbsp finely chopped fresh coriander leaves
1 heaped tbsp grated fresh; or frozen, defrosted, unsweetened coconut (optional)
1 tsp cayenne pepper powder or red chilli powder
salt to taste

## METHOD

Clean the fish and wash thoroughly. Pat dry with paper towels.

Mix the lime juice and tamarind in a small bowl and soak the green chillies and onions in it.

Put the oil in a skillet on medium heat. When hot, pan-fry the fish, till lightly cooked on both sides. Drain on paper towels.

Using tongs, roast each mackerel on an open flame or an outdoor grill or charcoal fire for 3-4 minutes, turning constantly.

Gently pound the fish with a pestle or a rolling pin. Roast each piece again for 1 minute.

Again, lightly pound the fish. Cool and remove and discard the bones and skin if you don't like crispy bits — I must admit I think these are the tastiest parts!

Flake the fish into small pieces but do not pulverise it.

Just before serving toss the fish with the remaining ingredients, including the soaked chillies and onions. Add salt to taste.

# GAAJRACHI KOCHIMBRI
## Carrot and Peanut Salad

*Bright orange and full of nutrition this is one of my favourite salads. The garlic is replaced with an extra pinch of asafoetida for religious holidays. Substitute the peanuts with crushed walnuts. Delicious!*

**4-6 SERVINGS**

### INGREDIENTS
500 gms carrots
4 tbsp finely chopped fresh coriander leaves
¼ tsp sugar
1 tsp salt or to taste
juice of 1 lime
1 cup crushed, unsalted, roasted peanuts (optional)

### TEMPERING
3 tbsp vegetable oil
½ tsp black mustard seeds
½ tsp cumin seeds
1½ tsp finely chopped garlic
a pinch of asafoetida powder
3-4 green chillies, 1½"- 2" long, finely chopped
10 fresh curry leaves

### METHOD
Scrape the carrots and shred them on a medium blade.

Toss the carrots with the coriander leaves, sugar and salt in a bowl and set aside.

Heat the oil for the tempering in a small skillet. Add the tempering spices and cook on medium heat for 30-60 seconds, till the spices splutter and turn fragrant and the garlic caramelises.

Cool and pour the contents of the pan over the carrots. Toss till the carrots are well coated. Add the lime juice and peanuts just before serving.

# VEGETARIAN ENTRÉES

## Vegetables and Lentils

### KONKANI CURRIES

In India, and particularly in the Konkan, there are different techniques, ingredients and names to prepare what is so easily labelled 'curry'. In the same way as the French may describe in great detail the differences between 'stews' such as a cassoulet, ragout, daube and a bourguignon, Konkani curries employ various methods. A randaayi is prepared without a tempering and always contains ground coconut, red chillies and garlic or triphala. Ghashi is tempered with mustard seeds and curry leaves and has a thick gravy. In contrast, alvatti is soupy and prepared with a leafy green such as spinach or colocasia leaves. A koddel is made with pulverised lentils, powdered nuts and chunks of root vegetables. A sasam or sasav is a fruit or vegetable pulp, a type of seasoned compote. A song, songta or saung is a starchy, spicy curry served as a relish with yogurt and rice.

# SHEVYA CHÉ SHEGYACHI AMTI
## Pigeon Peas with Drumsticks

### 4-6 SERVINGS

*This is a classic lentil preparation from Maharashtra. It has a broth-like consistency and is served hot with plain, boiled, white rice. You can add an extra 1 cup of lentils if you prefer a thicker curry.*

### INGREDIENTS

½ cup husked, split pigeon peas or toor/arhar dal
2 fresh green drumsticks, about 10" long
1 tsp turmeric powder
2 tsp grated jaggery or sugar
1 tsp salt or to taste

#### Spice paste

3 dried red Kashmiri chillies, seeds removed
2 tsp coriander seeds
¼ cup grated fresh; or frozen, defrosted, unsweetened coconut
1 tsp tamarind paste

#### TEMPERING

3 tbsp ghee or vegetable oil
4 dried round, red chillies or gol mirch
1 tsp black mustard seeds
a pinch of asafoetida powder
½" fresh ginger root, peeled, julienned
8-10 fresh curry leaves, torn

#### GARNISH

2 tbsp finely chopped fresh coriander leaves

### METHOD

Wash the dal and soak it in water for 1 hour.

Snip off the ends of each drumstick (do not peel them) and cut them into 3" pieces. Reserve.

Drain the dal and rinse well.

Transfer the dal to a heavy-bottomed pan that has a tight-fitting lid. Add the turmeric powder and 8 cups of water.

Cover and boil for about 40 minutes, till completely cooked.

Alternatively, pressure-cook it with 5 cups of water for 15 minutes on low heat after the cooker reaches full pressure. The dal must be completely pulverised.

Toast the Kashmiri chillies and coriander seeds for the spice paste in a dry skillet on medium heat for 2-3 minutes. Stir continuously.

Remove, cool and grind to a fine powder.

Add the coconut and tamarind to the powdered spices and grind again to make a smooth paste.

Stir the spice paste into the boiled dal with the drumsticks, jaggery or sugar and salt. Cook on high heat for about 15 minutes.

Put the ghee or oil for tempering in a small pan on medium heat. Add the round chillies and mustard seeds and then the asafoetida powder. Sauté for 30 seconds to a minute.

Add the ginger and curry leaves. Cook for 30 seconds.

Pour the contents of the pan into the dal and stir well. Taste and adjust seasonings.

Garnish with coriander leaves and serve.

# DAHICHI AMTI
## Yogurt Curry with Crisp Okra Fritters

### 4-6 SERVINGS

## INGREDIENTS

**Curry**

4 cups full-cream or low-fat plain yogurt

1½ tbsp gram flour or besan

2 tsp cayenne pepper powder or red chilli powder

a pinch of turmeric powder

1½ tbsp granulated sugar

1½ tsp salt or to taste

### TEMPERING

3 tbsp ghee or vegetable oil

1 tsp black mustard seeds

¼ tsp fenugreek seeds

8-10 fresh curry leaves, torn

a pinch of asafoetida powder

4 green chillies, 1½"- 2" long, finely chopped

1" fresh ginger root, peeled, julienned

### OKRA FRITTERS

12 whole, tender, green okra or bhindi

½ cup gram flour or besan

1 tsp turmeric powder

1 tsp cayenne pepper powder or red chilli powder

½ tsp salt or to taste

vegetable oil for frying

### GARNISH

2 tbsp chopped fresh coriander leaves

## METHOD

**Curry**

Whisk the yogurt, gram flour, cayenne pepper powder or red chilli powder, turmeric powder and sugar to a smooth paste with 1 cup of water.

Put the ghee or oil for tempering in a deep pan on high heat. When hot, add mustard seeds and fenugreek seeds and sauté on high heat for 30 seconds.

Add the curry leaves, asafoetida powder, green chillies and ginger and sauté for 30 seconds.

Reduce heat to low and add 2 cups of water. The mixture will bubble.

Stir in the yogurt mix and cook on low heat, stirring frequently, till it comes to a boil. Turn off the heat. Add salt to taste.

Add more cayenne pepper powder or chilli powder and sugar if you prefer a spicier, tangier flavour.

**Okra fritters**

Wash the okra and dry immediately. Lay out on a tray to dry.

Top and tail the okra.

Mix the dry ingredients in a bowl with ½ cup of water to form a smooth, thick, paste-like batter.

Pour 2" of oil in a small kadhai or wok on high heat. When hot but not smoking, reduce heat to medium.

Roll 1 okra in the batter to cover completely and fry for 4-5 minutes or till golden brown and crisp. Test for doneness and fry the remaining okra in the same way.

Drain in a colander lined with paper towels.

Then drop them into the hot curry, garnish with coriander leaves and serve with warm, plain, boiled, white rice.

# DALITHOI
## Garlic-Flavoured Pigeon Peas

*Another classic Konkani dish; eat it with plain, boiled, white rice.*

### 4 SERVINGS

### INGREDIENTS
250 gms husked, split pigeon peas or toor/arhar dal
½ tsp turmeric powder
2-3 green chillies, 1½"- 2" long, split lengthwise
1 tsp grated jaggery
1 tsp salt or to taste

### TEMPERING
2 tbsp ghee
½ tsp mustard seeds
2 dried red Byadgi or Kashmiri chillies, stalks removed
a pinch of asafoetida powder
8-10 fresh curry leaves, torn

### METHOD
Wash the dal and boil with the turmeric powder and green chillies in 6 cups of water till pulverised.

Melt the ghee in a small pan on high heat. Add the mustard seeds and red chillies and sauté for about 1 minute.

Add the asafoetida powder and curry leaves.

Pour the contents of the pan into the dal with the jaggery, salt and 4 cups of water. Cook on medium heat, till the dal is soft, thick and creamy.

Taste for salt.

Serve with plain, boiled, white rice or any flatbread.

# KARWARI SAMBHAR
## Lentil and Vegetable Stew

### 6 SERVINGS

*My favourite lentil preparation, this is more like a stew than a curry. This sambhar is much thicker than its famous south Indian cousin with a variety of vegetables including drumsticks, pumpkin, baby aubergine and okra. It's a wonderful, nutritious meal. Serve it with plain, boiled white or brown rice. Kolombyo is another Konkani-style sambhar with a thinner consistency and fewer vegetables.*

### INGREDIENTS
250 gms husked, split pigeon peas or toor/arhar dal
½ cup Karwari sambhar or Kumta masala powder
1 tsp turmeric powder
2½ tsp granulated or coarse sugar
2 tbsp tamarind paste
3 potatoes, diced into 1" cubes, soaked in water
250 gms peeled, diced red pumpkin
8-10 pearl or sambhar onions, peeled (optional)
5 okra or bhindi, washed, dried completely, sliced lengthwise
8 baby aubergines, stalks removed, quartered
¼ cup finely chopped fresh coriander leaves
200 gms baby grape tomatoes or chopped red tomatoes
1½ tsp salt or to taste

### TEMPERING
5 tbsp ghee or vegetable oil
2 tsp black mustard seeds
½ tsp cumin seeds
a pinch of asafoetida powder
4 green chillies, 1½"- 2" long, finely chopped
12 fresh curry leaves, torn
3 tbsp peeled, julienned fresh ginger root
½ cup finely chopped white onions

### METHOD
Wash the dal and drain. Put the dal in a large heavy-bottomed pan that has a tight-fitting lid with the sambhar or Kumta masala powder, turmeric powder, sugar, tamarind paste and 8 cups of water. Cover and boil for about 50 minutes on medium heat, stirring occasionally.

Alternatively, pressure-cook for 20 minutes with 6 cups of water on low heat after the cooker reaches full pressure.

Add the potatoes and pumpkin and boil for about 5 minutes or pressure-cook for 3 minutes with 1-2 additonal cups of water.

Add the remaining vegetables and simmer till they are tender and the tomatoes and dal have disintegrated, or pressure-cook for 10 minutes.

Put the ghee or oil for tempering in a skillet on high heat. Add the remaining ingredients, except the onions. Cook for 30-60 seconds, till the spices splutter and are fragrant.

Add the onions and sauté for 1 minute.

Pour the contents of the skillet into the hot dal and stir well.

Pour 1 cup of water into the skillet, mop up the spiced oil and pour it over the lentils. Simmer for another 10 minutes.

Mix in the salt. Adjust the spices and sugar.

Serve hot with plain, boiled, white or brown rice.

# KULITH KODDEL
## Horse Gram, Snake Gourd and Caramelised Garlic

*Also called kodyal, this dish is always prepared with whole, smashed, fried garlic in south Canara. Kulith or horse gram, a dark brown, round lentil has a mildly bitter taste, which is complemented by the addition of sour tamarind, sweet jaggery and coconut. The crisp gourd adds texture to the brothy lentil. Serve with plain, boiled, white rice and fritters or papad and a spicy pickle. I also like to serve this as a soup with a spoon of hung yogurt or sour cream as a garnish. Kulith or horse gram is a lesser known but nutritious lentil and resembles black Egyptian lentils or masoor, but tastes quite different.*

### INGREDIENTS
125 gms horse gram
¼ cup vegetable oil
8 large cloves garlic, smashed lightly with a rolling pin
250 gms snake gourd, diced into ½" pieces
1-2 tsp salt or to taste
1-2 tsp sugar or to taste
cayenne pepper or red chilli powder to taste

### Coconut paste
6-7 dried red Byadgi or Kashmiri chillies, stalks and seeds removed
⅓ cup grated fresh coconut
1 tbsp grated jaggery or to taste
2 tsp tamarind paste

### GARNISH
2 tbsp finely chopped fresh coriander leaves

### METHOD
Wash the gram, drain and soak it in water for 3-4 hours.

Drain the gram, rinse and cook it in 6 cups of water in a covered pan on medium heat, till soft and mushy.

Toast the red chillies and grind them to a fine paste with the coconut, jaggery and tamarind.

Put the oil in a large pan on high heat and sauté the smashed garlic, till golden but not burnt.

Add the gram and up to 2 cups of water if required. Cook for 10 minutes on high heat.

Stir in the coconut paste and gourd and cook for 2-3 minutes, till the gourd is tender, but crisp.

Add salt and sugar. Taste and add cayenne pepper or chilli powder if required.

Garnish with coriander leaves and serve with plain, boiled white rice or paan polé.

# VARAN
## Cumin-Flavoured Pigeon Peas

**4-6 SERVINGS**

### INGREDIENTS
500 gms husked, split pigeon peas or toor/arhar dal
1 tsp turmeric powder
½-1 tbsp grated jaggery
1-2 tsp salt or to taste

### TEMPERING
3 tbsp ghee
2 tsp cumin seeds
a pinch of asafoetida powder

*This is one of the oldest and most unchanged lentil recipe you will find in India and embodies Konkan cooking. It is always served at weddings and religious events.*

*Varan has a thick, pancake batter consistency, unlike amti, which is much thinner. It's best made with ghee and jaggery. You can use oil and sugar, but it doesn't taste the same. Always serve with hot, plain, boiled white rice, melted ghee and if possible a kokum curry. Fritters and usal are traditional accompaniments.*

### METHOD
Wash the dal and drain.

Pressure-cook the dal with 8 cups of water and the turmeric powder for 20 minutes on low heat after the cooker reaches full pressure. The dal should have a soft, mushy, thick consistency.

Alternatively, boil it in a covered pan on medium heat for 40-45 minutes.

Stir in the jaggery and salt.

Put the ghee in a small pan or tempering spoon on medium heat. When hot, add the cumin seeds, then the asafoetida powder and sauté for 30 seconds, till the cumin is golden and fragrant but not burnt.

Pour the contents of the pan over the dal and stir well.

Taste for salt and jaggery.

Serve hot.

# CURRIED VEGETABLES, FRUITS AND BEANS

## AMBÉ SASAV
### Seasoned Mango Curry

**6 SERVINGS**

**INGREDIENTS**
8 over-ripe mangoes
1½ tsp salt or to taste

**Spice paste**
2 black peppercorns
½ tsp cumin seeds
½ tsp coriander seeds
5 dried red Kashmiri chillies, stalks and seeds removed
4 tbsp grated fresh; or frozen, unsweetened coconut
1 tsp tamarind paste

*Mayapuri, Dussheri and Rajbhog mangoes, with a more watery flesh, give the curry a good consistency. The pulp is squeezed off the seeds, called 'bata' and left a little chunky. Traditionally the bata is returned to the curry and served as part of the portion.*

*In the Konkan, hot rice is often served with chilled curries such as sol or ambé sasav. Ambé halad, a root that looks like ginger but has the aroma of mangoes, hence also called mango ginger, is often ground and added to a sasav.*

**METHOD**
Toast the whole spices and chillies for the spice paste in a dry skillet on high heat for 1 minute.

Remove from heat, cool and grind to make a fine powder. Add the coconut and tamarind and grind to a fine consistency. Reserve.

Peel the mangoes and place them in a mixing bowl with 2 cups of cold water. Squeeze the pulp from the mangoes into the water in the bowl, till the seeds are bare.

Remove and reserve the seeds if you plan to add them to the curry, otherwise discard them.

Stir the spice paste into the mango pulp and add the seeds, if desired.

Cover and chill. Mix in the salt and taste. Serve cold over boiled, hot, white rice.

# PHULGOBI RASSA
## Stewed Cauliflower, Green Peas and New Potatoes

### 6 SERVINGS

*This classic, robust Karwari dish is a great way to enjoy fresh vegetables.*

### INGREDIENTS
250 gms baby potatoes
500-600 gms cauliflower
½ cup shelled fresh green peas
150 gms chopped red or plum tomatoes
2 tsp Malvani garam masala
¾ tsp turmeric powder
1 tsp cayenne pepper powder or red chilli powder
1-2 tsp grated jaggery or sugar
2 tsp salt or to taste

### Spice paste
2 tsp cumin seeds
½ cup grated fresh; or frozen, defrosted, unsweetened coconut
4½ fresh ginger root, peeled, roughly chopped
4 cloves garlic, roughly chopped
4 green chillies, 1½"- 2" long, roughly chopped

### TEMPERING
4 tbsp vegetable oil
1 tsp black mustard seeds
8 fresh curry leaves
a pinch of asafoetida powder

### GARNISH
1 tbsp fresh coriander leaves, finely chopped
juice of 1 fresh lime

### METHOD
Wash and scrub the potatoes, boil till tender, but firm and peel.

Remove and discard the outer leaves of the cauliflower. Wash the cauliflower and cut into small florets. Chop the stalks into small pieces.

Roast the cumin seeds for the spice paste in a dry skillet on medium heat and grind to make a smooth powder.

Toast the coconut in a dry skillet or tawa on medium heat for about 1 minute. Cool and grind to make a smooth paste with the powdered cumin, ginger, garlic and green chillies. Reserve.

Put the oil for the tempering in a small kadhai or pan on medium heat. Add the mustard seeds, curry leaves and asafoetida powder in the same order and sauté for about 1 minute.

Add cauliflower, green peas, tomatoes and garam masala powder and toss to coat with spices.

Stir in the turmeric powder, cayenne powder and 1 cup of water. Cook on medium heat for about 10 minutes.

Add the potatoes, sugar, spice paste, salt and 1-2 cups of water. Simmer till the vegetables are tender.

Remove from heat, garnish with coriander leaves and lime juice and serve warm with flatbreads such as phulka or bhakri.

# DABDAB MOONGACHÉ
## Sprouted Green Moong with Cashewnuts

### 6 SERVINGS

*A rich sprouted green moong bean stew, this is a Karwari delicacy. But the beans have to be peeled after they have sprouted, which is time consuming, so get a few friends together and you won't regret it. Karwaris prepare this with onions which would be omitted for a religious occasion.*

*Always served with flatbreads, this dish can be accompanied by another dry vegetable such as usal or fritters to make it a larger meal.*

### INGREDIENTS

200 gms sprouted green moong
½" piece fresh root ginger, julienned
50 gms finely minced white onions
40 gms unsalted, cashewnut pieces
1 cup thin coconut milk
2 tsp tamarind paste
2 tsp salt or to taste
½ tsp grated jaggery or to taste

#### Spice paste
2 tsp coriander seeds
4 dried red Kashmiri chillies, stalks removed
¼ tsp turmeric powder
½ cup grated fresh; or frozen, defrosted, unsweetened coconut
½" fresh ginger root, peeled, chopped

### TEMPERING

2 tbsp ghee or vegetable oil
½ tsp mustard seeds
6 fresh curry leaves
3 green chillies, 1½"- 2" long, chopped
a pinch of asafoetida powder

### GARNISH
juice of ½ a lime

### METHOD

Wash the moong sprouts and soak in 5 cups of boiling hot water for 10 minutes. Drain and peel off the outer coating. Set aside.

Toast the coriander seeds, cumin seeds and red chillies for the spice paste in a dry skillet on medium heat for about 1 minute. Stir continuously.

Switch off the heat and stir in turmeric powder.

Cool and grind to make a fine powder.

Add the coconut and ginger and grind to make a smooth paste. Reserve.

Put the oil for tempering in a deep pan on medium heat. When hot, add the mustard seeds, curry leaves and green chillies and sauté for 1 minute.

Add the asafoetida powder, ginger and onions and sauté, till soft but not brown.

Stir in the cashewnuts and sauté for 1 minute.

Add the spice paste, coconut milk, tamarind and sprouts and cook on medium heat, till tender.

Mix in the salt and jaggery.

Garnish with lime juice and serve with chapattis or phulkas.

# DUDDÉ RANDAAYI
## Curried Gourd with Whole Bengal Gram

**4 SERVINGS**

*If you cannot find triphala or Sichuan berries use garlic instead.*

### INGREDIENTS

100 gms whole Bengal gram or kala chana
500 gms bottle gourd or ash gourd, seeds removed, peeled, cut into 1" cubes
½ tsp turmeric powder
4-5 triphala or Sichuan berries, smashed but not powdered or 6-7 cloves garlic, smashed
1-1½ tsp salt or to taste

#### Spice paste

5-6 dried red Byadgi or Kashmiri chillies, stalks removed
½ cup grated fresh; or frozen, defrosted, unsweetened coconut
1 tsp grated jaggery
1 tsp tamarind paste

### METHOD

Wash the gram and soak it in excess water overnight.

Drain and rinse thoroughly.

Pressure-cook the gram with 3 cups of water on low heat for 25 minutes after the cooker reaches full pressure.

Alternatively, put the gram in a pan with 5 cups of water, cover tightly and cook on high heat for 35-40 minutes, till tender.
Drain and reserve.

Toast the red chillies for the spice paste in a dry skillet, till fragrant.

Cool and grind the red chillies with coconut, jaggery and tamarind to make a smooth paste. Add a little water to facilitate the grinding.

Add the gourd, turmeric powder, triphala or smashed garlic and spice paste to the cooked gram.

Add 1-2 cups of water to get the desired consistency and simmer, till the gourd is tender. Add salt to taste.

Serve with plain, boiled, white or brown rice.

# KONKANI CHANA GHASHI
## Stewed Chickpeas

**4 SERVINGS**

*Konkani cuisine calls for different kinds of Bengal gram; dried green peas and light brown chickpeas or Kabuli chana or garbanzo beans. This recipe is protein and fibre rich Serve it with plain, boiled, white rice or flatbreads.*

*Chickpeas need a lot of cooking time. So you can also use unflavoured canned beans. Crisp fruits or chewy vegetables are also added to the chickpeas: pieces of raw banana, gourds, gherkins, jackfruit or potatoes add texture to the buttery chickpeas.*

### INGREDIENTS
500 gms chickpeas or garbanzo beans
a pinch of baking soda
½ cup chopped vegetable of choice
1-2 tsp salt or to taste
red chilli powder to taste (optional)

### Coconut paste
6 dried red Byadgi or Kashmiri chillies, stalks and seeds removed
1 cup grated fresh; or frozen, defrosted, unsweetened coconut
½ tsp grated jaggery or sugar
1¼ tsp turmeric powder
3 tsp tamarind paste

### TEMPERING
3 tbsp coconut or vegetable oil
10 fresh curry leaves
a pinch of asafoetida powder
5 fenugreek seeds
1½ tsp cumin seeds

### GARNISH
2 tbsp chopped fresh coriander leaves (optional)

### METHOD
Wash the chickpeas and soak in water overnight in an oversized dish to accommodate the beans swelling. Change the water at least once. Drain the chickpeas and rinse thoroughly.

Cook the chickpeas with plenty of water and a pinch of baking soda in a pressure cooker on low heat for 25-35 minutes after the cooker reaches full pressure.

Alternatively, cook it in an excess of water in a covered pan on medium heat for 1½ hours, till tender and a little on the soft side.

If pressed between your fingers the chickpea should break easily. Drain and reserve 1 cup of the cooking liquid.

Roast the red chillies in a dry skillet on medium heat for 1-2 minutes. Cool and grind with the remaining coconut paste ingredients to make a smooth paste. Set aside.

Heat the oil for tempering oil in a large pan. Add the tempering spices and sauté for 2-3 minutes.

Add the vegetable of choice and stir well with the reserved 1 cup of chickpea water. Cook on medium heat for 2 minutes.

Add the coconut paste and chickpeas and simmer for about 10 minutes. Add salt and chilli powder for a spicier flavour. Garnish with coriander leaves, if you like and serve hot with chapattis or phulkas.

# MATKI UPKARI
## Stir-Fried Moth Bean Sprouts with Onions

### 2 SERVINGS

*Matki or moth beans, and sprouted green moong can both be used to make this upkari. You can also use chopped, fresh green string beans or chowli. It is an extremely nutritious dish packed with vitamins and fibre. I eat bowlfuls of this with chopsticks! It can be served as a main course with flatbreads, eaten as a midday snack or as a salad with a meal.*

### INGREDIENTS
250 gms sprouted matki or moth beans
4 tbsp vegetable oil
10 fresh curry leaves, torn
1½ tsp cumin seeds
a pinch of asafoetida powder
2-4 green chillies or to taste, 1½"- 2" long, finely chopped
½ cup finely chopped white onions
½" fresh ginger root, peeled, julienned
100 gms plum tomatoes, finely chopped
½ tsp turmeric powder
½ tsp cayenne pepper powder or red chilli powder or to taste
½-1 tsp grated jaggery or sugar
1-2 tsp salt or to taste

### GARNISH
½ tsp lime juice
2 tbsp finely chopped fresh coriander leaves (optional)

### METHOD
Rinse the sprouts and set aside in a colander to drain.

Heat the oil in a kadhai or wok on medium heat. Add the curry leaves, cumin seeds, asafoetida powder and green chillies and sauté for 30 seconds.

Stir in the onions and ginger and sauté, till the onions are translucent.

Add tomatoes and sauté for 2 minutes.

Mix in the sprouts, spice powders, jaggery or sugar and salt and toss well.

Pour in ½-1 cup of water, reduce heat, cover and cook, till the sprouts are tender.

Garnish with lime juice and coriander leaves. Serve warm with flatbreads.

# DRY
# **VEGETABLES**

## **BANGBANG BATATA**
## Crispy Potatoes with Chilli and Garlic

**3-4 SERVINGS**

*This hot, crisp potato dish is a childhood favourite. I make it with peeled, baby potatoes but you can also use the larger brown potatoes. A wonderful side dish with a dal and plain, boiled, white rice or curry, I also serve it as an appetiser with toothpicks.*

### INGREDIENTS

250 gms brown baby potatoes or medium-sized potatoes, washed
½-1 tsp salt or to taste
A pinch of sugar
½ tsp red chilli flakes
½ tsp turmeric powder
1 tbsp semolina or rava/sooji
1½ tbsp ghee or vegetable oil
2-3 green chillies, 1½"- 2" long, finely chopped
1½ tbsp finely chopped garlic

### GARNISH

2 limes, cut into wedges

### METHOD

Scrub the potatoes and steam them till tender but firm. Cool and peel.

If using baby potatoes, leave them whole; slice larger potatoes into thick wedges. Transfer to a large bowl.

Mix the salt, sugar, chilli flakes, turmeric powder and semolina in a bowl. Sprinkle this over the potatoes and toss, till well coated. Reserve.

Put the ghee or oil in a wide skillet on medium heat and sauté the green chillies and garlic for 10 seconds.

Throw in the spiced potatoes, reduce heat and cook for 6-8 minutes, tossing regularly to ensure even cooking, till the potatoes are browned and the semolina is crisp.

Taste for salt and garnish with limes wedges.

# FARASBI CHI USAL
## French Beans with Cashewnuts and Coconut

**4 SERVINGS**

*Buy fresh, smooth tender beans that snap easily between your fingers. Usals are a great way to eat firm, green vegetables because the technique calls for a modest amount of oil and light stir-frying that leaves the vegetable with its original texture and flavour.*

### INGREDIENTS

250 gms fresh, tender French beans or green beans
3 tbsp ghee or vegetable or corn oil
1 tsp cumin seeds
¼ tsp asafoetida powder
2 green chillies, 1½"- 2" long, finely chopped
4-5 fresh curry leaves
¼" fresh ginger root, peeled, finely chopped
½ cup finely chopped white onions
½ cup unsalted, raw, cashewnut pieces
¼ tsp cayenne pepper powder or red chilli powder
½ tsp sugar
1-1½ tsp salt or to taste

### GARNISH

2 tbsp grated fresh; or frozen, defrosted, unsweetened coconut (optional)

### METHOD

Wash the beans and drain. Top, tail and string the beans. Slice into three pieces, diagonally.

Put the ghee or oil in a large kadhai or wok on medium heat.

Add the cumin seeds and asafoetida powder and cook for 15 seconds.

Add green chillies, curry leaves and ginger.

Give it a stir and add the onions and cashewnuts. Sauté, till the onions are translucent, but do not let them change colour.

Add the beans and toss.

Mix in the cayenne pepper powder or chilli powder and sugar. Toss vigorously to coat the beans with the spices.

Reduce heat to low, add 1-2 cups of water and bring to a simmer. Cook till the beans are tender. Stir in the salt.

Garnish with coconut and serve piping hot with chapattis or phulkas or varan bhaat.

# PATTA GOBI CHI USAL
## Stir-Fried Green Cabbage

**4-6 SERVINGS**

*Cut the cabbage in half and slice very finely in long strips using a sharp, strong knife. Do not shred the cabbage in a machine; it may result in pieces that are too fine.*

### INGREDIENTS

700-800 gms green cabbage
4 tbsp ghee or vegetable oil
2 tsp husked, split Bengal gram or chana dal
a pinch of asafoetida powder
1 tsp black mustard seeds
3 green chillies, 1½""- 2" long, slit lengthwise
10 fresh curry leaves, torn
1" fresh ginger root, peeled, julienned
175 gms white onions, finely chopped
1 tsp turmeric powder
1 tsp cayenne pepper powder or red chilli powder
1-1½ tsp sugar or to taste
1-2 tsp salt or to taste

### GARNISH

¼ cup grated fresh; or frozen, defrosted, unsweetened coconut (optional)
3 tbsp finely chopped fresh coriander leaves (optional)

### METHOD

Slice the cabbage very finely, lengthwise by hand into thin, long strips.

Put the ghee or oil in a pan on medium heat. Add the dal, asafoetida powder and mustard seeds. Let them splutter for 15 seconds.

Add the green chillies and curry leaves and sauté for 30 seconds.

Mix in the ginger and onions and sauté for a few minutes, till the onions turn translucent but not brown.

Sprinkle in the spice powders and mix well.

Add the cabbage in batches and stir vigorously to coat the cabbage with spices.

Sprinkle ½ cup of water if too dry, and cook on low heat, stirring periodically, till the cabbage is tender but crisp and the water has evaporated.

Mix in sugar and salt.

Garnish with coconut and coriander leaves and serve.

## A NOTE ON OKRA

Okra, bhindi or lady's fingers is one of my favourite vegetables but it's not uncommon to find people who really dislike it. Most often they've grown up eating badly prepared okra that's slimy and chewy. Okra cooked the right way is delectable.

*Tips for cooking okra*: Use firm, tender okra. Buy them only if the tips snap off easily with a little pressure from your thumb and the skin is springy, smooth and green. If it is prickly to the touch or pitted with black spots, move on.

Always wash okra before cutting it. When water comes into contact with the insides it turns slimy. Immediately dry the okra completely with paper towels or a clean dish cloth before cutting them.

Lay the cut okra on a large white plate in a dry, sunny place for 20 minutes before cooking it. If you live in a humid climate, cook it immediately.

Okra is best cooked in oil, without too much liquid, or by dunking it completely in a gravy like a sambhar or a gumbo.

Cook okra in an oversized pan so it cooks evenly and quickly.

# BHENDÉ SAGLÉ
## Stir-Fried Okra

**4 SERVINGS**

*Saglé in Konkani is a vegetable stir-fried in a thick gravy. It is served in small portions with plain, boiled, white rice and lentils or yogurt. But you can also serve it as a main course with flatbreads, in which case you should double the quantities given here.*

### INGREDIENTS

250 gms tender, green okra or bhindi
½ tsp turmeric powder
cayenne pepper or red chilli powder to taste
1-2 tsp salt or to taste

#### Saglé Masolu

1 tbsp vegetable oil
¾ tsp husked, split black gram or urad dal
1 tsp coriander seeds
5 dried red Byadgi chillies, stalks and seeds removed, torn to pieces
⅔ cup grated fresh; or frozen, defrosted, unsweetened coconut
½ tsp grated jaggery
2½ tsp tamarind paste

#### TEMPERING

3 tbsp vegetable oil
1 tsp black mustard seeds
8 fresh curry leaves, torn

### METHOD

Wash the whole okra lightly in running water. Drain and immediately pat dry with a towel.

When the okra are completely dry, top and tail them. Slice into ¼" thick rounds. Lay out on a dry tray in a sunny spot.

Put the oil for the saglé masolu in a small skillet on medium heat. When hot, fry the dal and coriander seeds for about 30 seconds.

Add the red chillies and fry, till just golden.

Cool and grind the spices with the oil to make a smooth paste with the coconut, jaggery and tamarind. Reserve.

Put the oil for the tempering in a large kadhai or wok on medium heat.

Add the mustard seeds and curry leaves and sauté for 1-1½ minutes, till fragrant.

Add the okra and toss quickly to coat the vegetable with oil.

Add turmeric powder and toss again.

Reduce heat and cook uncovered for about 10 minutes, stirring periodically, till the okra is tender. Sprinkle in 1-2 tbsp of water at a time to prevent burning.

Stir in the saglé masolu and continue cooking for 3-4 minutes.

Raise the heat and add ½-¾ tbsp of water at intervals. Keep stirring and scraping the bottom of the pan for 6-8 minutes, till the okra is tender.

Mix in the salt. Add more cayenne pepper or red chilli powder and jaggery to taste.

Serve warm with yogurt and plain, boiled, white rice or dalithoi, or as a side dish with flatbreads.

# VAANGI BHARIT
# Smoked Aubergine

### 4-6 SERVINGS

*Bharit is a Marathi word used to describe any dish that involves puréed fruit and vegetable pulps such as pumpkin, squash, yam and aubergine. Bharta is Hindi for mashed. These mashes are cooked with spices and served as dips, relishes and also as main courses. In northern and southern India, smoked aubergine is always served as a main course.*

*Not all bharits require an open flame; pumpkin is boiled in water and ash gourd and tomato are sautéed in a pan. In my grandmother's home a 'dhuvan' or charcoal smoker that looks like a small wood fire built into a wall, was used to smoke vegetables, fruit and fish throughout the year. Smoking food is a common practice in Karwar and Goa. Whole vegetables like aubergine, coconuts, ramphul (bullocks heart), ash gourd, raw mangoes, long green chillies, capsicum, red pumpkin and fish, such as mackerel, are smoked inside a smoker or a piece of red-hot coal is placed in the middle of a pan of food, which is covered so that it can absorb the smoky flavour of charcoal and coconut oil. Coconut shells are also soaked in coconut oil, ignited and dropped into piles of chopped vegetables or rice, which are then covered and allowed to slow-cook.*

Turmeric roots are smoked, then finely sliced and added to a dish instead of the commercial, powdered turmeric. Paticho kando or green onions and young garlic are smoked and stirred into an amti or usal. Shengdané or raw peanut kernels are also smoked then peeled and eaten as a snack.

Aubergines are native to India and are also called eggplants or brinjal in India; the latter being a word of Portuguese origin.

Summer aubergines are the best. In India, good aubergines are available throughout the year unless there is a very long monsoon, in which case you will not get good aubergines in October. Look for an aubergine that weighs about 350-450 gms, not huge and not too small, with a dark purple skin and a springy body. If the body is soft, limp, discoloured or pitted, it means it has literally, gone to seed.

Smoked aubergine is prepared in India in different ways. In the north, tomatoes, onions and garlic are cooked in a garam masala with aubergine purée. In the southern Indian city of Hyderabad, mustard seeds, sesame and coconut enhance this delicious vegetable.

In the Konkan, bharit is served as a main course and as a side dish or salad. As a salad, raw ingredients such as onions and green chillies are stirred into it; and as a main course in Malvan, goda masala and curry leaves are mixed into the pulp, while in Kolhapur a more robust version is cooked with turmeric, garlic and tomatoes.

I like smoked aubergine any way but the Konkani version we make is a delicately flavoured, white-speckled aubergine mash where the focus is the flavour of the aubergine, spiked with green chillies. The yogurt helps to reduce the spiciness of the chillies and is added to the bharit when it's served as a salad.

This recipe can only be prepared if you have a gas stove top or a grill and don't mind making a mess.

## INGREDIENTS

1-2 large purple Italian or Indian aubergines, preferably with stalks intact (about 1¼ kg)
4 tbsp finely chopped white onion
1 tsp grated jaggery or sugar
3 tbsp chopped fresh coriander leaves
3 tsp tamarind paste
3 tbsp coarsely crushed, unsalted, roasted peanuts
2 tbsp plain yogurt (optional)
1-1½ tsp salt or to taste

## TEMPERING

2 tsp black mustard seeds
a pinch of asafoetida powder
12 fresh curry leaves, torn
4-5 green chillies, 1½"- 2" long, finely chopped

## METHOD

### To smoke the aubergines

Aubergines can be smoked over an open flame or on a charcoal grill. Baking them does not produce the same flavour. Line your stove top grids with aluminium foil.

Start a medium flame and roast the aubergine, till it is mushy and falls apart. Keep turning it with tongs to cook evenly on all sides. The aubergine skin will burn, the pulp will release oil and water and generally make quite a mess. But it's so worth it.

If using a charcoal grill turn the aubergine with a pair of tongs, till it's cooked through and falls apart. Put the battered aubergines on a plate to cool.

Then gently peel, scrape and discard the black charred skin with your fingers.

Pour 2 cups of water over the peeled aubergine mash, shake the bowl slightly (don't mash or stir it) and drain the water away. This helps remove any leftover bitterness from the charred outer skin.

### To prepare the dish

Mash the aubergine flesh coarsely with a fork. Stir in the remaining ingredients, except the tempering, briskly with a fork.

Put the oil for tempering in a small pan or tempering spoon on high heat. When hot, add the mustard seeds first. Then add the remaining spices. Allow 1-2 minutes for the spices to splutter and switch off the heat.

Pour the contents of the pan into the aubergine and mix well.

Serve hot with flatbreads. Konkani chana ghashi complements this meal with its thick coconut gravy.

# BHENDI TULSI
## Okra with Sweet Basil, Garlic and Onions

### 4 SERVINGS

*Basil (see glossary) is native to India and several varieties are available. This stir-fried okra with sweet basil has a delicious and unusual flavour. Serve with flatbreads and lentils like dalithoi.*

### INGREDIENTS

500 gms tender, green okra or bhindi
6 tbsp vegetable oil
1 tsp cumin seeds
½ cup finely chopped white onions
2 tbsp finely chopped garlic
3 red plum tomatoes, steamed, peeled, chopped
¼ tsp turmeric powder
1 tsp cayenne pepper powder or red chilli powder
8 large tulsi or sweet Italian basil leaves with stalks, finely chopped
1 tsp grated jaggery or sugar
1 tsp white vinegar
1-2 tsp salt or to taste

### METHOD

Wash the okra lightly in running water. Drain and immediately pat dry with a towel. Lay out on a tray to dry.

When the okra are completely dry, top and tail them and slice into ½" thick rounds. Lay out on a dry tray in a sunny spot.

Put the oil in an oversized pan, preferably non-stick on high heat. Add the cumin seeds and sauté for 30 seconds.

Add the onions and garlic and sauté for about 2 minutes, till the onions turn translucent and garlic is fragrant.

Mix in the tomatoes, turmeric powder and cayenne pepper powder or chilli powder and cook for about 2 minutes, stirring occasionally to prevent burning, till the tomatoes are pulpy.

Add the okra and mix well. Cook on low heat for about 25 minutes, turning and scraping the pan periodically, till the okra is tender, but crisp. Sprinkle in 2 tsp water if required to prevent burning.

Stir in the basil, jaggery or sugar, vinegar and salt. Serve warm with bhakri or phulkas.

# CRISPY KONKANI BABY POTATOES WITH GRAM FLOUR

## 4-5 SERVINGS

*This makes a great side dish but I also serve the potatoes as appetisers with little cocktail forks or picks. Unlike bangbang, this dish contains no garlic and green chillies, but you'll still get plenty of bang from your batata.*

### INGREDIENTS

250 gms baby potatoes, brown or red, skinned, washed
½ tsp turmeric powder
½-¾ tsp salt or to taste
½ tsp granulated sugar
2 tbsp gram flour or besan
1 tsp cayenne pepper powder or red chilli powder

### TEMPERING

3 tbsp ghee or vegetable oil
1 tsp cumin seeds
a pinch of asafoetida powder
10 fresh curry leaves, torn

### METHOD

Scrub the potatoes and steam them, till tender but firm. Cool and peel.

Combine the turmeric powder, salt, sugar, gram flour and chilli powder in a small bowl and mix well.

Sprinkle the spices over the potatoes and toss, till well coated. Set aside.

Put the ghee or oil in an 8"- 10" non-stick or heavy-bottomed pan on medium heat. When hot, but not smoking, add the cumin seeds, then the asafoetida powder and curry leaves and sauté for about 10 seconds.

Throw in the potatoes and toss, till well coated in the spiced oil.

Reduce heat to low and keep tossing gently, till the potatoes turn golden brown and crisp all over.

Drain with a slotted spoon and serve warm.

# MAAT USAL
## Sautéed Amaranth leaves

### 6 SERVINGS

### INGREDIENTS
½ kg green or red amaranth
or maat leaves
3 tbsp vegetable oil
1 tsp cumin seeds
2 green chillies,
1½"- 2" long, finely chopped
125 gms white onions,
finely chopped
2 tbsp finely chopped garlic
2 tsp golden raisins or manuka
juice of ½ a lime
1½ tsp salt or to taste
1 tsp grated jaggery
or sugar, or to taste

*Maat is amaranth leaf and is available in the Konkan as a red or green leaf. Considered a weed by many, hence cheaper than spinach or fenugreek, this very nutritious leaf is easy to prepare. It is also added to lentils in the same way as spinach. Like taro leaves, it is caustic. Wash and cook the leaves completely before eating them to avoid irritating your throat. Please note that if you are allergic to taro leaves or mildly caustic agents you should avoid this vegetable.*

*This makes a tasty side dish with roasted fish or meat.*

### METHOD
Remove and discard the thicker stalks of the amaranth leaves. Wash the leaves thoroughly and chop fine. Set aside.

Put the oil in a medium-sized kadhai or pan on medium heat.

Add the cumin seeds and green chillies and sauté for 1 minute.

Add the onions and sauté for 2-3 minutes, till they begin to caramelise.

Stir in the garlic and sauté, till fragrant. Mix in the amaranth leaves and raisins and cook till, soft and dry.

Sprinkle in the lime juice. Mix in the salt and jaggery or sugar and taste.

Serve warm with flatbreads and lentils.

# TENDLICHI BHAJI ANI GODA MASALA
## Ivy Gourd with Sweet Spices

*Goda, meaning sweet in Marathi, is a complex spice mix used only in Maharashtra, and is also called kala masalé for its smoky colour. If you are pressed for time, buy a good brand at the market. You can also use kumta masala. If you plan to use commercial coconut milk mix half a cup of thick coconut milk with half a cup of water.*

**6 SERVINGS**

### INGREDIENTS
500 gms ivy gourd or tendli
3 tbsp vegetable oil
½ tsp cumin seeds
6 fresh green curry leaves
a pinch of asafoetida powder
2 green chillies,
1½"- 2" long, finely chopped
¼ tsp turmeric powder
⅓ tsp cayenne pepper
or red chilli powder
¾ tbsp goda masala
1 cup fresh thin coconut milk
1-2 tsp salt or to taste
grated jaggery to taste

### GARNISH
juice of ½ a lime
2 tbsp finely chopped
fresh coriander leaves

### METHOD
Wash the gourds and cut them into quarters, lengthwise. Set aside.

Put the oil in a wide, thick-bottomed pan on medium heat. When hot, add the cumin seeds, curry leaves and asafoetida powder. Sauté for about 30 seconds, till the seeds splutter and add the green chillies.

Add the gourd and toss well. Add 1 cup of water. Cook on medium heat for about 4 minutes, tossing periodically and sprinkling in small amounts of water to prevent burning.

Add the spice powders. Stir and cover, till the gourds are cooked, but crisp.

Pour in the coconut milk and stir to coat the gourds. Cook for another minute and remove from heat. Mix in the salt and jaggery.

Garnish with lime juice and coriander leaves and serve with plain, boiled, white rice and amti or flatbreads.

# BAKAR BHAJI
## Red Pumpkin in a Spicy Curry with Peanuts and Coconut

### 4 SERVINGS

*Red pumpkin is also called lal kadoo or lal bhopla, but tastes different from the American red pumpkin. Many insist that bakar bhaji is a Vidharba speciality where poppy seeds, peanuts, tamarind and coconut are a popular combination. In the Konkan we use kokum as a souring agent and the peanuts are replaced with charoli or cudpah nuts which resemble pine nuts, to thicken the gravy.*

### INGREDIENTS

1 kg ripe red pumpkin
1 tsp tamarind paste or 3 soft, dried kokum fruit soaked in ½ cup of hot water
2 tbsp goda masala
1 tsp cayenne pepper powder or red chilli powder
½ tsp turmeric powder
1-2 tsp salt or to taste
grated jaggery to taste

### Coconut paste

⅓ cup cudpah nuts or charoli; or crushed, unsalted, roasted peanuts
⅓ cup grated fresh; or frozen, defrosted, unsweetened coconut
2 tsp white poppy seeds or khus-khus

### TEMPERING

¼ cup vegetable oil
½ tsp fenugreek seeds
1 heaped tsp black mustard seeds
a pinch of asafoetida powder

### METHOD

Wash the pumpkin, peel and cut into 1" cubes. Set aside.

Toast the coconut paste ingredients in a dry skillet till golden and fragrant.

Cool and grind to make a fine paste.

Put the oil for tempering in a pan on medium heat. When the oil is hot but not smoking, add the fenugreek seeds and mustard seeds, and then the asafoetida powder.

Add the pumpkin and sauté for 1 minute.

Pour in 1 cup of water and cook on high heat, till the water evaporates.

Stir in the coconut paste, tamarind paste or kokum water and spice powders.

Add a little more water if required and cook, till the pumpkin is tender. Mix in the salt and jaggery.

Serve with flatbreads.

# KONKANI KUMTA ALU DODKA
## Potatoes and Ridged Gourd in Kumta Masala

*Dodka, toori or ridged gourd and potatoes are cooked in a thin gravy with kumta masala. You can aslo use Goda masala and baby aubergines instead of ridged gourd. Serve this dish with bread rolls.*

### 4-6 SERVINGS

### INGREDIENTS
200 gms potatoes
10-12 cherry tomatoes
500 gms ridged gourd or dodka/toori
2 cups shelled fresh green peas
4 tsp kumta masala
1-2 tsp salt or to taste
1 tsp grated jaggery or sugar

### TEMPERING
3 tsp vegetable oil
1 tsp mustard seeds
a pinch of asafoetida powder
1 level tsp turmeric powder
8 fresh curry leaves

### TO SERVE
1 tbsp chopped fresh coriander leaves (optional)
2 lime wedges

### METHOD
Top and tail the gourd and dice into ½" pieces. If the skin is thick and pitted scrape it lightly. Scrub the potatoes and peel them. Cut into 1" cubes and keep them soaked in water.

Put the oil for tempering in a large pan on medium heat. When hot, add the tempering spices and sauté for about 30 seconds, till they splutter and become fragrant.

Add kumta masala, potatoes, tomatoes and 1 cup of water.

Cook for 5 minutes on high heat. Add the gourd and green peas and cook till the vegetables are tender.

Stir in salt and jaggery or sugar.

Garnish with coriander leaves, if you like and lime wedges. Serve with flatbreads.

# SEAFOOD, EGG AND **POULTRY** ENTRÉES

# Seafood Entrées

## BANGDA
## Fried Black Mackerel

**4 SERVINGS**

*Mackerel has a unique flavour, mildly bitter and salty. Go Indian and serve this fried fish with curd rice, or varan or dalithoi with plain, boiled, white rice and pickles. For a continental meal, a creamy sweet potato purée and a tangy salad creates good contrasting flavours.*

### INGREDIENTS

4 whole fresh black mackerel, 7"- 8" long
1 cup vegetable or corn oil for frying
1 cup fine semolina or rava/sooji; or rice flour

### MARINADE

1 tsp kitchen salt or to taste
juice of 1 lime
2 tsp turmeric powder
1 tsp cayenne pepper powder or red chilli powder
1 tsp ginger-garlic paste

### TO SERVE

2 limes, cut into wedges

### METHOD

Clean the fish, wash well and pat dry.

Combine the marinade ingredients in a bowl and mix, till well blended.

Rub the insides and outsides of the fish with the marinade. Cover and refrigerate for 4 hours or overnight.

Remove the fish from the refrigerator and bring to room temperature.

Put the oil in a pan on medium heat.

Dredge the fish on both sides with semolina or rice flour.

Fry the fish in hot oil, till the crust is golden brown and the fish is cooked through.

Drain on paper towels and serve warm with lime wedges.

# BOMBIL FRY
## Fried Fresh Bombay Duck

### 4 SERVINGS

### INGREDIENTS
8 fresh boneless Bombay duck fillets
2 tsp salt or to taste
1 tsp turmeric powder
1 tsp cayenne pepper powder
or red chilli powder
1 cup fine semolina or rava/sooji or
panko (Japanese style breadcrumbs)
vegetable oil for frying

### TO SERVE
2 limes, cut into wedges

*Bombil or Bombay duck fry is an immensely popular dish in Mumbai. Bombay duck is a small, local eel with fine, tiny bones and a larger central one. The latter can be removed during cleaning. The fish must be salted and drained before it is fried, like aubergine. Salt the fish on a perforated surface like a sieve or an oven rack over the sink. Place a heavy iron skillet or tray over it or press down on it with your fingers. This helps the water drain out faster and flattens the fish. Bombil comes in varying sizes so adjust portions according to the catch of the day.*

*When cooked, Bombay duck has a soft, moist consistency and breaks easily, so use a flat spatula instead of tongs to flip them while frying.*

### METHOD
Wash the fish and pat dry.

Rub it with salt, turmeric powder and cayenne pepper powder or red chilli powder.

Place the fish on a perforated surface and put a clean, heavy stone or cast iron pan on top to help force excess liquids out, for about 20 minutes.

Remove the weight and squeeze the fish using a clean absorbent cloth or paper towels to remove as much liquid as possible.

Coat the fish generously with semolina or panko.

Pour 1" of oil into a non-stick pan on medium heat. When hot, fry the fish on both sides, till golden brown.

Serve immediately with lime wedges.

Curd rice, lentils or prawn curry with plain, boiled, white rice are good accompaniments.

Fried Bombay duck is also served as a first course.

# BHARLELI HIRVI CHUTNEY CHI PAPLET

## Whole Pomfret Stuffed with Green Chutney

**4-6 SERVINGS**

*This fish tastes wonderful served with plain boiled vegetables, fried colocasia salad or Konkani potatoes. It can also be fried without egg. Pomfret can be substituted with trout or Atlantic sole.*

### INGREDIENTS

4 small pomfrets about 5"- 6" long, cleaned, kept whole
2 tsp salt or to taste
2 eggs, beaten
2 cups semolina or rava/sooji; or rice flour
10"- 12" of kitchen string
vegetable oil for frying

### Filling

¾ cup grated fresh; or frozen, defrosted, unsweetened coconut
4 green chillies 1½"- 2" long, roughly chopped
¾ cup fresh coriander leaves with stems, but no roots
¼" fresh ginger root, peeled, roughly chopped
3 cloves garlic, roughly chopped
juice of ½ a lime
salt to taste

### METHOD

Wash the fish well, drain and make a deep 3"- 4" slit along the base 2" below the fin for the stuffing. Pat dry.

Rub each fish with ½ tsp of salt. Cover and refrigerate.

Grind all the ingredients for the filling, except the salt, to make a smooth paste. Add salt to taste and mix well.

Stuff the chutney into the fish cavities and slits. Reserve some chutney for garnish.

Roll each fish in beaten egg and then in semolina or rice flour. Repeat once more. Tie the fish loosely with kitchen string to prevent the chutney falling out while frying.

Pour 1" of oil into a deep, wide frying pan on low heat. When the oil is hot but not smoking, fry the fish on both sides, till golden brown and cooked through. Reserve in the oven till ready to serve, if necessary.

Arrange the fish on a serving platter, remove the strings and spread the reserved chutney around it.

Serve hot with fried potatoes, a salad or boiled vegetables.

# VIMALA TAI'S FILLETS OF POMFRET FRIED IN MASALA BEER BATTER

### 4 SERVINGS

## INGREDIENTS
8 pomfret fillets, 5"- 6" long
1 tsp salt or to taste
½ tsp turmeric powder
1 tsp cayenne pepper powder
or red chilli powder
vegetable oil for frying

### MASALA MAYONNAISE
1 cup mayonnaise
3 large cloves garlic, roughly chopped
Juice of ½ a lime
½ tsp English mustard powder
1 tsp honey
¼ tsp cayenne pepper powder
or red chilli powder
salt to taste

### BATTER
2 cups refined flour or maida
¼ tsp salt or to taste
¼ tsp cayenne pepper powder
or red chilli pepper
¼ tsp black pepper powder
2 cups beer (Golden Lager)

*This recipe was recorded by my maternal grandmother during one of her visits to Mumbai. She would always visit my paternal grandmother, who she called Vimala Tai and they would exchange recipes. My Dadi, as we called her, was a sophisticated cook and had a dozen signature dishes that everyone who came to visit her in Mumbai wanted to eat.*

*The alu wadi you will find under appetisers, the green chilli and browned butter scrambled eggs (to be found in breakfast) and a glorious biryani, which I have saved for another cookbook, are all her recipes.*

*This dish, which can be made with trout or sole too, is delicious with her masala mayonnaise. But it can also be served with tartar sauce, wedges of lime, yogurt and plain, boiled, white rice or boiled veggies.*

## METHOD
Wash the fish and pat dry.

Combine the salt, turmeric powder and chilli powder in a small bowl and mix to blend well. Rub it into the fish and set aside for 30 minutes.

Blend all the ingredients for the masala mayonnaise in a blender to make a smooth purée. Remove to a bowl, seal tightly with plastic wrap to prevent a skin from forming and refrigerate.

Sift the dry ingredients for the batter into a bowl. Gradually add the beer and mix to make a smooth paste. Do not over blend.

Pour 2"- 3" of oil into a kadhai, wok or deep, medium-sized skillet on medium heat. When the oil is hot but not smoking, dip the fillets into the batter and deep-fry both sides, till golden brown and cooked through.

Serve immediately with masala mayonnaise and mashed potatoes.

# MANGALORE RED PRAWN CURRY

4 SERVINGS

## INGREDIENTS

250 gms medium-sized prawns
(size: 30-40 prawns/kg)
½ tsp turmeric powder
2 tsp salt or to taste
2 tbsp vegetable oil
¼ tsp black mustard seeds
2 tbsp finely chopped red
or white onions
3 green chillies,
1½"- 2" long, slit lengthwise
8 fresh curry leaves
400 ml extra thick coconut milk
¼ cup grated fresh; or frozen,
defrosted, unsweetened coconut,
ground to a paste

### Spice paste

1 tsp cumin seeds
¼ tsp fenugreek seeds
1 tsp coriander seeds
6 black peppercorns
10 dried red Byadgi or Kashmiri chillies,
stalks and seeds removed
2 tbsp finely chopped red
or white onions
2 tbsp chopped red plum tomatoes
1" fresh, ginger root, peeled,
roughly chopped
5 cloves garlic, roughly chopped
½ tbsp tamarind paste

### TO SERVE

1 lime, cut into wedges

*Though there are always exceptions, seafood curries are prepared differently in Mangalore, Goa, Malvan and Karwar and you can tell the difference even before you eat them, just by looking at the colour and texture, and often the fragrance.*

*Mangalorean curries use whole spices tempered in hot oil, while Karwari curries employ ground spices stirred into coconut milk. A Goan curry often includes tomatoes, garlic and vinegar, while a Malvan curry paste is a complex combination of various spices such as cinnamon and black pepper.*

## METHOD

Shell the prawns and devein. Wash thoroughly and drain well.

Combine the turmeric powder and salt in a bowl. Rub into the prawns, Cover and refrigerate.

Toast the whole spices for the spice paste in a dry skillet on medium heat for about 2 minutes, till fragrant. Remove, cool and grind to a fine powder. Add the remaining spice paste ingredients and grind to a fine consistency.

Put the oil in a deep skillet, kadhai or wok on medium heat. Add the mustard seeds and sauté for about 30 seconds. Add the onions, green chillies and curry leaves and sauté for 1 minute.

Stir in the spice paste and cook for 4-5 minutes, stirring continuously. Add a little water if required to prevent burning.

Mix the coconut milk with the ground coconut and ½ cup of water and pour it into the pan. Cook for 5-6 minutes on medium heat.

Add the prawns and cook for 2-3 minutes, till tender.

Taste for salt and tamarind. Serve warm with plain, boiled white rice and lime wedges on the side.

# AMBOTIK
## Goan Fish Curry
### 6 SERVINGS

*Ambat is sour and tik is spicy in Konkani. This classic Goan curry can be made with a variety of fish and prawns. Serve it with plain, boiled, white rice. It is best prepared the previous night to allow the spices to mellow.*

### INGREDIENTS
500-600 gms surmai or kingfish; or pomfret, cut into 6 steaks
¼ tsp turmeric powder
2 tsp salt or to taste
4-5 green chillies, 1½"- 2" long, sliced
1 tbsp tamarind paste
200 ml thick coconut milk
3 tbsp vegetable oil
1 tbsp chopped red or white onion
300 gms red plum tomatoes, chopped

### Spice paste
6 cloves
1" cinnamon stick
6 black peppercorns
½ tsp fenugreek seeds
2 tsp cumin seeds
12 dried red Byadgi or Kashmiri chillies, stalks and seeds removed
½ tsp white vinegar
10 cloves garlic
4 tbsp chopped red or white onions

### METHOD
Wash the fish and drain thoroughly.

Combine the turmeric powder and salt in a bowl. Rub into the fish. Cover and refrigerate.

Toast the whole spices for the spice paste in a dry skillet on medium heat. Cool and grind to make a fine powder.

Add the vinegar, garlic and onions and grind again to a fine consistency.

Stir the green chillies and tamarind into the coconut milk. Reserve.

Put the oil in a deep skillet and sauté the onion on high heat, till translucent.

Add the tomatoes and ground spice paste and cook for 3-4 minutes on medium heat, till the tomatoes are pulpy. Stir to prevent burning. Add water if required.

Stir in the fish and coconut milk with chillies and tamarind. Cook till the fish is tender.

Taste for salt and tamarind and serve with plain boiled white rice.

# RAWAS DABDAB
## Thick White Salmon Curry

### 4-6 SERVINGS

*Dabdab with onions is a Karwari speciality. When made vegetarian with sprouted beans, onions are replaced with a temper of cumin or mustard seeds. Dabdab is a thick curry that doesn't require much cooking and is served with flatbreads such as chapattis and wadé or rice polé. However, it tastes pretty good with plain, boiled, white rice as well.*

### INGREDIENTS
1 kg rawas or white salmon, cubed or a meaty white fish like ghol, halibut, swordfish
4 tbsp vegetable oil
75 gms white onions, chopped
1 heaped tbsp peeled, grated fresh ginger root
4 green chillies, 1½"- 2" long, slit lengthwise
1 tbsp sliced fresh coconut, white meat only
8 soft, dried kokum fruit, soaked in 1 cup hot water
1-2 tsp salt or to taste

### Spice paste
2 tsp coriander seeds
2" cinnamon stick
8 cloves
8 black peppercorns
10 dried red Byadgi or Kashmiri chillies, stalks removed
1 tsp turmeric powder
1 cup grated fresh; or frozen, defrosted, unsweetened coconut

### GARNISH
1 tbsp chopped coriander leaves

### METHOD
Wash the fish and soak it in water.

Toast the whole spices for the spice paste in a dry skillet on medium heat for 2-3 minutes, till fragrant.

Switch off the heat and stir in the turmeric powder. Cool and grind the spices finely. Add the coconut and grind again to a fine consistency, adding a little kokum water if required.

Put the oil on in a small kadhai or wok on medium heat. When hot, sauté the onions, ginger and green chillies for about 2 minutes, till the onions turn translucent.

Drain the fish and add it with the ground spice paste and coconut slices.

Squeeze the kokum and strain the water into the pan. Simmer on medium heat, till the fish is tender.

Add salt to taste and more kokum, if required.

Serve hot with chapattis.

# TISRI SUKKE
## Dry Curried Clams

### 6 SERVINGS

### INGREDIENTS
61.5 kg black clams
2 tbsp vegetable or coconut oil
75 gms white or red onion, finely chopped
3 green chillies, 1½"- 2" long, slit lengthwise
1" fresh ginger root, peeled, julienned
8 soft, dried kokum fruit, soaked in 1 cup hot water
2 tbsp sliced fresh coconut
2 kokum soaked in ¼ cup hot water
1-2 tsp salt or to taste

#### Spice paste
1 tbsp vegetable or coconut oil
2 tsp coriander seeds
½ tsp cumin seeds
2" cinnamon stick
6 cloves
8 dried red Kashmiri chillies, stalks and seeds removed
1 cup grated fresh; or frozen, defrosted, unsweetened coconut
½ tsp turmeric powder
1 tbsp tamarind paste

#### GARNISH
1 tbsp chopped fresh coriander leaves

### METHOD
Soak the clams in cold water and wash clean. Drain. Then soak in a large bath of warm water for ten minutes until the shells begin to open. Wash them in cold water again to remove any mud or residue on the insides of the shells. Any clams that don't open should be discarded. Drain opened clams again and reserve.

Put the oil for the spice paste in a skillet on medium heat. When hot, roast the whole spices, red chillies and coconut for about 3 minutes, till fragrant.

Switch off the heat and stir in the turmeric powder. Cool and grind with the tamarind paste to a fine consistency. Reserve.

Put 2 tbsp coconut oil in a large skillet on medium heat. When hot, sauté the onions, green chillies and ginger for about 2 minutes.

Squeeze the kokum and strain the water into the pan.

Add the ground spice paste and coconut slices and ½ cup of water. Simmer, 2-3 minutes.

Add the open clams to the pan. Toss well and cook till they are tender. Add more water if required.

Stir in the salt and taste.

Garnish with coriander leaves and serve warm with flatbreads.

# BANGDAYACHÉ AAMBAT
## Sour Mackerel Curry

**4 SERVINGS**

### INGREDIENTS

4 mackerels cut in half, horizontally
1 tsp salt + to taste
2 tsp vegetable oil
100 gms white onions, finely chopped
½ tsp turmeric powder
8 soft, dried kokum fruit soaked in 1 cup of hot water
½" fresh ginger root, peeled, julienned
3 green chillies, 1½"- 2" long, slit lengthwise
6 black peppercorns, lightly pounded

### Spice paste

½ cup grated fresh; or frozen, defrosted, unsweetened coconut
8 dried red Byadgi or Kashmiri chillies, stalks and seeds removed
½ tsp turmeric powder

### METHOD

Wash the fish and drain thoroughly. Sprinkle with 1 tsp of salt, cover and refrigerate for 1 hour.

Grind the spice paste ingredients with a little water, if required to a fine consistency.

Remove the fish from the refrigerator and bring to room temperature.

Put the oil in a deep skillet on medium heat. Add the onions and sauté, till translucent.

Mix in the ground spice paste and turmeric powder and sauté for 1-2 minutes.

Add the fish and stir.

Squeeze the kokum in the hot water. Discard the pods and strain the water into the fish curry. Stir in the ginger and green chillies. Cook till the fish is tender. Add salt to taste.

Finally, add the pounded black peppercorns.

Serve with plain, boiled, white rice.

# METHI SURMAI
## Kingfish with Fenugreek

### 6-8 SERVINGS

*This is my paternal grandmother's recipe and one of my favourites, not only because it's so unusual and delicious but because it can be served as an Indian main course with lentils and plain boiled, white rice or Continental-style with potato fingers, a tossed salad or sautéed vegetables. The mildly bitter flavour of fresh fenugreek leaves, available year round in India pairs well with the sweet, white fish and sour tomatoes.*

*You could use rawas, halibut or swordfish instead of surmai.*

### INGREDIENTS
1½ kg surmai or kingfish, cut into 8 steaks of the same size if possible

### MARINADE
1 tsp cayenne pepper powder or red chilli powder
½ tsp turmeric powder
1 tsp salt or to taste

### Fenugreek masala
½ cup vegetable oil
1 tsp cumin seeds
100 gms white onions, finely chopped
2" piece fresh ginger root, peeled, grated
10 cloves garlic, finely minced
2 green chillies, 1½"- 2" long, finely minced
400 gms fresh fenugreek leaves, without stalks and stems, chopped
2 tbsp coriander leaves with stalks, but no roots, finely chopped
¼ tsp turmeric powder
2 tsp cayenne pepper powder or red chilli powder
300 gms red tomatoes, chopped
½ tsp salt or to taste
½ tsp sugar
juice of ½ a lime

### TO SERVE
2 limes, cut into wedges

### METHOD
Wash the fish and drain thoroughly.

Combine the marinade ingredients and rub into the fish. Cover and marinate for 1 hour in the refrigerator.

Put the oil for the fenugreek masala in a skillet on medium heat. When hot, add the cumin seeds and sauté for 30 seconds.

Add the onions and green chillies and sauté for 1 minute. Add the ginger and garlic and sauté for 2 minutes, scraping the sides to prevent burning.

Mix in the fenugreek leaves and coriander leaves and sauté for 6-7 minutes.

Add the spice powders and tomatoes and a little water if required. Sauté for 5-7 minutes on high heat, stirring continuously to prevent burning, till the gravy is thick and no longer oozes water, only oil, when pressed against the sides of the pan with a spoon.

Stir in salt, sugar and lime juice. Taste and add seasonings as required.

Remove the fish from the refrigerator and bring to room temperature.

Preheat the oven to 180°C.

Place four fillets of fish one beside the other in a well-greased baking pan.

Spread both sides generously with fenugreek masala. Top with the remaining 4 fillets and cover with the remaining masala.

Cover the pan tightly with foil. Sprinkle 2 tbsp water on top of the foil.

Bake for 30-40 minutes in the preheated oven, till the fish is completely cooked.

Keep warm in the oven, till ready to serve.

Serve warm with lime wedges on the side.

# KARWARI FISH CURRY

## 6 SERVINGS

### INGREDIENTS

1 kg rawas or surmai,
cut into 6-8 steaks
1 tsp + 1½-2 tsp salt or to taste
2 tbsp vegetable oil
2½ tbsp finely chopped
white onion
½" fresh ginger root,
peeled, julienned
2 green chillies,
1½"- 2" long, slit lengthwise
1-2 tsp tamarind paste
400 ml thick coconut milk

### Spice paste

1 tsp coriander seeds
½ tsp fenugreek seeds
8-9 black peppercorns
8 dried red Kashmiri chillies,
stalks and seeds removed
1 tsp turmeric powder
4 green chillies,
1½"- 2" long, roughly chopped
½" fresh ginger root,
peeled, grated
2 tbsp roughly chopped
white onion
1 tsp rice flour

### GARNISH

juice of ½ a lime
2 tbsp chopped fresh
coriander leaves

### METHOD

Wash the fish and drain thoroughly. Sprinkle with 1 tsp of salt, cover and refrigerate.

Toast the whole spices for the spice paste in a skillet on medium heat for about 2 minutes, till fragrant.

Switch off the heat and stir the turmeric powder into the hot spices. Cool and grind to a fine powder. Add the green chillies, ginger, onion and rice flour and grind again to a fine consistency.

Remove the fish from the refrigerator and bring to room temperature.

Put the oil in a small kadhai or wok on medium heat. When hot, sauté the onion, ginger and green chillies for about 1-2 minutes, only till the onion is translucent. Do not brown.

Add the fish, ground spice paste, tamarind paste and coconut milk. Simmer for 5-8 minutes or till the fish is tender.

Add 1½-2 tsp salt and taste.

Garnish with lime juice and coriander leaves and serve hot with plain, boiled, white rice.

# Egg And Poultry Entrées

## HIRVI ANDI KARI
### Green Egg Curry

**6 SERVINGS**

*This simple egg curry has a faint green colour that comes from green chillies. A great main course when you need something quickly.*

### INGREDIENTS
8 eggs, hard-boiled
3 tbsp vegetable oil
1 dried bay leaf
5 cloves
150 gms potatoes, peeled, quartered
a pinch of turmeric powder
1½ tsp salt
400 ml thick coconut milk

### Onion paste
50-60 gms white onion, roughly chopped
4-5 green chillies, stalks removed, roughly chopped
1" fresh ginger root, peeled, roughly chopped
8 cloves garlic, roughly chopped
2 tbsp fresh coriander leaves with stems, but no roots

### METHOD
Peel the eggs, cut in halves and set aside.

Grind the onion paste ingredients to a fine consistency.

Put the oil in a pan on medium heat. Sauté the bay leaf and cloves for 30 seconds. Remove and discard the bay leaf and cloves.

Add the onion paste to the pan and sauté on medium heat for 4-5 minutes, stirring continuously, till golden but not brown.

Add the potatoes, turmeric powder, salt and 2 cups of water. Cook on medium heat, till the potatoes are tender.

Reduce heat and pour in the coconut milk. Simmer for another 2 minutes. Remove from heat.

Pour the hot curry into a serving dish and arrange the halved eggs over the gravy.

Serve with flatbreads or plain, boiled, white rice and lime wedges on the side.

# CHICKEN XACUTI
## Goan Chicken Curry

### 6 SERVINGS

*Also called shaguto in Konkani, xacuti is a rich, creamy curry. This is my great grandmother's recipe and tastes better the next day. It produces a thick gravy and is best eaten with phulka or paratha. Use potatoes for a vegan or vegetarian version.*

## INGREDIENTS

800-900 gms skinned chicken pieces with bone
4 tbsp vegetable oil
2 dried bay leaves
1 medium-sized red or white onion, finely chopped
2 tsp salt or to taste

### Spice Paste
2 tbsp vegetable oil
1" cinnamon stick
4 cloves
4 black peppercorns
1 tsp coriander seeds
2 tsp cumin seeds
5-6 dried red Byadgi or Kashmiri chillies, stalks and seeds removed
1 medium-sized white onion, roughly chopped
3 green chillies, 1½"- 2" long, roughly chopped
3" fresh ginger root, peeled, roughly chopped
8 cloves garlic, roughly chopped

### Coconut paste
2 tbsp vegetable oil
¼ cup raw, unsalted cashewnuts
2 tsp white poppy seeds or khus-khus
½ cup grated fresh; or frozen, defrosted, unsweetened coconut

## METHOD

Wash the chicken and set aside to drain.

Put the oil for the spice paste in a small, dry skillet heat on medium heat. Sauté the whole spices and onion for about 3-4 minutes, stirring constantly, till golden brown and fragrant.

Cool and grind coarsely. Add a little water if required to facilitate grinding.

Add the green chillies, ginger and garlic and grind again to a fine consistency. Reserve.

Put the oil for the coconut paste in the same skillet on medium heat. When hot, toast the cashewnuts, poppy seeds and coconut, till light golden brown and fragrant.

Cool and grind to a fine consistency, adding a little water, if required to facilitate the grinding. Reserve.

Heat 4 tbsp oil in a large pan. Add the bay leaves and sauté for 30 seconds. Add the onion and sauté for 2 minutes, till translucent.

Stir in the spice paste and sauté for 3-4 minutes on medium heat, stirring continuously, till the paste begins to thicken and release oil.

Raise the heat to high. Add the chicken and sear it in the spices for 2-3 minutes. Reduce heat to medium, add 1 cup of water, cover the pan and simmer for about 15 minutes.

Stir in the coconut paste and a little water if
required. Cook uncovered on medium-low heat
for 3-4 minutes.

Taste for salt. Cool and refrigerate overnight.

Reheat the curry the next day on low heat stirring
constantly. Serve hot with flatbreads or plain,
boiled, white rice.

# HIRVI KOMBDI
## Green Masala Roast Chicken

### 4 SERVINGS

*Serve this entrée with flatbreads, such as chapattis or bhakri, and lentils for a complete meal. Optionally, it works well with deep-fried or roasted potatoes and boiled vegetables like carrots and cauliflower. It will take 1½-2 hours to bake.*

## INGREDIENTS

1 chicken, kept whole (about 1¼ kg)
8 potatoes, kept whole
¼ cup vegetable oil

### Spiced yogurt

2 cups unsweetened, plain yogurt
1 tsp salt or to taste
½ tsp turmeric powder
1 tsp cayenne pepper powder
or red chilli powder

### Spice paste

¾ cup vegetable oil
1 tsp salt or to taste
a pinch of turmeric powder
3-4 green chillies 1½"- 2" long
2 tsp cumin seeds
1½ cups coarsely chopped white onions
1" fresh ginger root, peeled
9 cloves garlic
1 cup fresh coriander leaves
with tender shoots

## METHOD

Preheat the oven to 180°C.

Wash the chicken thoroughly inside and out. Pat dry. Make small cuts all over the chicken and set aside.

Scrub the potatoes, peel and toss in oil. Set aside.

Whisk the spiced yogurt ingredients with 2 cups of water in a small bowl to a smooth consistency.

Grind the spice paste ingredients to a fine consistency.

Rub the spiced yogurt all over the chicken. Spread a little into the cavities. Place the chicken in a greased baking dish. Spread ⅔ of the ground spice paste over it.

Arrange the potatoes around the chicken. Seal with aluminium foil, and put the dish in the preheated oven. After 30 minutes gently remove the foil. Baste the chicken with the remaining spice paste and return the dish to the oven for 30-40 minutes, till the chicken is golden brown and cooked through.

Transfer the chicken to a large serving platter.

Scrape all the cooked spices from the bottom of the pan over the chicken and arrange the roasted potatoes around it.

Serve warm.

# CHICKEN WITH PIGEON PEAS

*I prefer to make this dish with ghee because it adds a sweet richness to the lentils.*

**4-6 SERVINGS**

## INGREDIENTS
500 gms skinned chicken pieces with bone
1 cup husked, split pigeon peas or toor/arhar dal
2 cups chicken stock
5 tbsp ghee
150 gms finely sliced white or red onions
150 gms red or plum tomatoes, chopped
1½-2 tsp salt or to taste
2 tbsp tamarind paste

### Spice Paste
6 cloves
2" cinnamon stick
seeds of 1 green cardamom
2 tsp cumin seeds
10 dried red Byadgi or Kashmiri chillies, stalks and seeds removed
1¼ tsp turmeric powder
1½" fresh ginger root, peeled, roughly chopped
12 cloves garlic, roughly chopped

## METHOD
Wash the chicken and set aside to drain.

Wash the dal and drain.

Cook the dal in a pressure cooker with the chicken stock and 1 cup of water for 15 minutes on low heat, after the cooker reaches full pressure.

Alternatively, cook the dal in a covered pan with the chicken stock and 2 cups of water for 25-30 minutes, till the dal is soft and thick.

Mash the dal with a spoon or potato masher.

Grind the whole spices for the spice paste with the turmeric to make a fine powder.

Add the ginger and garlic and grind again to a fine consistency. Reserve.

Put the ghee in a pan on high heat. Sauté the onions, till translucent. Add the tomatoes and sauté for 2 minutes.

Raise the heat to high. Add the chicken and sear it for 2 minutes, to seal.

Add salt, tamarind, the ground spice paste and mashed dal with 1-2 cups of water.

Simmer together for 15 minutes on low heat, till the chicken is tender.

Serve hot with plain, boiled, white rice or flatbreads.

# SPINACH CHICKEN

*I love this dish. It makes a complete meal when served with flatbreads or rice.*

## 4-6 SERVINGS

## INGREDIENTS

### Spinach
400 gms spinach leaves with tender stems
4 tbsp ghee or vegetable oil
80 gms white onions, puréed
1" fresh ginger root, peeled, puréed
8 cloves garlic, puréed
200 gms red tomatoes, chopped
¼ tsp powdered green cardamom seeds
1 tsp cayenne pepper powder or red chilli powder
1 tsp coriander powder
½ tsp cumin powder
1 tsp garam masala powder
2 tsp salt or to taste
¼ tsp grated jaggery or sugar

### Chicken
500 gms boneless, skinned chicken pieces
4 tbsp ghee or vegetable oil
4" cinnamon stick
6 cloves
6 black peppercorns
1 dried bay leaf
salt to taste

## METHOD

### Spinach
Wash the spinach in several changes of water. Boil with 1 cup of water, till tender. Cool and purée with the cooking water.

Put the ghee or oil in a large skillet on high heat. When hot, add the onions and sauté for 3-4 minutes, stirring continuously to prevent burning, till light brown.

Add the ginger and garlic, reduce heat and sauté for 3 minutes. Add the tomatoes and spice powders and sauté for 3 minutes more.

Add 1 cup of water, the puréed spinach, salt and jaggery or sugar and simmer on low heat.

### Chicken
Wash the chicken and set aside to drain.

Put the ghee or oil in a pan on high heat. When hot, sauté the whole spices and bay leaf for about 30-60 seconds, till they sizzle and turn fragrant. Drain the spices with a slotted spoon and discard.

Add the chicken to the spiced oil and sauté on high heat for 1-2 minutes to seal the meat on all sides.

### To complete the dish
Spoon the chicken and oil over the spinach. Stir well and continue cooking on low heat, for 15-20 minutes, till the chicken is fully cooked.

Taste for salt. Serve warm with rice or flatbreads.

# BREAD BASICS
## TIPS

Polé are flatbread in Marathi and can refer to any kind of flatbread made without leavening agents. So a naan or rumali roti is not a poli.

Use fresh flour and knead it with warm water, unless the recipe specifies otherwise. In humid climates you will need less water to bind the dough.

Poli are generally made on a tawa, but you can also use a plain griddle or a flat non-stick pan.

Cool hot polé on a large plate before storing them to prevent them from sweating and turning soggy. Reheat bhakris and phulkas by turning them over a low flame with flat-edged tongs. Parathas can be warmed in an oven or on a griddle. It is best to refrigerate polé in an airtight container if you live in a warmer climate.

Please note that in many countries atta and wholewheat flour are not the same thing. Buy wholewheat flour that is ground specially for making Indian flatbreads.

If you want to make your phulkas and chapattis healthier, add a few tablespoons of millet flour or oat bran to the dough.

# BHAKRI
## Sorghum or Millet Bread

**MAKES 8-9 BHAKRI,
ABOUT 4½"- 5" ROUND**

*Bhakri made from ground millets is quintessential Konkani cuisine; the Maharashtrian farmer's food. After sunset when the first blanket of darkness falls over rural Konkan, if you climb a hill anywhere, the night is dotted with hundreds of coal and wood fires burning in mud huts and thatched cottages across the plains. The silence of an evening walk is punctuated only by cows mooing and farmer's wives slapping thick wads of dough between their hands before surrendering it to a hot cast iron griddle.*

*Jowar (sorghum), rice flour, ragi (finger millet) and bhajra (pearl millet) are packed with carbohydrates and fibre but are gluten free, low in cholesterol and cheaper than wholewheat. Millet dough does not form gluten bonds like wheat flour when water is added to it. The dough is putty-soft and impossible to roll. Village women are experts at patting them into thin, perfectly round breads in a matter of seconds by slapping a ball between their palms. But for urban housewives who have more experience with microwave popcorn, I suggest cheating: use a piece of plastic, thicker than saran wrap, such as a plastic bag, or the back of a steel plate or a banana leaf to pat down the dough.*

*This bread is very addictive. It has a heavy, chewy body and a robust flavour and if your body is accustomed to refined flour it takes a day or two to get used to it.*

**INGREDIENTS**

500 gms jowar or sorghum; or bajra or pearl millet flour; or an equal mix + more for shaping

¼ tsp salt or to taste

2 tsp ghee or vegetable oil (optional)

banana leaf or plastic sheet

**TO SERVE**

ghee or white butter

**METHOD**

Combine the flour, salt and ghee or oil (if used) in a bowl.

Gradually add 1½-2 cups of warm but not boiling water and mix to form a soft, earthy-smelling dough. Knead for 4 minutes.

Roll into a ball, cover and let it rest in a cool place for 1 hour.

Knead again for 2 minutes and divide into 8-9 round, smooth balls.

Dust a tbsp of flour on a clean banana leaf or thick plastic sheet.

Wet your palms with water and slap the ball of dough a few times between your palms to flatten it.

Place it on the banana leaf or plastic sheet and using your fingers, push the dough outwards into a ⅓" thick, more or less round piece of bread about 4½"-5" wide, or thinner if you prefer. You can also stretch and slap the dough between your hands to get the desired shape and thickness. (Bhakris tend to be imperfectly shaped and much thicker than a phulka or chapatti.)

Put a flat griddle on low heat. When it is warm but not smoking, peel the bhakri off the leaf or plastic sheet, on to the griddle and cook each side slowly, till evenly brown and fully cooked.

Add a dollop of ghee or white butter before serving or eat as is with jhunka, an usal, dabdab, bakar bhaji and peanut and coconut chutney.

# PATREL PARATHA
## Layered Wheat Flatbread

**MAKES 8-10 PARATHAS**

### INGREDIENTS
½ cup refined flour or maida
2 cups wholewheat flour or atta
+ more for rolling
1 tsp salt or to taste
½ cup cold ghee + more as required
½ cup cold full-cream milk

*This is not a traditional Konkan bread, but finds its origins in the Nizam's kitchens of Bijapur and Golconda, now in Karnataka. This recipe, perfected by my Grandma, produced a uniquely flaky flatbread that melted in your mouth. Patrel, refers to the layered, flaky quality of this bread. This is a master recipe and can be used for Nizami Parathas. You can also use it to make kathi kabab rolls or stir various spices and herbs; nigella seeds, dried fenugreek leaves, minced garlic and chopped green chillies into the dough.*

### METHOD
Sift both the flours with the salt into a large mixing bowl.

Mix in the cold ghee with your fingertips, till it resembles breadcrumbs.

Make a well in the centre and pour in the milk. Stir together with a fork.

Add cold water, a little at a time, to form a soft, smooth dough.

Knead for 5-6 minutes. Cover and leave in a cool, dry place for 30 minutes.

Knead again for 8-10 minutes and let it rest covered for another 15 minutes.

Divide into equal-sized balls. Cover.

Sprinkle a flat, clean surface with a little wholewheat flour. Roll out a ball of dough into a small circle. Spread ¼ tsp of ghee over the top. Using your palms knead the dough into a smooth ball again.

Place the ball between both palms and start rolling the dough lengthwise, as if forming a rope or snake. When the dough is about 8" long, place it on the rolling surface. Curl the dough into a flat spiral. Tuck the ends in well.

Using a rolling pin, roll the spiral upwards and outwards from the centre to form an even 6"- 8" disc.

Put a griddle on very low heat. When warm, toast each side very slowly, pressing down the sides with a piece of cloth or a flat spatula to ensure even cooking.

When both sides are golden, but not brown, spread about ¼ tsp of ghee on each side and continue to brown the paratha, till it turns a shade darker.

Repeat for the remaining parathas.

Serve warm. Traditionally, the paratha should be gently crushed between both palms before serving, to expose the layers.

# PHULKA
## Puffed Wheat Flatbread

**MAKES 18 PHULKAS**

*Phulka or phul in Marathi means to swell or puff up. These light and healthy breads are best eaten immediately with bhaji, usal and dabdab preparations.*
*You need a gas burner to cook phulkas; it cannot be prepared on an electric one.*

### INGREDIENTS
4 cups wholewheat flour or atta + 2 cups for rolling
½ tsp salt or to taste (optional)
ghee or butter to serve (optional)

### METHOD
Sift the flour and salt (if used) into a large mixing bowl.

Make a well in the centre. Slowly add 1 cup of water at room temperature into the well and using your fingertips blend the ingredients together.

Add a little more water to form a soft, tight, smooth dough.

Knead the dough vigorously for 8 minutes into a ball. Cover and leave in a cool place for 2-3 hours. The dough should not be sticky.

If using a food processor, pour a cup of water into the food bowl, and then pour in the flour. Process to crumbs, and then add a little more water to form a firm dough. Keep pulsing for a few minutes then remove the ball of dough and knead manually for a few minutes.

Make 2" balls of the dough.

Dust some flour on a flat, clean surface or rolling board. Flatten a ball of dough in your palm and place it in the centre of the rolling surface. Apply the rolling pin to the middle of the dough and roll gently outwards, away from you, and then in the opposite direction, towards you. Form a perfect circle about ¼" thick.

If you are unable to form a perfect circle use a cookie cutter or a lid with sharp edges to cut a circle out of the dough.

Put a flat tawa or griddle on low heat. When warm, place or slap the phulka in the centre and cook both sides lightly.

Switch on the adjacent burner and keep it on a high flame. Using tongs, pick the phulka off the tawa or griddle and place it over the open flame. Cook both sides till they turn brown and puff up.

Serve immediately, plain or with a little ghee or butter.

# WADÉ
## Wheat and Millet Flatbread

### MAKES 16-18 WADÉ

### INGREDIENTS
3 cups wholewheat flour
or atta + 2 cups for rolling
1 cup finger millet
or ragi/nachni flour
½ tsp salt or to taste
2 tbsp ghee or vegetable oil
vegetable oil for deep-frying

*Wadé not to be confused with fritters or candy is also a coarse, puffy, somewhat crunchy deep-fried bread, prepared with whole wheat and ragi/nachni or finger millet flour, very typical of the Konkan region. Malvané wadé are similar breads made with black gram or urad dal batter and served with chicken curry. Wadé work very well with curries and gravy dishes as they are thicker and coarser breads that absorb liquids. They look much like puris but are less puffy, and unlike the latter, are not made from refined flour.*

### METHOD
Combine both the flours with the salt and ghee or oil in a large mixing bowl.

Make a well in the centre and pour in a cup of warm, but not hot water. Using your fingertips, blend the ingredients together. Add a little more water if required, to form a soft, tight, smooth dough.

Divide the dough into two portions and knead each portion vigorously for 8 minutes into a smooth ball. Cover and leave in a cool place for 2-3 hours.

If using a food processor, pour a cup of water into the food bowl, and then pour in the flour and salt. Process to crumbs, and then add a little more water to form a firm dough. Keep pulsing for a few minutes then remove the ball of dough and knead manually for a few minutes.

Make 1" balls of the dough.

Dust some flour on a flat, clean surface or rolling board. Flatten the ball of dough in your palm and place it in the centre of the rolling surface. Apply the rolling pin to the middle of the dough and roll gently outwards, away from you and then in the opposite direction, towards you. Form a perfect circle about ¼" thick and about 3½"- 4" wide.

If you are unable to form a perfect circle use a cookie cutter or a lid with sharp edges to cut a circle out of the dough.

Roll out as many wadé as you can and place them on a dry, flat platter. Keep them covered with a clean, slightly damp towel.

Heat 2" of oil in a small kadhai or wok. Fry each wada, till puffy and golden brown. Ladle hot oil over it. As it begins to puff, turn it over to ensure even cooking. They do not puff up as much or as evenly as puris, because wholewheat flour is denser.

Serve immediately.

# PURAN POLI
## Lentil and Jaggery Flatbread

**MAKES 10 POLIS
6"- 7" ROUND**

### INGREDIENTS
**Filling**
250 gms husked, split Bengal gram or chana dal
2 tbsp ghee
200 gms jaggery, grated
1 tsp freshly powdered seeds of green cardamoms
½ tsp salt or to taste

**Poli**
400 gms wholewheat flour or atta + more for rolling
1 tbsp ghee + more for rolling

*Puran poli is to the Konkan what pizza is to the Italians. We worship it and a woman who can make it well is considered a supremely gifted cook. Puran refers to the filling of lentils and jaggery.*

*Puran poli is generally served as a dessert during festive holidays. The broth from the cooked chana dal is used to make katachi amti, (see glossary) or can be added to any lentil or pulao dish. Puran poli can be stored in an airtight container and refrigerated for up to seven days. Cover and warm in a microwave oven before serving.*

### METHOD
**Filling**
Wash the dal and soak it in water for about 6 hours. Drain and rinse the dal well.

Boil the dal with 8 cups of water in a large pan on high heat, stirring periodically, till soft.

Alternatively, pressure-cook it on low heat for 40 minutes after the cooker reaches full pressure.

Drain the dal completely and reserve the broth for another dish. It can be added to vaangi bhat, usals or Karwari sambhar instead of water.

Mash the dal with a fork or potato masher, till it is completely smooth.

Stir in the ghee and cook in a pan on low heat, stirring continuously, till the dal moves away from the sides of the pan and comes together as a ball of dough. It must form a thick, dry dough. It will dry and thicken further when it cools.

Transfer the dal to a food processor and purée to a fine consistency.

Return the dal to the pan with the remaining filling ingredients and cook on low heat, stirring continuously. The filling must be dry and free of any liquid. Remove from heat and cool completely.

### Poli

Sift the flour with the salt into a large mixing bowl. Add the ghee and rub it into the flour with your fingertips.

Make a well in the centre. Add up to 2½ cups of warm water, a little at a time and knead to form a firm dough. In a dry climate you may need to use more water while in a humid one you will need less.

Knead for 3-4 minutes and shape the dough into a ball. Cover and keep in a warm place for a few hours.

Knead the dough again and divide into 10 equal portions. Roll into small balls. Rub the balls with a little ghee. Cover with a damp cloth.

### To assemble and cook the puran poli

Divide the filling into 10 portions.

Sprinkle 1 tsp of flour on a flat, clean surface. Place a ball of dough in the centre. Roll the dough into an even 3" circle.

Place a ball of filling in the centre of the dough. Wrap the dough around the filling by bringing the ends towards the centre so that it is completely enclosed. Press down on the disc gently to seal the ends.

Sprinkle with a little flour and then roll out the stuffed dumpling. Start in the centre and move first upwards and outwards away from you. Then repeat the movement in the opposite direction towards you to form a ⅛"- ¼" thick, round patty. Do not press the dough too hard because the surface will break and force the filling, out. The skin of the bread dough should be thin enough for you to be able to see the filling inside.

Put a tawa or griddle on low heat. When warm, gently slap a polya on it. Cook both sides slowly, till golden brown. Then spread 1 tsp of ghee on each side and cook till golden and fragrant. Avoid flipping this bread too much because it will break.

Repeat with remaining dough and filling.

Drizzle melted ghee over the warm puran poli or serve with a bowl of cold milk.

# RICE

## DAHI BHAAT
## Curd Rice

### SERVES 6

*A versatile entrée, you can serve curd rice with a variety of fried fish, sol kadi, amti, saar, aubergine or mango pickles, papads, koshimbris and usals for a complete meal.*

### INGREDIENTS
#### Bhaat
6 cups warm plain, boiled medium-grained white rice
1 cup chilled full-cream or skimmed milk
3 cups chilled fresh (not sour) full-cream or low-fat plain yogurt
2-3 tsp salt or to taste
200 gms peeled and finely diced cucumbers (optional)

### TEMPERING
4 tbsp ghee or vegetable oil
1 tsp mustard seeds
12-14 fresh curry leaves, torn
5-6 green chillies, 1½"- 2" long, finely chopped
a pinch of asafoetida powder

### METHOD
Mash the cold rice thoroughly with a potato masher or a large fork.

Stir in milk and mash again. Mix in ½ cup of chilled water.

Add yogurt and mix thoroughly. Stir in salt to taste.

Put the ghee or oil in a small skillet or tempering spoon on high heat. When hot, add the mustard seeds, curry leaves, green chillies and finally asafoetida. Sauté for 1 minute, till fragrant.

Cool and stir the tempering into the curd rice.

Stir in the cucumbers, if desired.

Cover and chill, till ready to serve.

You may need to thin the rice with a little milk or water before you serve it, as it thickens in the refrigerator.

# MASALÉ BHAAT
## Spiced Rice Pulao

**4-6 SERVINGS**

### INGREDIENTS
4 cups plain, boiled, white,
short-grained rice
juice of ½ a lime
1 tsp grated jaggery or sugar
1 tsp cayenne pepper powder or more
2 tbsp finely chopped fresh
coriander leaves (optional)
⅔ cup ghee or vegetable oil
1 tsp black mustard seeds
¼ tsp fenugreek seeds (optional)
12 fresh curry leaves
3 green chillies, 1½"- 2" long,
finely chopped or to taste
a pinch of asafoetida powder
1 cup finely sliced white onions
1 tsp turmeric powder or more
½ cup unsalted, raw peanuts
salt to taste

### GARNISH
¼ cup grated fresh; or frozen,
defrosted, unsweetened coconut
(optional but yummy)

*This is a tasty, quick and easy dish that's prepared with leftover plain, boiled white rice. You can also use brown rice. Serve it for breakfast or lunch. You can add green peas or finely diced carrots to it as well. My grandmother made this in a large, cast iron griddle and allowed the rice at the bottom to turn slightly crisp and brown. Delicious!*

### METHOD
Toss the cooked rice with lime juice, jaggery or sugar, cayenne pepper powder and coriander leaves. Reserve.

Put the ghee or oil in a pan on high heat.

Add the mustard seeds and fenugreek seeds, then the curry leaves, green chillies and asafoetida powder.

When the spices sizzle, add the onions, turmeric powder and peanuts. Sauté on medium heat, till the onions turn golden and soft.

Add the rice and toss well on high heat for about 2 minutes.

Add salt and sugar to taste and garnish with coconut.

Serve warm with papads.

# KARWARI FISH BIRYANI

### 4-5 SERVINGS

*This biryani can also be made vegetarian with deep-fried potatoes and hard-boiled eggs. Serve it with papad and a coconut, yogurt and ground mustard relish. It pairs well with a slightly sweet white wine or cold beer.*

## INGREDIENTS

### Spice Paste
1 tbsp ghee or vegetable oil
2 tsp coriander seeds
1 tsp cumin seeds
2" cinnamon stick
5-6 cloves
3 black peppercorns
seeds of 1 green cardamom

### Coriander Paste
3 green chillies, 1½"- 2" long
7 cloves garlic
1" fresh ginger root, peeled
1 cup fresh coriander leaves
and their tender stems

### Onion Paste
1 tbsp vegetable oil
¼ cup chopped onions
¼ grated fresh; or frozen, defrosted,
unsweetened coconut
4-5 black peppercorns

### Fish
10 slices surmai or kingfish;
or pomfret
1 tsp salt or to taste
½ tsp turmeric powder
½ tsp cayenne pepper powder
or red chilli powder
juice of ½ a lime
vegetable oil for frying
1 cup rice flour

### Rice
3 cups medium-grained white rice
3 cups thick coconut milk
2 tbsp + 2 tbsp ghee or vegetable oil
1 cup finely chopped red or
white onions
3 red plum tomatoes, chopped
2 dried bay leaves
5-6 black peppercorns
¼ cup grated fresh; or frozen, defrosted,
unsweetened coconut

## GARNISH
Fresh coriander sprigs

## METHOD

### Spice Paste
Heat the ghee or oil for the spice paste in a small skillet and sauté the spices on medium heat, till fragrant.

Cool and grind the spices and oil to a fine consistency. Reserve.

### Coriander Paste
Grind all the coriander paste ingredients to a smooth consistency. Reserve.

### Onion Paste
Heat the oil for the onion paste and sauté the onions, till light brown. Add the remaining ingredients and sauté on medium heat, till light brown.

Grind to a smooth paste. Reserve.

**Fish**

Wash the fish slices and pat dry. Sprinkle with the salt, turmeric powder, chilli powder and lime juice.

Combine all three spice pastes.

Rub 2 tbsp of the combined spice mix into the fish, cover and refrigerate.

**Rice**

Wash the rice and set aside to drain.

Add the coconut milk to the remaining spice mix, stir and reserve.

Heat 2 tbsp of ghee or oil in a pan. Sauté the onions on medium heat, till golden.

Add the tomatoes and stir for 2-3 minutes to pulp them completely.

Stir in the spiced coconut milk. Cook for 5 minutes on low heat and remove from heat.

Heat 2 tbsp of ghee or oil in a pressure cooker or heavy-bottomed pan with a lid. Add the bay leaves and peppercorns and sauté on medium heat for about 30 seconds.

Reduce heat to low and add the drained rice. Sauté gently for about 1 minute.

Pour in the cooked spiced coconut milk, stir well and pressure cook for 8-10 minutes or cover and cook on low heat, till the rice is tender and fluffy.

**To assemble the biryani**

Remove the fish from the refrigerator and bring it to room temperature.

Heat the oil for frying the fish in a frying pan.

Pat the fish steaks in rice flour and fry in hot oil, till golden brown. Drain.

Fluff up the biryani with a fork, taste for salt and ladle it into a serving dish.

Decorate with fried fish pieces and fresh coriander sprigs.

# MARATHA CHICKEN PULAO

### 6-8 SERVINGS

### INGREDIENTS
### Rice
3 cups basmati rice
½ cup ghee or vegetable oil
1 dried bay leaf
4 cloves
2 cups hot chicken stock

### Chicken
1½ kg boneless, skinned chicken
3 tbsp ghee or vegetable oil
3 black peppercorns
2 cloves
1 black cardamom
2 green cardamoms
1 dried bay leaf
1" cinnamon stick
1½ cups finely chopped white onions
3 green chillies,
1½"- 2" long, chopped
3" fresh ginger root, peeled, puréed
6 cloves garlic, puréed
4 plum or red tomatoes, chopped
2 cups full-cream, plain yogurt
3 heaped tbsp Malvani garam masala
6-7 saffron strands
salt to taste

### To assemble and serve the pulao
1 cup cubed potatoes, fried
½ cup finely sliced onions, fried
2 hard-boiled eggs, peeled, quartered
2 tbsp chopped fresh coriander leaves

*This is not typical Konkani fare but it was a dish for special occasions and I had to include it in this book. Aurangabad, famed for the Ellora and Ajanta caves and named after Mughal Emperor Aurangzeb, has a delicious culinary history where Maratha cooking and Mughlai technique provide a rich, sensory experience. This dazzling dish is worth the effort. It makes for a complete, hearty meal and tastes even better on the second day. Serve it warm with a cold vegetable raita and a deep, full-bodied red wine or chilled beer.*

### METHOD
### Rice
Wash the rice and soak it in water for 2 hours.

Rinse the rice and drain completely.

Heat the ghee or oil in a large heavy-bottomed pan that has a tight-fitting lid.

Add the bay leaf and cloves and sauté on medium heat for about 1 minute.

Add the drained rice and gently sauté for about 30 seconds.

Pour in hot chicken stock and 3 cups of hot water. Stir, cover the pan and cook on medium heat for about 6 minutes, till the rice is fluffy.

Switch off the heat and keep the pan covered so the rice continues to cook in its own steam.

Fluff up the rice with a fork and spread on a large plate to cool.

**Chicken**

Wash the chicken and it cut into 1" cubes.

Heat the ghee or oil in a large, deep pan. Add the whole spices and sauté on high heat, till they sizzle and rise to the surface. Drain the spices and discard.

Add the onions and green chillies to the spiced oil and sauté on medium heat, till soft. Stir in the ginger and garlic and sauté for another minute.

Add the tomatoes and sauté on high heat for 3-4 minutes, till they are completely pulped.

Mix in the yogurt and Malvani garam masala and continue to cook for about 5-7 minutes, stirring constantly, till the yogurt thickens, splits and releases its oil. Add the chicken and stir well. Cook on medium heat, till the chicken is tender.

Sprinkle in the saffron and salt to taste. Switch off the heat and let it rest for about 10 minutes.

**To assemble the pulao**

Spoon half the cooked rice into the bottom of a bundt pan or a large ring-shaped mould about 4" deep. If you don't have either of these use a round, heat-proof dish that sits inside your pressure cooker.

Pat down the rice and dot with some fried potatoes and onions.

Spoon all the chicken with its gravy evenly over the rice bed.

Cover with the remaining rice, pat down and seal tightly with aluminium foil. Refrigerate overnight.

Remove from the refrigerator and bring to room temperature.

Reheat either by steaming in a pressure cooker for 10 minutes, or place it in a bain marie (warm water bath) in an oven heated to 150°C for 1 hour.

Turn out on to a large serving platter. Garnish with the remaining fried potatoes and onions and the hard-boiled eggs and coriander leaves.

Serve hot.

# VAANGI BHAAT
## Rice Pulao
## with Aubergine

### 6 SERVINGS

*An absolute must for aubergine lovers. The lentils and seeds give this dish a nutty, earthy flavour. You can also replace the spice mix here with goda masala for a change. Serve it with thick, plain yogurt or kakdi dahi koshimbri and papad for a complete meal. A sweet, fruity white wine or limbo pani, pairs well.*

## INGREDIENTS

### Vaangi bhaat spice mix
2 tbsp husked, split Bengal gram or chana dal
2 tbsp husked, split black gram or urad dal
2 tbsp husked, split moong beans or moong dal
½ tbsp white sesame seeds
2 tbsp coriander seeds
1¼ tsp cumin seeds
4" cinnamon stick
1 tbsp ghee or vegetable oil
10 dried red Byadgi or Kashmiri chillies, stalks and seeds removed
8 cloves or marati moggu if you can find it
2 tsp grated jaggery or sugar

### Rice
2 cups medium-grained white rice
10 Indian baby or 3 long Japanese aubergines
4 tbsp ghee or vegetable oil
1 tsp black mustard seeds
10 fresh curry leaves
3 green chillies, 1½"- 2" long
½ cup finely chopped red or white onions
2 tsp tamarind paste
¼ tsp turmeric powder
2 tsp salt or to taste
½ cup unsalted, roasted peanuts, coarsely crushed, fried (optional)
½ cup grated fresh; or frozen, defrosted, unsweetened coconut (optional)

## METHOD

### Vaangi bhaat spice mix
Roast the dals, sesame seeds, coriander seeds, cumin seeds and cinnamon in a dry skillet on medium heat for 3-4 minutes.

Remove, cool and grind to a fine powder.

Heat the ghee or oil in the same skillet. Sauté the red chillies and cloves or marati moggu on medium heat for about 1 minute.

Cool. Add to the ground spices and grind again with the jaggery or sugar to make a smooth, slightly moist powder. Reserve.

### Rice
Wash the rice and set aside to drain.

Wash the aubergines and remove the stalks.

If using baby aubergines quarter them lengthwise. Cut the Japanese aubergines into 1" thick round slices.

Put the ghee or oil in a large heavy-bottomed pan that has a tight-fitting lid on medium heat.

Add the mustard seeds, curry leaves and green chillies and sauté for 1 minute.

Add the onions and aubergines and sauté for 4-5 minutes, stirring constantly to prevent burning.

Reduce the heat to low and add ¼ cup of water to prevent the aubergines from sticking to the bottom of the pan. Cover and cook till the aubergines are soft but not fully cooked.

Stir the rice into the pan.

Add 3 cups of boiling water. Mix gently.

Add the tamarind, vaangi bhaat spice mix, turmeric powder and salt and stir.

Cover the pan and cook for 7-8 minutes on low heat.

Switch off the heat and let the rice cook in its own steam for 5-7 minutes.

Fluff up the rice with a fork and taste. Add some lime juice, salt and sugar if required.

Stir in the peanuts and coconut, if you like. Serve warm.

# SPICE MIXES, CHUTNEYS, PICKLES AND JAMS

## GODA OR KALA MASALA

### MAKES ABOUT 2 CUPS

#### INGREDIENTS
10 tsp vegetable oil
⅓ cup cumin seeds
1 tsp black mustard seeds
¾ cup coriander seeds
¼ tsp asafoetida powder
1 tsp black cumin seeds or shahi jeera/kala jeera
6 cloves
3" cinnamon stick
½ cup stone flower/lichen flower or dagadphool
4 dried red Byadgi or Kashmiri chillies, stalks and seeds removed
1 dried bay leaf
¼ black cardamom

#### For dry-roasting
2 cups grated fresh; or frozen, defrosted, unsweetened coconut
¼ cup white sesame seeds
½ tsp turmeric powder

*Goda means sweet in Marathi and kala means black. This sweet, smoky spice mix is the most complex one you will find in Indian cooking. Unlike other spice mixes, that require a light toasting, spices for goda masala are individually roasted slowly, till they are golden brown, to produce a dark colour. Stone flower is a unique ingredient used in this spice mix and is crucial to its taste. Goda masala is added to a long list of dishes: usals, stuffed aubergines, vaangi bhaat and amti.*

*Do not heat the oil before adding the spices.*

*Combine cold oil with the spices in the skillet and cook on low to medium heat. Keep stirring to avoid burning the spices.*

*You can quarter this recipe to produce just enough for a few dishes.*

## METHOD

Put a cast iron skillet on low heat.

Begin with 3 tsp of oil along and the cumin and mustard seeds. Roast for about 3 minutes, till fragrant and golden. Remove and scrape into a medium-sized mixing bowl.

Add 3 tsp of oil to the same skillet with the coriander seeds and asafoetida powder. Roast for 2-3 minutes. Remove from heat and scrape into the bowl with the cumin seeds.

Add another 2 tsp of oil with the black cumin seeds, cloves, cinnamon and stone flower. Roast for 2 minutes. Scrape into the same bowl.

Heat 2 tsp of oil and sauté the red chillies, bay leaf and black cardamom for about 2 minutes. Scrape into the bowl.

In the same skillet, but without adding oil toast the coconut on low heat, stirring occasionally, for about 4-5 minutes, till the coconut browns and dries up.

Add the sesame seeds and continue toasting for about 4-5 minutes, till the seeds are golden.

Stir in the turmeric and switch off the heat.

Combine all the spices and the coconut. Cool them and grind to a slightly wet powder.

Store in the refrigerator in an airtight container. This spice mix, if kept moisture-free, will last 2 weeks in the refrigerator.

# KARWARI SAMBHAR MASALA POWDER

**MAKES ABOUT ½ CUP**

## INGREDIENTS
8 cloves
12 black peppercorns
12 dried red Byadgi or Kashmiri chillies, stalks and seeds removed
¼ tsp fenugreek seeds
1 tsp coriander seeds
1 tbsp husked urad dal
1 tbsp cumin seeds
4" cinnamon stick
¼ cup desiccated coconut
1 tbsp vegetable oil
1 tsp mustard seeds
a pinch of asafoetida powder

*Sambhar masala is one of India's most well-known spice mixes and every housewife has a recipe. Called kolombyo pitto in the Konkan, it is made with a variety of ground lentils such as husked, split Bengal gram or chana dal and pigeon peas or toor/arhar. In Karwar, we made it with coriander seeds and husked, split black gram or urad dal.*

*Stir the masala into lentils, sprinkle on fresh idlis, coconut chutneys and polé and mix it into clam batter.*

## METHOD
Toast the cloves, peppercorns, red chillies, fenugreek seeds, coriander seeds, dal, cumin seeds and cinnamon in a dry skillet on medium heat for 2-3 minutes. Add coconut and stir till golden, about 3 minutes.

Cool completely and grind to a fine consistency.

Put the oil into the same skillet on high heat. Sauté the mustard seeds and asafoetida powder, till fragrant. Cool and grind again with the powdered spices and coconut.

Refrigerate in an airtight container for up to 2 weeks.

# KUMTA PITTO
## Kumta Masala

**MAKES ABOUT 6 TBSP**

**INGREDIENTS**
10 cloves
3 dried red Kashmiri chillies,
stalks and seeds removed
3" cinnamon stick
2 tbsp coriander seeds
1 tbsp fennel seeds or
badi saunf/badishap
½ tbsp cumin seeds

*Pitto means powder in Konkani. Kumta on Karnataka's western coast (north Canara) is about a four-hour drive from Goa. Known for its beautiful beaches and important temples it has an excellent local cuisine, also called Kumta. Locals down Kumta masala pohé with shunti soda, a fizzy fresh ginger root drink. This dried spice mix can be used in a variety of dishes including curries, relishes and snacks. For variety, add some to pohé, rassas, home-made chiwda, missal pao and bhajji batter.*

**METHOD**
Toast all the ingredients in a dry skillet on medium heat for 2-3 minutes.

Cool the mix completely and grind to make a fine powder.

Store in an airtight container for up to 4-6 weeks.

# MALVANI GARAM MASALA

*Stir this robust spice mix into vegetarian and non-vegetarian pulaos, biryanis, usals and bhajis, also kothimbri vadé.*

## MAKES ABOUT ½ CUP

### INGREDIENTS

2 tbsp ghee or vegetable oil
2 tsp white poppy seeds or khus khus
2 tsp white sesame seeds
1 cup grated fresh; or frozen, defrosted, unsweetened coconut
2 dried red Byadgi or Kashmiri red chillies, stalks and seeds removed
6 cloves
2" cinnamon stick
1 tsp cumin seeds
1 tsp turmeric powder
½ tsp coriander seeds
¼ tsp seeds of green cardamom

### METHOD

Put the ghee or oil in a pan on low heat. When hot, add all the spices and roast them for 4-5 minutes, tossing continuously, till golden and fragrant.

Cool and grind to a clumpy powder.

Refrigerate in an airtight container for 3-4 weeks.

# METHKOOT

*A flavourful combination of roasted lentils, grains and spices. Mix it into clam batter, Karwari sambhar lentils or eat with thalipeeth.*

### INGREDIENTS
½ cup raw, milled wheat grains
½ cup raw, short or medium-grained rice, washed and completely dried
2 tsp husked, split Bengal gram or chana dal
2 tsp husked, split moong beans or moong dal
2 tsp husked, split pigeon peas or toover/arhar dal
2 tsp urad dal
1 tsp white sesame seeds
2 tsp coriander seeds
2 tsp cumin seeds
1 tsp fenugreek seeds
½ tsp turmeric powder
¼ tsp white pepper powder
6 dried red Byadgi or Kashmiri chillies, stalks and seeds removed
1 tbsp vegetable oil
½ tsp mustard seeds
¼ tsp asafoetida powder
2 tsp salt
1 tsp sugar

### METHOD
Roast the wheat and rice grains in a dry skillet on medium heat for about 6-8 minutes, till golden. Set aside to cool.

Add the dals to the skillet and roast them on medium heat for 6-8 minutes till golden. Set aside to cool.

Add the remaining ingredients, except the oil, mustard seeds, asafoetida powder, salt and sugar to the same skillet and roast them on medium heat, till fragrant and golden. Set aside to cool.

Grind the cooled grains to a fine powder. Add the dals and grind again to a smooth powder.

Add the remaining roasted ingredients and grind once more to a smooth powder.

Put the oil in a small pan on medium heat. When hot, sauté the mustard seeds and asafoetida powder for about 30 seconds.

Cool and add the contents of the pan to the powdered mix with the salt and sugar and grind again.

Taste for salt. The mixture must be slightly salty as it is eaten with plain, unsalted, boiled, white rice.

Store in a clean, dry airtight container. Refrigerate for up to 1 month.

# COCONUT, YOGURT AND GROUND MUSTARD RELISH

## MAKES ABOUT 3 CUPS

*This is one of my favourites. It's chilled, creamy and spicy. Excellent with rice entrées, it can also be served as a dip with crackers and papad if you use hung yogurt instead of plain yogurt.*

### INGREDIENTS

2 cups plain yogurt
2 green cucumbers, peeled, finely chopped
1 tsp sugar or more
1 tsp salt or more
1 tbsp ghee or vegetable oil
1 tsp black mustard seeds

### Spice paste

1¼ tsp black mustard seeds
2-3 green chillies, 1½"- 2" long, roughly chopped
3 tbsp grated fresh; or frozen, defrosted, unsweetened coconut

### METHOD

Grind the spice paste ingredients to a fine consistency.

Stir it into the yogurt with the cucumbers, sugar and salt.

Put the ghee or oil in a small skillet on medium heat. Sauté the mustard seeds, till they splutter.

Remove from heat and add ¼ cup of cold water.

Stir into the relish.

# QUICK VEGETABLE RELISH

**MAKES ABOUT 4 CUP**

## INGREDIENTS

3 cups plain yogurt
Juice of 1 lime
1 tsp salt or to taste
1½ tsp sugar
¼ cup shredded carrots
¼ cup shredded green onions
(white bulbs only)
3-4 green chillies,
1½"- 2" long, finely chopped
8-10 fresh mint leaves, chopped
1 tbsp chopped fresh coriander leaves

### Garnish

2 red tomatoes, finely chopped

## METHOD

Whisk the yogurt in a bowl with the lime juice, salt and sugar.

Stir in the remaining ingredients.

Taste for salt and sugar.

Top with tomatoes.

Serve as a condiment with rice entrées.

# COLD BANANA YOGURT RELISH WITH TAMARIND

## MAKES ABOUT 3½ CUPS

### INGREDIENTS
2 large yellow bananas
2 cups full-cream, plain yogurt
2 tbsp date and tamarind chutney
¼ tsp cayenne pepper powder or red chilli powder
½ tsp powdered, roasted cumin seeds
1 tsp salt or to taste

### METHOD
Peel the bananas. Dice 1 banana and set aside.

Purée all the ingredients together except the salt and diced banana.

Stir in the banana pieces and season with salt.

# MINT CHUTNEY

## MAKES ABOUT ¾ CUP

### INGREDIENTS
1 cup fresh mint leaves, stalks removed
1 cup fresh coriander leaves, with some of the stalks
1 tsp sugar
1 tsp salt or to taste
juice of ½ a lime
¼" fresh root ginger, roughly chopped
1-2 small green chillies, 1½"- 2" long, roughly chopped

### METHOD
Purée all the ingredients with ½ cup of water.

Keep chilled.

# KARWARI WHITE COCONUT CHUTNEY

**MAKES ABOUT 1¼ CUPS**

## INGREDIENTS
1 tsp husked, split black gram or urad dal
3 small green chillies about 1½"- 2" long
2 cups grated fresh; or frozen, defrosted, unsweetened coconut
1 tsp tamarind paste
1 tsp salt or to taste
1½ tbsp ghee
1 tsp black mustard seeds
2 dried red Kashmiri chillies, stalks, seeds removed, kept whole
6 fresh curry leaves
a pinch of asafoetida powder

## METHOD
Toast the dal in a skillet on medium heat for about 30-60 seconds till fragrant.

Cool and grind to a powder.

Add the green chillies, coconut, tamarind paste and salt and grind again to a fine consistency.

Heat the ghee in a small skillet on medium heat and sauté mustard seeds, red chillies, curry leaves and asafoetida in the same order for about 1 minute. Cool and stir into the chutney.

Taste for salt and serve at room temperature. Can be kept refrigerated for 2-3 days.

# KARWARI RED COCONUT CHUTNEY

**MAKES ABOUT ½ CUP**

## INGREDIENTS
4 dried red Byadgi or Kashmiri chillies, stalks removed
1 cup grated fresh; or frozen, defrosted, unsweetened coconut
½ tsp salt
1½ tsp tamarind paste

## GARNISH
1 tbsp very finely chopped red onion

## METHOD
Toast the red chillies in a dry pan for 2-3 minutes on low heat.

Cool and grind to make a fine powder. Add the remaining ingredients, except the garnish, and grind again to a fine consistency. Taste for salt.

Garnish with the onion.

# DRY COCONUT CHUTNEY WITH PEANUTS

## MAKES ABOUT ¾ CUP

*Serve this with fritters, flatbreads, puris, polé, idlis; the list is endless.*

### INGREDIENTS

15-16 fresh curry leaves
1 tbsp white sesame seeds
½ cup grated fresh; or frozen, defrosted, unsweetened coconut
½ cup unsalted, roasted peanuts
1 tbsp tamarind paste
2 tsp freshly ground cayenne pepper powder or red chilli powder
1 tsp salt or to taste

### METHOD

Toast the curry leaves and sesame seeds in a dry skillet on medium heat for 2-3 minutes, till golden, dry, crisp and fragrant. Remove and set aside to cool.

In the same skillet, roast the coconut on low heat, till light brown. Cool completely.

Using a rolling pin or a large mortar and pestle, pound the coconut lightly to release its flavours. Add the peanuts and pound again to a coarse powder. Add all the remaining ingredients and pound again to make a slightly moist powder.

Store in an airtight bottle for up to 1 week at room temperature or 1 month refrigerated. Serve this chutney with fritters, thalipeeth and polé.

# CORIANDER COCONUT CHUTNEY

## MAKES ABOUT 1½ CUPS

### INGREDIENTS

1 cup fresh coriander leaves, with tender stalks but no roots
1 cup grated fresh; or frozen, defrosted, unsweetened coconut
1 tsp salt or to taste
juice of ½ a lime
¼" fresh ginger root, peeled
2 green chillies, 1½"- 2" long, stalks removed

### METHOD

Grind all the ingredients together with a little water to a smooth consistency. Bottle and refrigerate for up to 1 week.

As a variation stir in 1-2 tbsp of chinch khajur chutney.

# CHINCH KHAJUR CHUTNEY
## Date and Tamarind Chutney

**MAKES ABOUT 1½ CUPS**

*A tremendously useful chutney to have around. It is used in curries, snacks such as sev puri, as a dipping sauce for samosa or chamunchas and fritters and in lentil and bhaji preparation, also in banana yogurt relish.*

**INGREDIENTS**

500 gms dates pitted, chopped coarsely
½ cup tamarind paste
6 cloves garlic (optional)
2 tsp cayenne pepper powder or red chilli powder (optional)
1 tsp salt or to taste
½ tsp freshly roasted powdered cumin seeds (optional)

**METHOD**

Soak the chopped dates in 2 cup of hot water for about 20 minutes.

Put the dates and water in a blender with the remaining ingredients. Purée till smooth. Add more water if required.

Bottle and refrigerate for 4 weeks.

# BATATÉ DAHI CHUTNEY
## Potato, Yogurt and Peanut Chutney

**MAKES ABOUT 1½ CUPS**

### INGREDIENTS

2 potatoes
1 cup full-cream-milk plain yogurt
+ ½ cup cold water
2 tbsp grated fresh; or frozen, defrosted, unsweetened coconut
1½ tsp tamarind paste
1 tsp salt or more
1 tsp jaggery or more
2-3 green chillies, 1½"- 2" long
2 tbsp unsalted, roasted peanuts, crushed

### TEMPERING

1 tbsp ghee or vegetable oil
8 fresh curry leaves, torn
1 green chilli, 1½"- 2" long, finely chopped
a pinch of asafoetida powder

### METHOD

Wash the potatoes and boil, bake or steam them, till tender but firm.

Peel and dice the potatoes into ¼" cubes.

Purée the yogurt and water with the coconut, tamarind, salt, jaggery and green chillies, to a fine consistency.

Put the ghee or oil for tempering in a small skillet on high heat and sauté the curry leaves, green chilli and asafoetida for 30 seconds.

Cool and stir the tempering into the spiced yogurt.

Stir in the potatoes and peanuts. Serve chilled.

# DOUN LAAT JHUNKA
## Two-Kick Jhunka

### 6 SERVINGS

### INGREDIENTS
1 cup gram flour or besan
¼ tsp coriander powder
¼ tsp cumin powder
¼ tsp turmeric powder
2 tsp cayenne pepper powder
or Guntur Saanam
red chilli powder
salt to taste
½ cup finely chopped
white onions
6 cloves garlic, finely chopped
juice of ½ a lime
1 tbsp chopped fresh coriander leaves
grated jaggery to taste

### TEMPERING
½ cup vegetable oil
6 fresh curry leaves
½ tsp black mustard seeds
a pinch of asafoetida powder

*Laat is kick in Marathi, which is exactly what you get when you eat this. As if the first kick from the spicy Guntur Saanam chilli (one of India's spiciest red chillies) is not enough, the second one is provided by the raw onion and garlic. Only for the adventurous with no planes to catch!*

*A jhunka is like a saung, a condiment to be eaten in small quantities with bhakri. Made with inexpensive ingredients, it is a staple in rural Maharashtra. Pithla is a similar dish, but is less dry, cooked with green chillies and tomatoes and served over plain, boiled, white rice.*

### METHOD
Whisk together the gram flour and spice powders with 1 cup of water. Add salt to taste. Reserve.

Put the oil for tempering in a medium skillet on high heat. When hot, add the curry leaves, mustard seeds and asafoetida powder.

Stir in the onion and garlic and sauté till translucent and fragrant.

Add the gram flour mix and cook on medium heat, stirring continuously.

The gram flour will begin to dry and come together in a ball. Keep breaking it up and stirring, till it has the consistency of mashed potato.

Stir in the lime juice and coriander leaves.

Taste and add jaggery and more salt, if required.

Serve immediately with millet or rice flatbreads and curried vegetables.

# VAANGI LONCHÉ
## Aubergine Pickle

**MAKES ABOUT 2½ KGS**

### INGREDIENTS
2 kg firm, large purple aubergine
or brinjal/baingan
3¼ cups sweet oil or a mild,
unflavoured vegetable oil
4" fresh ginger root, peeled, julienned
15 green chillies, 1½"- 2" long,
stalks removed, slit
2½ cups white vinegar
½ cup sugar or to taste
2-3 tsp salt or to taste

### Spice paste
12-14 dried red Kashmiri chillies,
stalks removed
½ tsp fenugreek seeds
1½ tsp black mustard seeds
1½ tsp cumin seeds
2 tbsp white vinegar
15 cloves garlic, roughly chopped

*This is one of the best pickles I've ever eaten. It's so lip-smacking, you'll want to spread it on toast but its best served with any kind of rice dish, especially curd rice or as a condiment with flatbreads and vegetables. It's also good with roasted or steamed fish.*

*Use a pan with a heavy bottom: enamel-clad cast iron or copper-clad stainless works well. Make sure the pan's surface is in good shape; exposed metals react with vinegar. Keep sterilised pickle jars ready.*

### METHOD
Wash the aubergines and wipe well. Remove and discard the stalk but do not peel. Cut into 1½" cubes. Set aside.

Remove seeds from half the dried Kashmiri chillies. Reserve chillies only.

Grind all the red chillies and whole spices for the spice paste to a fine consistency. Add the vinegar and garlic and grind again to a smooth consistency.

Put the oil in a deep, heavy-bottomed pan on medium heat. Sauté the ginger for about 1 minute.

Add the spice paste and sauté well for about 4-5 minutes, stirring all the while to prevent burning. The spice paste should be fragrant, oily and bubbly. Add the green chillies, vinegar, sugar and aubergines. Stir well. Cook open on low heat for about 1 hour, turning occasionally.

The aubergines will release water, so keep cooking, till all the water has evaporated.

Add salt and taste.

This is a sweet and spicy pickle so if you want it tangier, add more vinegar. For a sweeter taste, add more sugar. Stir well and cook longer.

Pour into sterilised pickle jars while the pickle is still hot. Cap tightly. When cooled refrigerate for up to 30-40 days.

# GUAVA JAM

## MAKES 400-500 GMS

### INGREDIENTS
1 kg ripe guavas (about 8-10)
½ cup peeled, cored and finely
diced red apples
1½ cups sugar or to taste
strained juice of ½ a lime
¼ tsp freshly powdered green
cardamom or more for a stronger
flavour (optional)

### METHOD
With a potato peeler, peel 4 guavas and discard
the peel. Cut into 4 pieces lengthwise and remove
the centre pulp and seeds. Reserve pulp and seeds.

Cut the peeled guavas into 4-5 pieces. Reserve.

Slice the remaining guavas finely with their peel.
Reserve.

Put the flesh, pulp and seeds from the 4 peeled
guavas with the apples and 3 cups of water in
a heavy-bottomed pan on medium heat. Cook,
stirring all the while for about 25 minutes.

Strain the cooked fruit through a seive to collect,
about 1-1½ cups of juice. Reserve.

Pulse the residue from the strainer in a grinder
for 30 seconds only, so that the seeds are not
completely pulverised.

Strain this residue through a seive again to fill
about 1-1½ cups. Reserve. Discard the residue.

Place the strained juice, strained pulp, the sliced
guavas and half the sugar in a pan. Cook on low
heat for about 10 minutes, stirring all the while.

Add the remaining sugar and continue to stir on
low heat, till the mixture is very thick.

Remove from heat and add the strained lime juice
and cardamom.

Fill bottles while the jam is still hot. Cool and
screw on the lids. Refrigerate for 6-7 weeks.

# TOTAPURI MANGO JAM

### MAKES ABOUT 1½ CUPS

*This is more a relish than a jam and is excellent with any pulao, bhaat, curd rice, with plain flatbreads and a vegetable dish. It's also excellent with fresh cheese and crackers, roast chicken and grilled fish.*

### INGREDIENTS

4 unripe Totapuri mangoes
1 cup white granulated sugar
6 large cloves garlic, lightly smashed
3" cinnamon stick
salt to taste

### METHOD

Wash the mangoes. Grate them with the skin. Discard the seeds.

Steam the grated fruit for 5 minutes in a pressure cooker, rice cooker or steamer, without water. Reserve.

Boil the sugar with 1 cup of water in a pan, till thick and syrupy. Stir continuously and do not let the sugar brown.

Stir in the garlic and cinnamon. Continue cooking.

When the syrup is very thick, add the steamed mangoes. Cook on high heat, till thick, stirring periodically to prevent burning.

Remove from heat and add salt and a little water if you prefer a thinner consistency. Return jam to high heat. Bring to a boil, reduce heat and simmer again for 10 minutes.

Bottle in a clean, airtight, sterilised jar while the relish is still hot.

Keep refrigerated for 1 month.

# COOLING OFF:
# **ICED BEVERAGES**
# FOR HOT SUMMERS

## **AAM PANNA**
## Chilled Raw
## Mango Beverage

### MAKES 12-14 CUPS

*Mango panna is a magnificent sweet and sour drink with a light green colour that comes from raw mangoes. It can be made with almost any variety of inexpensive raw mango. If you prefer a more golden colour add a semi-ripe mango. Panna will keep well refrigerated for about a week. It makes an excellent mixer with vodka, gin and white rum. Rim the glasses with coarse salt for a salty after taste.*

### INGREDIENTS

5-6 large raw green mangoes, Dassheri, Langda, Totapuri, South American, washed
1 large semi-ripe mango, washed (optional)
1½ cups sugar or to taste

### Spices (optional)

12-15 saffron strands
½ tsp cayenne pepper powder or red chilli powder
¼ tsp freshly powdered green cardamom seeds
½ tsp powdered, freshly roasted cumin seeds
¼ tsp salt or to taste

### GARNISH

fresh mint leaves or lime slices

### METHOD

Coarsely chop the raw mangoes and place them in a large heavy-bottomed pan that is well lined. Avoid unclad cast iron, aluminium and non-stick.

Using a sharp knife make 1-2 slits in the ripe mango (if used) and add it to the raw ones. Fill the pan with 7 litres of water.

Cover and simmer for about 45 minutes on medium heat. Stir occasionally. The water should reduce to about 3 litres and turn a pale, yellow-green colour. Press down gently on the ripe mango to release its flavours and pulp into the water.

Strain the liquid, discard the fruit, then add the spices and cool.

Chill and serve in tall glasses filled with ice. Garnish with mint leaves or lime slices.

# LIME WATER WITH SAFFRON AND CARDAMOM

*This twist on the traditional limbu pani or fresh lime has a lovely golden colour from the saffron.*

## 4 SERVINGS

### INGREDIENTS
¾ cup sugar or more
¼ tsp salt
juice of 3 limes
4-6 saffron strands, crumbled
⅛ tsp freshly powdered green cardamom seeds
600 ml chilled club soda or water

### METHOD
Put the sugar and salt with 1 cup of water into a small skillet on high heat. Reduce to half its volume. Cool completely. Add lime juice, saffron and cardamom. Chill.

Fill 4 highball glasses with 3-4 ice cubes and divide the lime-saffron mixture equally. Top with chilled club soda or water. Stir in more sugar or salt to tase,

Serve immediately.

# SPICED WATERMELON CUCUMBER COOLER

*Ruby red watermelons and peridot green cucumbers flood the market in summer. The perfect fruit and vegetable combination to beat the heat.*

## 4 SERVINGS

### INGREDIENTS
2 puneri or similar mild, tender, 6" long cucumbers, peeled, finely diced
⅛ tsp salt or to taste
1 litre fresh puréed watermelon

### GARNISH
½ tsp chaat masala powder
fresh mint leaves

### METHOD
Purée the cucumber with the salt in a food processor. Add the watermelon and give it a whirl, to blend well.

Chill and divide the juice between 4 highball glasses. Sprinkle with chaat masala and garnish with a sprig of mint.

# ICED TEA WITH MINT AND LEMON GRASS

## 6-8 SERVINGS

*The leaves of the lemon grass plant are called gilli chai and have a more delicate flavour than the lemon grass root, making it ideal for beverages.*

### INGREDIENTS

1 cup sugar
4 tbsp coarsely chopped lemon grass leaves or gilli chai
8-10 fresh mint leaves, torn
2 tbsp black CTC Assam tea

### GARNISH

2 limes, cut into wedges

### METHOD

Combine all the ingredients, except the black tea with 8 cups of water in a deep pan and put it on medium heat. When the water reaches a boil, switch off the heat. Add the tea leaves and cover.

Set aside for 10 minutes. Strain and chill the liquid.

Serve over ice in glasses of your choice with lime wedges.

# TAAK
## Spiced Buttermilk

*Also called mattham this is the most commonly drunk beverage in the Konkan. Freshly ground cumin makes all the difference.*

### 4 SERVINGS

### INGREDIENTS

2 green chilli, 1½"- 2" long, stalks removed
1 tsp peeled, julienned fresh ginger root
1 litre plain buttermilk
1½ tsp freshly ground cumin seeds
1 tsp powdered sugar
tsp finely chopped, fresh coriander leaves
salt to taste

### GARNISH

1 tbsp chopped, fresh coriander leaves

### METHOD

Purée the green chilli, ginger and buttermilk.

Stir in the remaining ingredients. Add salt to taste.

Chill and pour into highball glasses. Garnish with coriander leaves and serve.

# SWEET ENDINGS:
# DESSERTS

The Konkan, like the rest of India has a plethora of rich desserts made from milk, in various forms, and sugar, such as kheer, a thickened rice pudding and carrot halva. But there are sweets, unique to the Konkan also: puran poli, gulachi poli, sanjori — stuffed flatbreads, modak — steamed coconut dumplings, karanjias — filled and deep-fried empanadas; and others made with grains; vegan desserts such as oundo ravo — rice dumplings in sugar syrup, jilbi — deep-fried spirals of dough soaked in sugar syrup; and a variety of boiled sweets made with coconut, sesame, peanuts and cashewnuts.

Baked desserts like bread pudding, chilled ice creams made with local fruits, layered custards like the Goan bebinca and crème caramels, legacies of a colonial past, live on in homes and restaurants.

## BASUNDI
## Saffron Milk with Almonds and Pistachios

*Basundi is slightly thickened milk served as part of a meal with flatbreads, such as phulkas and puris. It can also be served as a beverage dessert.*

### 8 SERVINGS

### INGREDIENTS
1 litre milk
1½ cups granulated sugar or to taste
¼ tsp freshly grated nutmeg
1 tsp freshly powdered green cardamom seeds
8 saffron strands, crumbled
2 tbsp crushed unsalted pistachios
3 tbsp slivered almonds

### METHOD
Combine the milk, sugar, nutmeg and cardamom in a pan and bring to a boil on medium heat. Continue to boil, till the sugar has dissolved. Cook for 5 minutes longer, stirring constantly.

Remove from heat and cool.

Add the remaining ingredients and refrigerate.

Serve chilled in low ball glasses or vati.

# SITAPHAL RABDI
## Custard
## Apple Dessert

### 3-4 SERVINGS

*Sitaphal is commonly called custard apple but is in fact a sugar apple. It has a short shelf life so consume this dessert quickly — I promise you, it won't be difficult. Rabdi is easy to make but time consuming. You can also buy it ready-made and stir in the custard apple.*

### INGREDIENTS
6 ripe custard apples
2 litres full-cream milk,
cow or buffalo
1¼ cups sugar

**METHOD**

Pull open the custard apples and peel the flesh off the black seeds. Scrape the flesh off the shells gently with a spoon.

Discard the seeds and outer green shells. Cover and refrigerate the white pulp.

Put the milk and sugar in a large, heavy kadhai or non-stick wok on medium heat.

Use a wooden, heatproof plastic or silicon stirring spoon with a somewhat sharp edge, so it's easier to scrape off the milk fat as it thickens on the sides and bottom of the pan.

Stir constantly to prevent burning. Cook the milk till it is reduced to one-third of its original volume. This will take 40 minutes to an hour.

If you feel confident, you can raise the heat and complete the reduction faster. But make sure you don't burn any of it because you will have to discard all the milk and start again.

When the milk resembles a thick cake batter, remove it from the heat. Pour into a bowl and cover with plastic wrap. Press the wrap close to the thickened milk to prevent a sikn from forming. Chill.

Stir the custard apple fruit into the thickened, chilled milk. Cover again tightly with cling film. Press the wrap on to the milk's surface to remove any air bubbles. Chill again.

Before serving check the consistency of the dessert. If it's too thick, add some cold milk to it. Taste for sugar.

Spoon it into small bowls or dessert cups and serve chilled.

# AAMRUS
## Chilled
## Mango Pulp

### 6 SERVINGS

*This is a delicious, simple, mango dessert, best served cold. Use a good quality mango with fibreless and sweet pulp.*

### INGREDIENTS

8 overripe langda, mayapuri, rajbhog or dusheri mangoes, peeled
1-2 tbsp granulated sugar or to taste
½ tsp freshly powdered green cardamom seeds (optional)

### METHOD

Cut all the flesh off the mango seeds and put it in a bowl.

Then using your hands scrape the remaining pulp on the mango seeds off and squeeze it into the bowl.

Soak the seeds in ½ cup of water in another bowl and continue to squeeze off as much pulp as possible.

Discard the seeds and pour the liquid into the bowl containing the mango pulp.

Mix in the sugar and cardamom. Taste and add more sugar.

Mash the pulp with a potato masher. The consistency should be thick and pulpy, with pieces of mango for texture. Do not blend in a food processor.

Chill and serve with puris or whipped cream.

# KESAR SHRIKHAND
## Hung Saffron Yogurt

### 6-8 SERVINGS

*This classic Konkan dessert is made with hung yogurt. It can be eaten as is, or served with port-poached pears, fresh berries, pound cake, sliced mangoes, grilled pineapple or traditionally with salted, deep-fried puris. The whey that is released while draining the yogurt can be used to prepare taak. It can also be added to lentil dishes like amti or stirred into a varan or kadi. The yogurt thickens when chilled so you can add a little cold water and whip it with a whisk before serving. The desired consistency is light, fluffy and creamy.*

### INGREDIENTS
1 kg plain yogurt
¾-1 cup powdered sugar or to taste
1 tsp freshly powdered green cardamom seeds or lemon zest
6-8 saffron strands, crushed in ½ cup cold water

### GARNISH
2 tbsp blanched, peeled, slivered almonds
1 tbsp slivered pistachio nuts

### METHOD
Pour the yogurt into a mixing bowl and blend thoroughly with a whisk.

Lay a cheesecloth over a strainer or fine colander and place it over a deep bowl to facilitate drainage.

Pour the yogurt into the cheesecloth.

Refrigerate overnight.

Squeeze the cheesecloth periodically, to facilitate draining. Empty the bowl if the drained fluid rises too close to the cheesecloth.

Scrape the thick yogurt off the cheesecloth into a mixing bowl.

Use an electric beater to whip the yogurt on medium speed for about 2-3 minutes or with a hand whisk for about 4 minutes.

Slowly, add the sugar and keep whipping the yogurt.

Add the cardamom or lemon zest and saffron with its soaking water to the yogurt and blend in thoroughly.

Spoon the yogurt into a glass bowl and cover tightly. Chill till ready to serve.

Garnish with nuts and serve.

# SHEERA
## Semolina Pudding with Almonds

### 6 SERVINGS

*This dessert is called sheera in Konkani, sanja in Marathi, kesari bhaat in Kannada and sooji halva in northern India. The preparations vary a little in their use of milk and water and the consistency of the pudding. It can be served as is or with whipped cream, vanilla ice cream and if you add eggs you can bake it into a cake.*

*You can use this sheera without raisins and nuts as a filling for sanjori. Traditionally, this dish is prepared with ghee but my mother uses butter which gives the dish a sweet and salty flavour. You can also go vegan by using water and margarine.*

### INGREDIENTS
1½ cups milk or water
1 tsp freshly powdered green cardamom seeds
1 cup powdered sugar (more for a sweeter sheera)
200 gms butter, ghee or vegetable margarine
2 cups medium-coarse semolina or rava/sooji
6-8 saffron strands
2 tbsp seedless golden raisins (optional)

### GARNISH
2 tbsp toasted, slivered almonds (optional)

### METHOD
Combine the milk or water, cardamom and sugar in a pan. Add 1 more cup of water and place on low heat to keep warm.

Melt the butter, ghee or margarine in a skillet on medium heat and sauté the semolina for 3-4 minutes. Stir constantly, till the semolina is hot, fragrant and lightly toasted. Do not brown.

Remove the pans with the milk and semolina from heat.

Add saffron and raisins to the milk and stir well. Slowly pour the milk into the semolina. The mixture will spit and bubble. Stir immediately and vigorously to make sure no lumps are formed.

Transfer the pan back to medium heat. Stir for 2-3 minutes, till the semolina is dry and crumbly. Switch off the heat and let it cool for 2-3 minutes.

Garnish with almonds and serve warm as is or with hot phulka, puri, whipped cream or vanilla ice cream.

# LANGDA MANGO ICE CREAM

## 12-14 SERVINGS

*If you can't find langda mangoes, use Alphonso or any other flavourful, tender mangoes. This method does not require an ice cream machine.*

### INGREDIENTS

2 cups full-cream milk
3 egg yolks
1 heaped tbsp white sugar, powdered
2 ripe, langda mangoes, peeled, finely chopped
2 cups heavy or double cream
3 egg whites
a pinch of cream of tartar

## METHOD

Whisk the milk and eggs yolks together. Strain to remove lumps. Whisk in the sugar and pour into a double boiler or heavy-bottomed pan.

Stir continuously on very low heat for about 10-12 minutes, till the mixture thickens to the consistency of a custard. This process takes patience. If the heat is too high the custard will curdle.

Remove from heat and pour into a bowl.

Wrap in cling film, pressing the wrap close to the surface of the custard, to prevent the formation of a skin. Refrigerate for 4 hours.

Remove the custard from the refrigerator and stir in the mangoes gently with a fork. Wrap in cling film and return to the refrigerator.

Whip the cream till stiff peaks form.

Remove the mango custard from the refrigerator again and gently fold in the whipped cream. Cover again and chill.

Whisk the egg whites with cream of tartar, till stiff peaks form.

Remove the mango custard from the refrigerator. Fold in the egg whites gently using a fork.

Immediately pour into a clean, dry air tight, sandwich or ice cream box. Cover and freeze overnight.

Remove five minutes before serving. To loosen the frozen ice cream, place the container in a pan of lukewarm water for a minute then turn out, slice and serve.

**BIBLIOGRAPHY**

Aigal, G. R. *The Ancient History of South Canara.*

Cairnes, Reverend, *History of the Konkan.*

*Cochin Tribes and Castes.*

Dellon, Gabriel and Archibald Bower, Edward, Peters, *Inquisition.*

Existence of Saraswati River: Evidences from Remote Sensing and GIS: Digital Enhancement Studies of IRS-1C data (1995)

*Forme De Cury* (Medieval text).

Gopalakrishnan, T. R., *Horticulture Science Series.*

Hunter, W. W., A Brief History of the Indian People.

Kalidasa, *Abhijnan Shakuntalam.*

Keni, Chandrakant, *Saraswats in Goa and Beyond.*

Khatre, S. M., *The Formation of Konkani.*

Khobarker, Dr, *Konkan from the Earliest to 1818 AD.*

Kudva, V. N., *History of the Dakshinatya Saraswats.*

Kulkarni, Uday, Solstice at Panipat.

*Larousse Gastronomique.*

*Le Viandier de Taillevent.*

McGee, Harold, *The Science of Cooking.*

Nabar, S. M., *Konkan Economy and Society in Transition (1818-1920); With Special Reference to Ratnagiri, Malvan and Vengurla.*

Panda, H., *Herb Cultivation and Medicinal Uses.*

Pradeep Kumar, T., *Management of Horticultural Crops*, Vol 11.

Ranade, Vinayak, *A Social Economic Survey of a Konkan Village.*

Saraswats in Kanara, *Kanara Gazetteer*, 1883.

Sharma, G. R., *Saraswat-Bhushan.*

Singh, Kumar Suresh, *People of Maharashtra* Volume 2.

Singh, Suresh, *People of Maharashtra*, Volume 2.

Skanda-Purana Sahyadri Khanda (Uttarardha 1-3).

Zimler, Richard, Guardian of the Dawn.

**WEB REFERENCES**

http://irfc-nausena.nic.in

Imperial Gazetteer of India Volume 8

Wikipedia

www.bharat-rakshak.com

**GLOSSARY OF KONKAN CUISINE**

A
Aambadé: A sour leafy green, also called Indian roselle, it is cooked into lentils.

Aambodé: Flattened fritters with onions, husked, split Bengal gram or chana dal and rice flour, it is also prepared as fluffy wadé with husked, split black gram or urad dal. Biscuit Aambodé is popular fare at Konkani weddings.

Aamboli: A Konkan speciality, this dosa is made with rice, husked, split black gram or urad dal, husked, split Bengal gram or chana dal and wheat batter. The dosa is spongy and soft.

Adgai: A dark brown-black pickle made with raw mangoes, raw green jackfruit and burnt cayenne.

Adolee: A wooden vegetable chopper and grater consisting of a sharp sickle-like blade attached to a small wooden board, to be placed on the floor.

Airawat: A sweet and spicy chutney made for festive occasions like Satya Narayan puja, it is a combination of coriander seeds, dates, tamarind and ginger.

Ajmoda: Celery root.

Ajwain: Carom seeds, used in spice mixes.

Ajwain flower:  Also called thymol, it is used to make sautéed vegetables and fritters.

Akola: *Capsicum annuum* variety from Thane near Mumbai.

Akrod: Walnuts.

Alambé: It is the Konkani word for mushrooms. Mushrooms are cooked into xacuti as a vegetarian option and also as dabdab, upkaris, ambats and bhuthi. It is also called khumb, kuttryachi chattri (dog's umbrella).

Aldona: A variety of blackish red Goan chilli used in vindaloo.

Allh: Fresh ginger root in Marathi; adrak in Hindi; sunth is dried ginger.

Alsi: Hindi for flax seeds.

Alu: Potato in Hindi but in Marathi, alu are the leaves of the colocasia plant.

Alu bhukara: Dried plums from Central Asia.

Alvati: A soupy curry with a cooked leafy vegetable.

Amba: A general Marathi term for mango. Mango trees find mention in the Ramayana. Mango (*Mangifera indicus*) is native to India, and the national fruit of the country where more than 50 cultivars are produced in different states.

Ambadé: Konkani or tulu for hog plums. Used as a souring agent when the fruit is still raw. From the cashew family, these plums sweeten as they ripen; called Spanish plums and makok in Thailand.

Ambat: Marathi for sour. It is used to describe dishes with a souring agent.

Ambat chukka: Green sorrel; khatti palak (sour spinach) in Hindi. It looks like spinach but has a lemony flavour and smaller leaves. High in oxalic acid, it is boiled before eating in large quantities. Ambat chukka bhaji is a curried Konkan speciality with peanuts and jaggery.

Ambé halad: Ginger mango, or *Curcuma amada*, a variant of the turmeric root, also called manganari. Ground into sasavs and chutneys.

Amla: Indian gooseberries used to make curries, soups, pickles, chutneys and syrups.

Amrood: Guava fruit available as a green and light pink variety.

Amsul: Dried, hardened kokum or mangostein fruit.

Anarsa: Shallow-fried biscuits made with jaggery, rice flour and poppy seeds.

Anjeer: Brown figs, eaten fresh, pickled and dried.

Appé: A cross between an idli and a pancake, this round fluffy cake is made from husked, split black gram or urad dal and fried in a special pan called an appé patr that resembles the Swedish ebelskiver.

Arandi: Castor plant from which castor oil is extracted.

Arhar dal: Husked, split yellow pigeon peas or toover/ toor. This gram is used all over the country to make dal preparations; sometimes called harada in the Konkan.

Avla: A green-yellow Indian gooseberry that has many ayurvedic properties and is used in hair and other cosmetic products. Also used for pickling and chutneys.

B

Badishep: Marathi for aniseed and fennel; also saunf in Hindi.

Bael: Stone apple or Bengal quince, this fruit is native to India. A large, hard-shelled fruit with an extremely sweet pulp it is used to make sherbets, bael papad, a fruit leather and is also eaten fresh.

Bagadé: Brown cowpeas. Used to make usals and dals.

Bajji:  A technique used to prepare a boiled or smoked and pulped vegetable such as potato, ridged gourd or aubergine. Spices are seasoned separately and poured over the dish. Sometimes the mashed vegetable is stirred into yogurt or puréed with the seasoning. This is a variation of a bharit.

Bajra: Pearl millet, used to make flatbreads all over the Konkan.

Bangalore torpedo: A spicy green pepper with a hooked tip that ripens to a bright red and becomes spicier as it matures.

Barnee: A tall porcelain container with a lid meant essentially for storing food and pickles.

Basic masolu:  Masolu is Konkani for masala or spice mix. A basic or mother masala in the Konkan is a combination of coconut, roasted red chillies and tamarind, ground to a fine or coarse paste.

Bassaru:  Kannada, for the stock drained after cooking vegetables with spices. This stock is used as a soup for dumplings and rice and is similar to kat.

Batata dosa: A thick crêpe made with mashed potatoes, eaten as a snack or for breakfast.

Bathua: Also called chakkavarti or wild spinach, this is a weed that grows in wasteland areas. A dull green colour the leaves are waxy and consumed for their nutritional value by boiling with spices.

Beedacha tawa: A cast iron pan resembling a tart tatin pan used for making polé, flat cutlets and pancakes.

Bengal gram/chana: It is a chickpea and is used in different forms in Konkan cuisine. The 'desi' or Indian variety are smaller and are called harabhara in their fresh green form in Marathi, while the hard, dark brown one is called kala chana. These are soaked and boiled and cooked with beets, pumpkin and potatoes to make curries. The Indian chickpeas are higher in fibre content and lower in sugar than the Kabuli or Afghan variety, which is a larger pulse with a lighter colour. Kabuli chana, garbanzo beans or chickpeas are used to prepare dishes like chholé bhatura in north India. The husked, split Bengal gram is sold as yellow chana dal, which is added to usals, ground to make puran poli and modaks or simply cooked as a lentil curry in the Konkan. It is ground to make besan or gram flour, which has exhaustive uses in Indian cuisine. India is the largest producer of chickpeas and with good reason: it's a wonder food. Low glycaemic, high in zinc and protein and contains mostly polyunsaturated fats.  •

Benné dosa: A Konkan polé in Karnataka, served with a palya, soft, spicy potatoes.

Ber: Indian jujube cultivated all over India, it is an inexpensive fruit, eaten dry and fresh, turned into sherbets. Also used to make food colour and for medicinal purposes.

Besan: Gram flour, also called harbharyach or daliché peeth.

Betel nut: Tall areca palms are cultivated in plantations all over Dapoli, Guhagar and Ratnagiri. The fruit of this tree is called supari, betel nut or areca nut and is added to paan and supari mixes.

Bhajnee: A mix of several flours like millets, wheat and rice, it is used for the preparation of thalipeet or bhakris and mixed grain dosas.

Bhakur: Bengal carp, also called catla, this is a river fish.

Bharlelé tor: Whole raw mangoes called tor in Goa are slit, stuffed with a spice paste, then tied up with string and stored in porcelain containers full of warm sweet oil.

Bhein: Lotus stems, deep-fried, sautéed and pickled in the Konkan.

Bhing: Chinese herring or shad. An endangered fish, popular all over South East Asia.

Bhoothi: A vegetable or bean curry with a thick gravy, it is sometimes called dabdab. Dried coriander and fenugreek are added to a basic masolu.

Bhopala: Red pumpkin; lal kadoo in Hindi. The Indian variety differs in flavour and texture from the American red pumpkin.

Bhopli Mirchi: Green bell pepper or capsicum.

Bhuthi: Vegetables with high water content like gherkins, boiled spinach, cucumber are cooked with garlic till they release their liquids, to make a moist, slightly overcooked main course and is generally seasoned with a masolu of fenugreek and coriander.

Bhutta: Corn on the cob; hurda, makai in the Konkan.

Bibbo/bibbé: Tender, raw, unsalted cashewnuts, available only during the harvest season.

Bilimbi: A sour fruit and close cousin of carambola or star fruit. It resembles a small green gourd and its evergreen tree is called a cucumber tree. In Kerala, it is pickled while in Konkani cuisine, it is added to curry pastes.

Birandé: A wild berry found in Maharashtra, it is used as a souring agent and to prepare cold beverages.

Black toree: The black-brown seed of yardlong beans, it is sold as a dried bean.

Bobshi: A small fish peculiar to the Konkan, usually dried and stored for use during the monsoons, and is added to stir-fried vegetables and thick coconut gravies.

Bogalé: Konkani-style cast iron wok for stir-frying vegetables on high heat.

Bombay duck or bombil: A lizard fish, popular in the Konkan, abundant in the Arabian Sea and the Ganga delta, it is called tenaga-mizutengu in Japan. Fresh, it is deep-fried to make bombil fry. Dried, it has a strong smell and is added to curries and vegetables.

Bor: Meaning berry in Marathi, this refers specifically to jujube.

Broad beans or horse beans: A kind of fava bean, it is possibly the world's most well known one. In the Konkan, they are sold dried and boiled to make vegetables and curries. In Italy, they are puréed to make appetisers, while the fresh beans are sautéed as a side dish. In China, they are combined with other beans to make fermented bean pastes.

Byadgi/Bedgi chillies: They are popular all over the Konkan and are cultivated in Haveri, Karnataka. Used for their excellent colour and mild spice, these chillies have fewer seeds and are called kaddi in Kannada for slender. They are red or chocolate brown when dried.


C
Cafreal: Goan green curry made with ground coriander leaves and spices.

Cassava: Also known as yucca, this tuber is grown all over Andhra Pradesh and parts of the Konkan. High in starch, its leaves in contrast are high in protein. Both plant parts are used in Konkan cooking (see khatkhaté).

Catfish: Sangot in Konkani.

Cayenne: The most commonly used powdered red pepper in India along with Guntur, called lal mirch, even though lal mirch, mirchi are different varieties. Cayenne was originally cultivated by the Tupi Indians in French Guyana. Many different red peppers are dried and powdered and used all over India, and erroneously labelled lal mirch.

Chaha: Marathi for tea and chai in Hindi, it is prepared in a vessel called chahaci bhandi, a small heatproof pot with a spout and a long handle. Drinking tea is a complex and personal ritual in India. Some drink it from a metal glass or an earthen mug; others from a teacup and many pour hot tea from a cup into a saucer. They blow at the liquid to cool it and then tip the saucer into their mouths. In Sikkim, tea is mixed with yak butter, and in the Konkan, lemon grass or gilli chai is boiled with the tea leaves. References to tea are made in the epic Ramayana (750 BC); Hanuman, the Monkey God travelled to the Himalayas to find Sanjeevani, a medicinal tea plant for the king's ailing brother. Whether tea drinking began in China or India has never been established but the East India Company was the first to grow tea commercially in the north-east plains of India. The first English tea plantation opened in 1840 in the State of Assam. The British had so much success, they took it to Africa. Black, green and oolong teas are processed differently but they come from the same tea plant, Camilea sinesis. Chamomile, rooibus, peppermint are not teas but infusions of herbs and flowers. The French call them tisanes. First blush or flush are the youngest and most flavourful leaves of the tea plant, picked just after winter. The champagne of all teas, Darjeeling is unique to India and grows at elevations of 6,000 feet. Muscatel is often used to describe its perfumed flavour. Queen Catherine of Braganza and Anna, Duchess of Bedford popularised the drinking of tea in the 1800s by serving it in the afternoons to friends with elaborate ceremony and cakes, crumpets, sandwiches and biscuits. Afternoon and high tea became an integral part of British culture, till tea bags were introduced in New York in 1950. America drank tea till the Boston Tea Party, where huge quantities of it were jettisoned off ships as a protest against monopolistic trade practices by British colonists.

Chaimui: Indian cottage cheese with sugar, cardamom and pistachios, it is made from split milk in the hot Konkan summers.

Chakko: Konkani term for a dry side dish with shredded bamboo shoots, jackfruit and breadfruit mixed with coconut.

Chakli: Generic terms for spiral-shaped, deep-fried savoury cookies. They are made with rice, millet, refined wheat flour, gram flour and a variety of spices.

Chakra magi: Marathi for dried star anise.

Chakulli: A brass appliance for making gram, rice and wheat flour chaklis and sev — deep-fried farsan.

Chakwat: Also called orach, a leafy vegetable sautéed with spices and millet flour.

Chanya manya bor: Indian Jujube; Konkani ber and Jhar beri. These berries are sold fresh and dry and can be eaten as a fruit or turned into sherbets.

Chasli: White kidney beans.

Chawli/Chowli: Black-eyed beans; lobia or safed chola in HIndi. Fresh chowli is a long green bean also called Chinese long bean that is chopped and sautéed as upkari.

Chettinad: The cuisine from the Chettiar community of Tamil Nadu. It shares some unique ingredients like marati moggu and dagadphool with Konkan cuisine.

Chewda/chivda/chiwda: General Indian name for a huge variety of crunchy, fried, American-style trail mix of sev, peanuts, cashew nuts, fried flattened or parched rice, dried coconut and spices.

Chikoo (sapota/sapodilla): A soft, extremely sweet, heart-shaped fruit that resembles a brown potato, grows on an evergreen tree, and is cultivated in huge quantities in India.

Chinch: Marathi for tamarind; imli in Hindi; chincbot in Konkani. It is a dark brown, sour fruit described by some as Indian dates. This pod-like fruit is used extensively in Konkan cuisine as a souring agent.

Chippi: Mussels in Marathi.

Chironji/charoli: A pinenut-like seed, it is used instead of almonds in desserts like kheer and sheera.

Chiroti: A sweet, deep-fried pastry made with poppy seeds, flour and jaggery.

Chitni: Konkani for chutney; it can be dry or wet.

Churmunda: Wheat flour and ghee ladoo.

Churmura: Puffed white rice used to make trail mixes like bhadang and a variety of ladoos.

Cuncolim: Goan green pepper.

D

Daav: A spoon traditionally made from a coconut shell, it is used to measure rice and lentils and is polished to a shine when used to stir curries.

Dabbi chilli: A crinkled, small red pepper, this is fiery with plenty of seeds. In Marathi they are called harekala.

Dabeli: A buttery panini with tamarind chutney, potatoes, pomegranate seeds and onions.

Dagadphool: Lichen flower and black stone flower in English; kalpasi in Tamil. This is a rare dried flower and an ingredient unique to Konkan and Chettinad cuisine.

Dal gotni: A wooden masher for pulverising lentils.

Dalichi nivli: Whey; chenna paani; paneer paani.

Dalimb/dalintri: Pomegranate; anar in Hindi.

Dalimbya: Marathi for hyacinth beans.

Dhaval: A spoon used to stir curries; it is long with an oval-shaped cup at the end. Dhaval is also Marathi for stir.

Dhemasé: Marathi for tinda or apple gourd, it is eaten less frequently in the Konkan but is extremely popular in northern India.

Dhobalé Mirch: Bell peppers.

Dhodak: Whole mackerel marinated in red chilli paste and triphala. It is baked in banana oil and banana leaves. Whole plantain is used in the vegetarian version.

Dhodhak: A kind of thalipeet with semolina.

Dhokla patra: A compartmented steamer used to steam lentil cakes.

Dhondas: Dhondas is a sweet cucumber cake, a speciality of Malvan. It is made with a large, long, green cucumber, much like zucchini; the cucumber is often referred to as dhondas kakdi. Also called tavsali, this cucumber is puréed and grated to make dosas, wadis and kheers.

Dhondshi: A small Konkan fish hung out to dry in the sun; it is used to make pickles.

Dink: Edible gum in Marathi. Antu in Kannada, it comes from the Acacia plant and is added to ladoos for crunch.

Dodak: Cured and smoked or baked mackerel.

Duddali: Konkani version of pannacotta, cut into squares, it is made with coconut, milk and arrowroot flour.

Dudhi/duddé: Bottle gourd; ghia and lauki in Hindi; garduddhé in Konkani. It is stir-fried to make usals, randaayi and ghashi. It is also added to lentils and shredded to make sweet halva and pickles.

Dudya kalé: Tender pumpkin or squash buds sautéed to make upkaris and usals.


E
Eeril: Yardlong beans; val in the Konkan, not to be confused with val papdi. A common bean, it is stir-fried with tempered spices.

Ekpanni: Brahmi or Indian pennywort, this leafy herb is a cure for many ailments.

Ekshipi: Ek in Marathi is one. Ekshipi means shellfish served in an open shell. Oysters and mussels are opened fried or steamed and served on the half shell; a Karwari speciality.

Ellachipur sanman chillies: Pungent, dried red peppers grown in Amravati, Maharashtra.


F
Farsan: A general term used in Maharashtra and Gujarat to describe a variety of snacks such as sev, chakli, fried papdi and chewdas.

Feni: A strong-smelling Goan liquor produced from the sap of the toddy palm or the fruit of the cashew tree. The first distillation of toddy sap is called urrak, a mild version of feni, and is used to mix cocktails. Feni is distilled in an earthen boiler called a bhatti. The juice extracted from cashew apples is called neero. This is fermented in a pot by burying it for several days.

Fodnichi pali: A large, deep ladle made from cast iron, it is placed on an open flame with oil in it. Whole spices like curry leaves, cloves, cumin and cinnamon are tempered and poured over cooked foods.

G

Gabbé/gabbo Green plantain, available seasonally.

Gaddo: Edible plantain stem, chopped up and stir-fried with mustard and fenugreek seeds.

Gaj: A cup used as a measure. Could be 9 or 12 ozs.

Gajbajé: A mixed vegetable stew with mogge and triphala served at ceremonial occasions.

Gharya: A thick, soft deep-fried flatbread where a fruit or lentil pulp is added to the dough.

Ghashi: A thick vegetable, sprouted bean or whole dried bean curry made by roasting coconut with red chilli and the addition of a souring agent. Green chilli and coriander leaves are not employed in a traditional ghashi which has a tempering of mustard seeds and karbev leaves. Cauliflower, black chickpeas, plantains and fresh green peas are commonly used.

Ghavan:  A gluten-free pancake made with jungle rice, and also with white rice flour in Malvan.

Ghetu: Vinegar; sirka in Hindi. Red and white vinegar are used in Konkan cooking as souring agents and for marinades, but mostly in Goan food where it was first introduced by the Portuguese.

Ghewda: A type of broad bean in Marathi.

Ghol: A meaty fish with large bones used to make curries and semolina fry.

Gholé: Purslane.

Ghosalé: A variety of collard greens.

Gilli chai: Lemon grass leaves used in the preparation of masala tea.

Gobro: A variety of cod called reef.

Godé val: Light, yellow-green hyacinth beans, sweeter than their brown counterparts, they are used to make vaalaché birdé, a curried vegetable and val khichdi, a kind of risotto.

Gojju: Konkanis in Karnataka call a heavily spiced vegetable stew with sesame seeds and a variety of lentils, seasoned and cooked in butter or ghee, a gojju and the variations are innumerable. It is eaten in small quantities; generally a tablespoon is mixed into rice. It is often confused for a rassa or randaayi but is in fact a kind of pickle or chutney.

Gongura: Also called ambadi, a leafy green vegetable not to be confused with ambadé or hog plums.

Gul/gud: Jaggery or unrefined molasses in Marathi.

Gulla: A small green aubergine grown in Udupi.

Guntur saanam: Not to be confused with Guntur, this thick-skinned red chilli is spicier than the Guntur or Andhra chilli.

Guvar: Cluster beans, it has a unique mildly bitter flavour; often cooked with sweet coconut or apricots.


H
Haddo: Rock bream.

Halad/haldi: Turmeric, a rhizome cultivated for its root and leaves, it thrives during the monsoon. Haldi is used copiously in Indian cooking. The rhizome is sold commercially as a strong-smelling yellow powder. It can also be bought as a fresh rhizome in any Indian market. In the Konkan, turmeric leaves are used to steam, smoke and bake a variety of different polé, fish and idlis. Turmeric leaves are considered sacred by Konkanis; they are used instead of a mangalsutra, a bridal necklace that signifies betrothal. The tubers are tied to a groom's wrists in a ceremony called Konkana bandhana.

Halwa: Black pomfret.

Handvo cooker: A steamer used to make among other dishes, lentil cakes called handvo, a Gujarati speciality and kothimbri and gobi wadis.

Harmal: A Malvani green pepper.

Hing/hinga: India's most notorious and foul-smelling spice is in fact a herb called *Ferula asafoetida*; devil's shit in Turkish. Asafoetida is a yellowish powder used all over the Konkan in vegetables, curries and lentils. A member of the Apiaceae family from which, come other herbs — celery, parsley, coriander anise and hemlock — it is the milk of a caudiciform root which is dried, powdered and sold in small plastic jars. It is used in miniscule quantities and must be boiled or tempered in hot oil to be palatable. It has a flavour reminiscent of onion and garlic and is used copiously by Jains, who don't eat roots and tubers, to replace their absence. Commonly used in Iran and the Mediterranean countries many centuries ago, with mentions in the Talmud, it is exclusively used in India now. It is believed that Prometheus secretly carried stolen fire in the asafoetida root, hence the name 'ferula' which means carrier in Latin. Medicinally, the herb is used to reduce flatulence and in medieval Europe, it was sprinkled outside homes to keep rats away. Rock asafoetida is pure asafoetida sold in small pieces, but commercially, the spice is sold as compounded asafoetida, a combination of asafoetida, rice or wheat flour and gum, and is easier to use than pieces.

Hitto/khotte: This is a pyramid-like idli, steamed in jackfruit leaves and served with a vegetable randaayi.

Horse gram: Kulith in Maharashtra. It may sound unfamiliar, since it is used as cattle feed but is a commonly used bean on the western coast and in southern India to make ladoos, koddel, ghashi, upkaris and saars. Crêpes, soups, lentils, spice mixes, chutneys, pithla and ladoos are all prepared by soaking the beans overnight. Ulava charu, a dark sweet and spicy condiment is one of Telugu cuisines shining stars. It is an excellent source of iron.

Huli: Curried vegetables cooked with tamarind, ground lentils and coconut in Karnataka.

Humman: Vegetables boiled in a spice paste and then seasoned with whole fried spices.

I

Idli patra: A multi-layered, sieve-like vessel used to steam batter.

Imli: Tamarind; chinch in Marathi.

Indian flat beans/val papdi/avarekai: These are actually the seeds of hyacinth beans, a type of field bean. Often confused with broad beans the val papdi somewhat resembles the shape of a snow pea. The plant is bright purple and often grown for ornamental beauty. The dried beans must be boiled before consumption. Once boiled, they are called sugatu. In stores the beans are sold as Surti papdi lilva.

Ingalo: Konkani for hot charcoal pulled out of a smoker.

J
Jaiphal: Nutmeg.

Jamun/jambhul: Mistakenly called a plum because it closely resembles a purple damson, this fruit is native to south Asia and belongs to the Syzgium genus while plums come from the Prunus genus.

Jardalu: Indian apricots, light brown, they taste very different from the Turkish variety. Their nut contains an aromatic, edible seed.

Javitri/jopatri: Mace.

Jawas tel: Linseed oil; the seed is called alsi.

Jeer mirya kadi: A Konkan gravy with garlic prepared like a kat and served with plain boiled rice.

Jhinga: General Marathi term for a variety of prawns; sungta in Konkani.

Jhunka: A spicy condiment made with ground gram or millet flour, it is eaten in small quantities with bhakri.

Jowar/jwari: Sorghum or great millet in English; jola in Kannada. It is a grass harvested to make molasses and used as a flour in the Konkan for flatbreads, sweetmeats and vegetable dishes.

K
Kaalé alvaa maddi: The root of the taro plant and the paan or leaves are commonly used in Konkan food.

Kaap: Round vegetables such as potatoes and aubergines are finely sliced horizontally, to expose a large surface area.

Kabba rosu bhakri: Flatbread dough with millet flour and sugarcane juice.

Kabit:  Marathi for wood apple; bael in Hindi. This sweet and sour fruit has a woody exterior, and is used to make sherbets, jams and chutneys.

Kacra: arrowroot.

Kadamb: A rectangular cucumber idli steamed in turmeric leaves.

Kadavé val: Bitter, brown hyacinth beans, generally sprouted, peeled and cooked with spices.

Kadgee: Jackfruit; phanas in Marathi; kathal in Hindi; halasu in Kannada; gujjé in Tulu. It is a large green fruit available all over the Konkan and finds mention in the Mahabharata in the region of Saraswati.

Kadi patta: Curry leaves; karibevu in Kannada. It is from the citrus family.

Kadlé bajil: A popular Mangalore dish, kadlé is garbanzo beans and bajil is flattened rice in Tulu.

Kaileoli: A Goan-style polé or dosa.

Kairas:  A Konkani staple, this rich curry is made with green bell pepper, powdered sesame and lentils and fried nuts.

Kairi: Raw young mango which is tart and hard.

Kaju: Cashewnuts.

Kakdi: Marathi for a light green, thin-skinned cucumber, also called Poona kheera.

Kala draksh: Large black currants or grapes.

Kalonji: *Nigella sativa*, a black seed also called charnushka in Russia.

Kalva: Large oysters found closer to the shore.

Kanchi: A dry pickle prepared with only ginger, salt and green chillies.

Kand: Purple yam, used in undiyo and gajbajé.

Kanda: Marathi for onion; also called pyaaz.

Karamaré: Carambola or starfruit.

Karambi: A method of curing mangoes; also called ambuli and tor.

Karanji: A deep-fried empanada stuffed with coconut and sugar.

Karela: Bitter gourd in Marathi and Hindi; karaaté in Konkani.

Karkara: Tiger perch found in shallow waters.

Karwanda: Conkerberry. Thorny berries, sour and astringent that are native to India. They are excellent for jams, beverages and pickles and are often grown as a decorative hedge in parts of India.

Kasuri Methi: Dried Fenugreek leaves. Added to lentils and flatbread dough, it has a pleasantly bitter taste.

Kat: A vegetarian broth ladled over cooked vegetables. Kolhapuri misal employs this technique. The sprouted beans are cooked separately and the broth is poured over them just before serving. Also called tarri.

Katachi amti: A broth-like lentil made from husked, split Bengal gram or chana dal stock.

Kati: Anchovy.

Keerlu: Young bamboo shoots; vasotya in Marathi. It is an acquired taste. Stir-fried with spices it is prepared as a curry.

Kekra: Marathi for black or red crabs.

Keli: Banana. One of the Konkan's most important crops; nendran, dwarf Cavendish, red banana, naine and robusta are some varieties.

Kesar: Stamens of the crocus flower, it is used to make desserts such as kesari bhaat, shira, kheer and ladoos; a highly prized and expensive spice.

Kewra: Screwpine leaves.

Khajoor: Brown dates. Also called chhuara.

Khajuri: Barramundi; betki in West Bengal. Also called Asian sea bass, this differs from the Australian barramundi cod.

Khalbatta: Mortar and pestle.

Khamang kakdi: Konkani version of a kakdi chi koshimbri.

Khamen: Yeast.

Khampi: Pony fish.

Khatkhaté: The avial of the Konkan. A simmered vegetable stew with 15-18 different vegetables and beans including pumpkin, sweet potato, corn on the cob, cassava, carrots and hyacinth beans. Similar to gajbajé and kandamool, it is always cooked during Ganesh puja. Saraswats cook it without tomatoes, since red is not a colour offered to Lord Ganesh but add plenty of onions and garlic to create a thick gravy. The Konkanasth community who cook without onions and garlic on religious occasions use tomatoes, tephala and asafoetida and prepare the vegetables in a thinner gravy.

Khava: Mava or khoya in Hindi. Reduced, crumbled milk solids, stirred into halvas and mithais.

Khichdi: Stewed lentils and rice served with a dahi kadi or yogurt.

Khotee: A small container made with jackfruit leaves, used to steam idlis.

Khuman: Kashmiri apricots, dark brown and small, they are sweeter than Turkish apricots but less sweet than jardaloo, Indian apricots.

Kismuri/kiskis: A very traditional method of Konkani cooking, it is a dry side dish that resembles a salad, usually prepared by cutting, roasting or frying a vegetable or fish and tossing it with fresh coconut and spices.

Kisni: Handheld grater; a flat, rectangular tool made from brass or aluminium, now from stainless steel, used to shred vegetables.

Kodbolé: Deep-fried, savoury rice pastry.

Koddel: Konkani and Kannada for gravy but also refers to a south Canara dish prepared with garlic, lentils like horse gram and chunks of green jackfruit, plantain, yam or bamboo shoots.

Kohala: Ash gourd in Marathi; kuvale in Konkani. In north India they call it safed petha.

Kokum/amsul: The most popular souring agent in the Konkan after tamarind. This fruit grows on the ratambi tree, also called mangostein. During the drying process the skin of the kokum is repeatedly soaked in kokum juice and dried. It produces a dark red colour when soaked in water.

Kolombyo/kolombo: A north Canara lentil dish with vegetables akin to sambhar but thicker and more yellow.

Koncar: Long-fin cavalla.

Koorka/kooka: Called Chinese potato it is actually native to Sudan. A dark, misshapen potato, it is wrapped in a jute bag and smacked around to break the tough skin, then soaked and peeled. Commonly used in south Canara to make upkaris, talasani and bhajjis, it is also very popular in Kerala.

Koot/podi: Marathi for manual grinding with a large mortar and pestle. Koots are lentils, nuts and spices, in some cases vegetables, powdered or pounded together and served as dry or wet chutneys or added to a dish to flavour it. Methkoot or menthe hittu, kadgi koot, sambhar podi are some examples. In Konkani is can also be a cooked yam pickle made for special occasions.

Koshimbri: In Marathi, it is a raw, chopped and seasoned salad.

Kotla/kochla/hindee/nonché: A dry shredded pickle made with raw mango or other sour raw fruit.

Kubbé: Smooth, soft-shelled clams with a clear shells.

Kulfi saacha: A conical mould made from aluminium used to set eggless Indian ice creams called kulfi.

Kuttu: Buckwheat.


L
Ladoo: Undé in Kannada. Desserts or sweets in the shape of a ball.

Lady fish: Murdusha in Marathi. Also called nagli and kané.

Lahya: Jowar, a millet, is popped like popcorn and eaten as a snack.

Lepas/lep: Malabar sole, a delicate fish, generally coated in semolina and pan-fried.

Loni: Traditionally refers to white butter made from churned cream but can also mean commercial yellow butter.


M

Madgané: A husked, split Bengal gram or chana dal and jaggery dessert

Maggé: Chinese cucumber also called orange cucumber, it is used to make huli and polé.

Mahaseer: Also called mahi or tiger fish.

Majjigé huli: Majjigé or sour buttermilk is cooked with ash gourd or beans and coconut in Karnataka.

Malvani chicken curry: A spicy chicken gravy with chicken on the bone.

Malvani wadé: Puffed, deep-fried breads made with lentil and rice flours, it is served with Malvani chicken curry or black gram curry.

Mandakki: Also called bhadang or churmuri, with variations, a non-fried, healthy version of chewda.

Mandé: A wheat and ghee dessert rolled like a papad, it is served with warm milk and ghee.
Manuka: Marathi for brown raisins or kishmish.

Marati moggu/mokku: Shemul in Hindi; kapok in English. A spice that resembles a black clove but is more astringent, it is actually a variety of dried caper. Used in Konkan and Chettinad cuisine, it is ground into bisebele baath and coconut saagu.

Masala dabba: A round, flat tin with tiny cups or compartments to store spices.

Masolu: A mother masala or a multi-purpose spice mix used commonly in Konkani cuisine. A basic masolu has coconut, red chillies and tamarind, but it is adapted for various dishes by adding fenugreek, cumin and curry leaves.

Masoor (lal): Husked, split Egyptian lentils.

Massaru: Kannada for a soup prepared by cooking and puréeing leafy greens and lentils.

Matki/moth bean: It is from the same family as horse gram and is very popular all over the western coast because it is drought-resistant and a very good source of protein for vegetarians. Often confused with moong, another bean from the Fabaceae family, it is brownish red in colour and is cooked whole or soaked and sprouted to make amtis, usals, kochimbris and curries.

Matt: Amaranthus leaves in red or green; denté in Konkani; also called hinn choy. This is a very nutritious vegetable, cooked for Ganpati puja. Green matt is also called rajgira.

Methkoot: A complex, roasted powder of three grains, three lentils and eight spices. Meth is methi or fenugreek, the dominant flavour in this podi. It is sprinkled over ghee rice, polé and idlis.

Milagai: Also called gunpowder, a popular Telugu podi or koot made by powdering red chillies, sesame seeds and chana dal. Eaten with idlis and ghee rice.

Mirsaangé/mirsanga: Indian green chillies in Konkani; mirchi in Marathi and Hindi.

Moira keli: A variety of plantain.

Molavees: A smooth yellow lentil curry with black pepper.

Moong/mung: Small, oval-shaped, green beans, moong is indigenous to the Indian subcontinent and one of India's oldest cultivated species of beans. High in protein and starch, they are cooked whole with the husk to make curries and vegetables. When husked, they have a light yellow colour. The whole beans are sprouted to prepare usals, upkaris and amtis. In Asia, cellophane or glass noodles are made from moong starch.

Moriché tel: Black mustard oil. The leaves of the mustard plant, also called saag or moharaché patra, are sautéed with spices.

Mosambi: Indian orange, it is a lemon coloured fruit with a unique citrus flavour. A variant of key lime, it is mellower and less sour than the well-known Florida key lime. Consumed as juice all over the Konkan.

Mrigal: Marathi for a type of non-oily, white river carp, called rohu in West Bengal, it is extensively farmed.

Muday: This originates in Mangalore and differs from other idlis because it contains yellow lentils.

Muddo: Konkani term for mixing wet and dry spices together.

Muleek: Sweet jackfruit fritters.

Mumbri: Pan-fried rice batter cooked on a banana leaf.

Murabba: A jam-like sweet preserve made with shredded mangoes served with flatbreads.

Murdi: Indian or northern whiting, also known as smelt.

Murukka/mudukku: A deep-fried savoury gram flour biscuit served as tanek mané.

Mushroom: Kukun mutté, a variety of bella mushrooms, used to make dabdab and xacuti.

Mushti: The Konkani word for fistful. A common measure employed in old Konkani recipes.


N
Nagkesar/nagchampé/nagpushpa: This dried flower is called cobra saffron in English and comes from the Ceylon ironwood tree. It is used in traditional medicine and in the Konkan to balance heavy, aromatic spice mixes.

Nal shingala: Catfish. Shingala means horns in Marathi referring to the whiskers of this fish. A nocturnal bottom feeder, it varies greatly in size. Several kinds of catfish are found on the west coast. Etta are salt water while muzhi are found in ponds.

Naral: Coconut in Marathi, essential to Konkan cooking, it is cultivated all over the coast. Many strains and varieties are available including singapuri, guhagari and banavalli.

Naspatti: Asian pear.

Navalkolé: A root vegetable known as Knolkhol in the West.

Neer phanas: Bread fruit in Marathi; videshi panas and pala phanas in Hindi; jeev kadgee in Konkani and Kannada. It looks a lot like a jackfruit from the outside but contains a meaty pumpkin-like white interior which is cut into chunks to prepare talasani, phodi and upkaris. Its latex is used to waterproof boats.

Neivedya: The first morsel of every dish cooked during Ganesh puja, which is offered to the deity of Lord Ganesh and his vahan or vehicle, a mouse. It must include several desserts like modaks, ladoos and kheer.

Nendra: A variety of Konkan plantain.

O
Olé: Wet in Marathi, used as a prefix to describe something moist or steamed.

Olé mirsangé: Chillies are fried in oil and dunked in a liquid to soften them. Taka mirsangé, fried chillies in buttermilk is served with a Konkani thali.

Oos: Sugarcane in Marathi.

Oova: Carom seeds.

P
Paan polé: A Konkan speciality, this is a fluffy dosa made from a thin fermented rice and coconut batter similar to neer dosa.

Paays/payasa/payasam: A stewed dessert similar to a kheer. Shredded gherkins, pumpkins and lentils are cooked in coconut milk with jaggery and spices.

Pacchadi: Raw mangoes seasoned with a temper of asafoetida and ground coconut.

Paddu patra/appé patra: A pan with round compartments, to fry appé, a kind of idli.

Padwal: Snake gourd with a striped green and white outer skin, it grows on a vine and is also called chirchunda and serpent gourd. A very popular vegetable, it is usually cooked with husked, split Bengal gram or chana dal, coconut and onions in the Konkan.

Paej/pej: A breakfast soup or gruel made with brown rice.

Pala: Hilsa fish is a delta fish but larger ones, considered less flavourful are also caught at sea.

Palu: A fish similar to perch.

Palya: A thick spicy curry made with a root vegetable like potato or yam served with flatbreads or polé.

Pandal: The area around a havan or holy fire, set up specifically for a wedding ceremony. Generally consists of four pillars in a square area decorated with strung flowers and leaves.

Panta bhaat: Rice soaked in water and cooked to a sticky consistency with lime juice and onions.

Papad: A lentil cracker in Marathi and Hindi, it is called appalam and pappadam in south India. These wafers are made from potato, lentils, rice and spices. Lijjat papad, India's largest papad making company with a three billion rupee turnover was started by seven semi-literate women in Mumbai in 1959 with a start-up capital of one dollar and fifty cents. Uncooked papads have a long shelf life if stored in airtight containers. Do not refrigerate fried or uncooked papads. Cooked papads are best eaten immediately but their crispness remains for 24 hours if packed in dry airtight containers. In Punjab, papads are often sprinkled with cayenne, salt, cilantro, onions and tomatoes and served as snacks. Thick, fried, rice pappadams can be served with salsa and cheese dips. Papads can be crushed and sprinkled over curry and rice for crunch. They can be rolled and cut into different shapes to make cups, cones and slivers. In the Konkan, papads are roasted or deep-fried, then broken into pieces and stirred together with onions, spices and sauces and served as a salad or appetiser. Khakra, sometimes mistaken for papad, is a delicious Gujarati-style flatbread with a crisp papad-like texture, made with spiced wheat flour that's already pan-roasted in oil and ready to eat. Papads are generally roasted over an open flame by rapidly turning them with a pair of tongs. They can be cooked in a microwave as well. Rice papads taste best when fried in hot oil. Once the oil is hot, a papad takes less than 10 seconds to turn golden brown.

Papanas: Pomelo or Chinese grapefruit; chakodra in Hindi; batobi nimboo in Bengali. A variety of grapefruit, but less bitter than the breakfast grapefruit popular in the US. It is a green fruit, the largest in the citrus family. Papanas wadi in Mumbai is named after the trees you find there in Gamdevi.

Paplet/pomfret: A delicate flavoured fish, also known as butterfish. Three varieties are found abundantly in the Konkan area. Silver (pomfretor in Chinese; chandawa in Marathi); white (suragat in Konkani); and black (halwa in the Konkan and slade in Australia). Steamed, stuffed, fried and curried this is an expensive fish and prized above all others in the Konkan.

Parwar: Pointed gourd, also called green potato in the Konkan, it is used like other gourds for stews, usals, dals and pickles.

Pasphonus: A smaller variety of jackfruit with tiny seeds. It is pickled with raw mango or brined and then stir-fried with green chillies.

Patal: Literally means thin in Marathi. Used to describe curries with a watery gravy. Aluchi patal bhaji, are taro root leaves cooked in a thin yogurt gravy.

Patholi: Rice pancakes steamed in turmeric leaves stuffed with coconut and jiggery; made for Naag Panchmi.

Patodi/rasaajé: Steamed gram flour cakes from Vidharbha soaked in a kat or spicy gravy.

Patta gobi: Green cabbage.

Peedavan/patrado: A steamer for patrel or rolled and stuffed colocasia leaves.

Peeth: A term used to describe ground flour, but also used to describe dough.
Peru/amrood: Green guava.

Phagil: Teasel gourd, a spiny gourd erroneously called wild melon and wild cucumber, it is a member of the Dipsacus family.

Phanna polo: A seasoned wheat flour dosa that doesn't require fermentation.

Phasa: Anchovies.

Phenori/chiroti: Sweetened, deep-fried biscuits made for Diwali.

Phodi: A vegetable or fish that's been deep-fried or pan-fried.

Phodni: Marathi for tempering spices; vaghar in Gujarati; tadka In Hindi; phanna in Konkani. A tempering spoon, a deep ladle made from cast iron with a long handle is used for tempering spices all over India.

Phulgobi: Cauliflower.

Pithla: Lentil flours such as husked, split Bengal gram or chana dal and bean flours like kulith are cooked with spices to make a paste-like curry eaten with bhakri and rice.

Pitho: Similar to a podi, a combination of ground spices, nuts and coconut but slightly moist and oily.

Pitté nonché: A variety of chopped vegetables — lime, lemon, bilimbi, raw green mangoes, dhodlé — are coated with a dry spice mix and marinated in jars.

Pohé: Parched or flattened rice in Marathi; phovu in Konkani; avalakki in Kannada. This is a very popular food in the Konkan. The rice is stir-fried with spices and garnished with lime and peanuts.

Poli: General term for a flatbread.

Policha dabba: A round, flat, stainless or aluminium-lined, brass tin used to store flatbreads.

Pomegranate: Dalimb in Marathi; anar in Hindi.

Pongal baath: Prepared all over the Konkan and the South this risotto-like dish is made sweet or salty.

Pood or podi: A ground spice; hittu in Kannada.

Post dana: White poppy seeds; khuskhus in Marathi and Hindi.

Pudina: Mint leaves.

Puran poli: Ubbati in Konkani; holigé in Kannada. This is a lentil and jaggery stuffed flatbread, a speciality of Maharashtra.

Puran yantra: A food mill to pulverise cooked chana dal.

R

Ragda: Ragdo in Konkani; paata varvanta in Marathi. It is a large flat granite slab with a pestle resembling a granite rolling pin, to manually grind spices.

Ragi: Finger millet.

Rajma: Red kidney bean, shaped like the human organ, it is a member of the common bean family and is consumed all over northern India but less frequently in the Konkan.

Ramphal: Bullock's heart, this is a green, smooth-skinned fruit with a delicate custard apple flavour. There are many cultivars grown all over Asia and Australia.

Randaayi: A Kannada word also used in Konkan families to describe a thick brothy curry.

Randekayee nonché: A mixed vegetable pickle with ivy gourd, cauliflower, green chillies, cayenne pepper and lime.

Randhuni: Parsley.

Rashi: Not to be confused with rassa, a northern Maharashtrian delicacy made from lentil broth with millet dumplings.

Rassa: A Marathi word for a broth made with vegetable stock, thickened with ground coconut, tomatoes and onions.

Ratalé: Indian sweet potato.

Rawa: Semolina in Marathi. It is available in fine and coarse textures.

Rawas:  Marathi for black salmon. A popular and expensive fish in the Konkan, it has a meaty texture and is cooked with coconut curries.

Rawi: A wooden buttermilk churner.

S

Saagu: A coconut curry with mixed vegetables from North Canara. Saagu is also used to describe vegetables with thick coconut gravies.

Saar/saaru: Marathi and Konkani words for soup.

Saatkaapyache ghavané: A sweet, seven-layered Malvani pancake.

Sabudana: Pearl sago, made from tapioca, the starchy extract of the cassava plant. Gluten-free and high in carbohydrates (see sabudana wadi), it is used to make desserts, stir-fries and snacks in the Konkan.

Sabut moong: Green moong beans.

Safarchand: Red apple in Marathi; seb in Hindi.

Safed watné: Dried white peas.

Saglé: A south Canara Konkani dish. Coriander seeds are added to a basic masolu to spice this vegetarian dish. Vegetables are stir-fried first and then a thick coconut gravy or stuffing is added to it. It is generally prepared with pulpy vegetables like okra that need to be cooked dry to prevent them from getting gummy, or vegetables like drumsticks, green aubergines and sugarcane that need extra cooking time.

Sagoti: A Malvani chicken curry served with finger millet bread.

Sai: The cream that accumulates on top when milk is boiled.

Samsaar Paadvo/Samvatsradi: Also called Ugadi in the south and Gudi Padwa in Marathi, it is the first day of the Hindu New Year based on the lunar calendar. It is celebrated by traditional Hindus by honouring their ancestors, cooking special foods and visiting temples.

Sandan: Not to be confused with sanna, this is a sweet, steamed coconut, semolina and milk cake made by Konkani Muslims and Kolis for the high holidays.

Sandgé: Deep-fried and sun-dried moong bean dumplings.

Sanna idli: A fluffy rice idli fermented with toddy that requires larger, deeper containers called gindlan, for steaming than other idlis.

Sanna polo A crêpe made with rice batter, fermented with toddy.

Santra: A common name for a variety of oranges.

Sapota: Chikoo fruit.

Sarupkari: A combination of the words saar and upkari, this is a garlicky soup made with whole beans.

Sasav/saasam: A simple, sweet curry made with the pulp of a fruit like mango or jackfruit. Lightly spiced with salt, coconut and asafoetida, the idea is to enhance the flavour of seasonal fruit.

Saung: Vegetables like potatoes are cooked in coconut oil and tamarind and the onions are lightly browned to sweeten them to balance the souring agent.

Sepu/shepu: Fresh dill.

Shahi jeera: Caraway seeds.

Shalgam: Turnip.

Shankarpali: A deep-fried sweetened pastry cut into oblong shapes with a serrated pastry wheel.

Shengdana: Peanuts in their shells. The shells are steamed and the peanuts are removed. They have a thin skin, which if steamed, is edible. For dried peanuts, the shells are cracked open and the nut is harvested for consumption or oil pressing.

Shetur/tuti: The sweet fruit of the mulberry plant.

Shev/sev: A kind of farsan. Deep-fried bits of gram flour, plain, or spiced with chilli, are eaten as a snack or used as a garnish over misal pav, yogurt raitas and bhel puri.

Shevand: Lobster.

Shevya chya shenga/mashingaa saang: A long green drumstick, chopped into 3"- 4" pieces and added to lentils. The seeds are a roasted snack and drumstick leaves are sautéed with garlic. The white buds, called phool, are also eaten. Finds mention in the Mahabharata.

Shevya danteey: A manual brass appliance for processing rice paste into string noodles. The rice paste is rolled into balls, lightly steamed and then run through the danteey. Shevaya or rice vermicelli is used for savoury and sweet desserts (see rice vermicelli upama).

Shiblo: Shallow baskets, also used as lids, made from natural plant fibres.

Shimpla: A deep, round sieve, which has a 1"- 2" thick wooden or stainless steel ring with a nylon or plastic sieve.

Shirvali: Vermicelli noodles cooked in coconut milk — a Malvani dessert.

Shriphal: Wood apple.

Sil batta: A large, heavy mortar and pestle. The mortar is a flat piece of stone and the pestle is a long piece with rounded edges, used like a rolling pin to grind wet and dry spices.

Sindhav/saindhava lavanam: A fasting salt used during upwas. It is unrefined, unprocessed rock salt and available colourless, pink or red. It is believed that this salt was mined in the Indus Valley, where it was first used as a culinary aid. It is considered pure because it doesn't contain free flow agents and additives.

Sitap: Blue fin treevally, a fast swimming predatory fish, considered excellent table fare.

Sitaphal: Sugar apple or sweetsop, commonly mistaken for custard apple, is a pine cone-like fruit from the semi-evergreen tree annona. High in calories it is also a good source of iron.

Song: Pronounced 'soung', it is a thick, spicy chutney-like curry always made with onions and served as a flavour enhancer with
a plain dal like varan or dalithoy and rice.

Songoda/singhada: Water chestnuts, roasted, sautéed and ground
to make chutneys and chestnut bread flour.

Soonth: Dried ginger.

Sukké: A curry with a dry gravy that clings to the vegetables or meat and is always eaten with flatbreads. A tablespoon each of fried coriander seeds and husked, split black gram or urad dal is added while grinding the basic masolu and it is given a seasoning
of mustard seeds and curry leaves.

Sukké mirsangé: Chillies are fried in oil to a crisp with salt and served as a side dish or sprinkled on a vegetable as a garnish to keep them crisp.

Sukkil: Sun-dried fish. This is a very popular method of preserving and eating shrimp, fish and eel in the Konkan. The fish is either hung to dry in the same way laundry is on a clothesline, spread out on straw sheets or brass thalis or weighed down by rocks to release water.

Surali: A savoury rolled gram flour pasta, similar to khandvi.

Suran: Elephant foot yam.

Surmai: Marathi for Indo Pacific king mackerel; iswaan in Konkani. This is a popular and expensive Konkan fish.

Surnali: A sweet dosa with jaggery, rice and yogurt.

Susal: A dry coconut curry, similar to a sukké but vegetarian. It is made with jackfruit, breadfruit and gherkins.


T
Tadgola/targula: Marathi for a variety of small, heart-shaped palm fruit about the size of a lemon that grow in clusters, also called ice apple. The flesh is white and jelly-like, similar to a lychee and has a thin, light brown skin that is peeled off before the fruit is eaten. Like a coconut, the inside of the fruit contains a small pocket of sweet juice. Available in the summer, these are chilled, manually peeled and popped into ones mouth whole.

Tadi: A fermented palm liquor, also called toddy, kallu and palm wine, it is consumed along the Konkan coast and in Tamil Nadu and Kerala. The unfermented sap is a sweet non-alcoholic drink called neera. Toddy is also used to ferment rice batters for sannas and sanam idlis.

Taikilo: Coffee or cassia taro leaves cooked in buttermilk or coconut milk.

Talasanna: A technique that involves searing garlic with fish or vegetables in a very hot pan and then cooking them in water.

Talegaon potatoes: A local potato, also called jumping jack, ideal for deep-frying.

Taleigao: A local Goan green pepper.

Talwarmashé: Swordfish.

Tamal patra: Marathi for bay leaf; tej patta in Hindi.

Tambli: A culinary term for a purée of vegetables, generally leafy, with yogurt and spices.

Tambusa: Incorrectly called red snapper in India, it is in fact a different snapper called tomato snapper.

Tandla mané: A 12-oz measuring cup.

Tandul: Marathi for raw rice; cooked rice is bhaat. Ground rice flour is tandulachi peeth.

Tannek mané: Konkani term for dishes like pohé, bhajjis and fried pastries that can be served for both breakfast and tea.

Tanni anna: A sticky boiled rice seasoned with green chillies and served cold.

Tarbuj: Marathi for watermelon.

Tarsulo: Rainbow sardines.

Tausalli: A steamed cucumber idli.

Tendli/tondli: Ivy gourd. A small, oval, light green vegetable, it grows on a vine and is considered an invasive weed in some countries. Very popular all over India as a sautéed vegetable, it is recommended to diabetics to help regulate blood sugar.

Tentuli patra: Tender shoots of the tamarind tree.

Thecha: A spicy paste made with herbs and garlic, added to cooked dishes or served as a condiment.

Thoi: An overcooked lentil preparation spiced with garlic and cumin; a classic Konkan recipe.

Til: White sesame, used as whole seeds, oil and as a powder in Konkan cooking. It is a religious requirement for holidays like Makarsankranti.

Tingalore: A white bean commonly known as northern beans.

Tisri: Small, striped, yellow or black, hard-shelled, river clams.

Tonki: Indian barracuda, it is an elongated scavenger fish. Eaten smoked in parts of the Konkan. Also called ooza and jaban tal.

Toop/ghee: Marathi for clarified butter; ghee in Sanskrit, a word for saturated milk fat from buffalo or cow's milk. In the Vedas, hymns are dedicated to the importance of ghee in Hindu life. Ghee, honey, milk, sugar and yogurt are the five elements of panchamrut, a holy offering made to the gods during religious holidays. Panchamrut is believed to be the liquid that emerged from the Vedic churning of the seas. During Diwali it is traditional to light lamps with ghee to welcome Lakshmi, the Goddess of Wealth into your home. Ghee, unlike olive, corn, vegetable, seed and fruit oils, has great tolerance to heat and is therefore considered the best medium to temper spices and sauté foods that need to be cooked at high temperatures or for long periods. I don't recommend deep-frying in ghee because it's expensive, very rich and the flavour is overpowering. French drawn or clarified butter is similar in quality to ghee, but prepared differently. Ghee is also produced in Egypt and Brazil. In Morocco, it is buried in the ground for weeks to ferment before it is eaten. In Ethiopia, it is boiled with spices like sumac to give it a smoky, brown colour. In India, police raids are frequents on stores, selling spurious ghee. Asli or shudhh, meaning pure, ghee is made entirely of milk fat from cow or buffalo milk and has a golden colour. Dalda vanspati is a vegetable product made from hydrogenated oils containing trans-fats and used mostly for deep-frying.

Torai: Ridged gourd also called luffa, tori, shirale and dodka in Maharashtra. There are two kinds: the smooth ghosavala or gossalé in Konkani; and the rough or ridged gourd. In the Americas, it is called Chinese okra. Interestingly, the mature dried fruit is used to make loofahs or bath sponges.

Torli/hairde: Indian oil sardine.

Trifal/teppal/triphala: A small berry-like Sichuan pepper used exclusively in the Konkan. Also called jummana kayi. Not to be confused with trifalla, an ayurvedic medicine.

Tulsiché bee: Marathi for sweet basil seeds. Sweet basil has a strong association with Italian food, but is native to India where it has been grown for 500 years. Also called subja in Hindi the variety called holy basil is found in many traditional Hindu homes. Sweet basil seeds are used to make sherbets, desserts and ground into spice mixes.

U

Udak: The stock extracted by boiling seafood, vegetables or poultry. This technique is employed to make brothy gravies with leftover shrimp or vegetables, then seasoned with spices and served with spongy idlis, white rice or bhakris. Like a bouillabaisse, they are sometimes thickened with millet flour or ground coconut.

Uddamethi: A mango-fenugreek curry, similar to a sasav.

Udupi: A southern region in Karnataka. It is not a coastal town but has a large Konkani-speaking population and is an important pilgrimage spot for Hindus. It has a unique and pure vegetarian cuisine that is inextricably woven into the worship of Krishna, one of Vishnu's reincarnations.

Udupi mattu gulla gulla: A thorny green aubergine that grows in Udipi, Karnataka.

Ukad: Marathi to boil or simmer. Is also used to describe a mellow, boiled rice soup eaten for breakfast; similar to pej.

Ukadpendi: A cabbage, powdered peanut and wheat porridge.

Ukdo tandul: A variety of Konkan brown rice that is often sold parboiled.

Ulthané: Marathi for a flat spoon with a square head used to turn flatbreads.

Upkari: Similar to a Marathi usal, a lightly stir-fried vegetable or bean, but unlike usal which is always dry, an upkari can sometimes have a little gravy. The vegetable is cooked in its own moisture and served slightly undercooked to retain shape and texture. Garnished with coconut.

Uppi pullé dosa: Dosa batter with tamarind (pullé) and uppi (salt) in Udupi.

Upwas: The term for fasting. Satvik or pure vegetarian food is prepared for a variety of fasts. Some restrict the consumption of grains, onions, garlic and fruits. Sautéed tapioca and potatoes with peanuts are a popular fasting food in the Konkan.

Urad dal/kali dal: Often called black gram and not be confused with black beans, it is one of India's most prized beans and is an annual, trailing herb. Without the husk it is sold as a white lentil called urad dal and is used to make wadas, dosais, papads and added as part of a tempering to a variety of chutneys. With the husk it is black and used to prepare lentil curries, the most famous being the creamy kali dal.

V

Vaalaché birdé/dalimbya usal: A mildly bitter vaal or hyacinth bean, also called Surti, kewda, are sprouted and stewed with spices.

Vaali bhaji/Malabar spinach: A variety of the common spinach with a higher oxalic content. It is stir-fried with papaya or cooked in yogurt.

Vaam: Salt water eel.

Vaangi: Marathi for brinjal or aubergine. Native to India, this member of the Solanaceae family is related to the tomato and is cultivated as a perennial and an annual. Some varieties have a bitter flavour and require leaching or smoking. There are dozens of varieties and colours grown in China, Thailand and Sri Lanka.

Valaché birdé: A Konkan classic of curried field beans made with coconut and ground spices.

Valval: A Konkani speciality from South Canara, it is a coconut broth with mixed vegetables similar to avial but contains no lactose.

Van tulsi: Marjoram.

Vari tandul/jungle rice: It is actually a grass seed like American wild rice. It grows among rice crops in paddy fields in India and is often called samo. In other countries, this grass is considered a weed and is removed using weedicides, but in arid and poor rural areas anything edible is harvested and cooked.

Vatamba: A sour fruit from the gamboge tree, also called Malabar tamarind. The tree produces a dark yellow pigment used as a textile dye. Vatamba finds mentions in the Ramayana.

Vati: Marathi for a small bowl made of brass, stainless steel or silver to serve saar, dals, kadi and other gravy dishes.

Velchi kela: *Cardamus bananas*, a small cardamom-scented banana, popular all over the Konkan.

Velchi pud: Ground green cardamom seeds.

Vilayati chinch: Vilayati meaning foreign and chinch meaning tamarind. This flowering pea is called Madras thorn; it is not related to the tamarind family and is native to South America. The sweet seeds of this pod are roasted, steamed and also made into sherbets.


W
Wadé: Not to be confused with cutlets, Wadé are deep-fried puffy finger millet breads.


Y
Yelavni: A spicy Sholapur curry made with lentil broth.


Z
Zatuh dantey: Jaata and dantey in Marathi. A traditional round milling stone for masalas and chutneys. Two heavy discs placed one over the other are turned manually to grind grains.